101
THOUGHTS
FROM THE
WORD:

Volume Five

101 THOUGHTS FROM THE WORD:

Volume Five

DAVID PECKHAM

authorHOUSE®

AuthorHouse™ LLC
1663 Liberty Drive
Bloomington, IN 47403
www.authorhouse.com
Phone: 1-800-839-8640

Published by AuthorHouse 08/13/2014

ISBN: 978-1-4918-5601-7 (sc)
ISBN: 978-1-4918-5600-0 (e)

Library of Congress Control Number: 2014902065

Cover photo by : J. C. Ryle, 1816-1900,Bishop of Liverpool

All poems are by the author unless otherwise credited.
Unless otherwise indicated, Scripture quotations are from the New King James Version of the Bible, copyright 1979, 1980, 1982, 1990. Thomas Nelson, Inc., Publishers.
Quotes credited to KJV are from the King James Version.
Quotes credited to NASU are from the New American Standard Bible.
Quotes credited to the SNB are from the Sacred Name Bible.
Quotes credited to the TLB are from The Living Bible.

CONTENTS

ALL THINGS SERIES

LEVITICUS SERIES

INTRODUCTION

I quote from, and recommend your reading of "How Readest Thou?" by J. C. Ryle, 1816-1900, Bishop of Liverpool, whose picture graces the cover of this book.

"No book in existence contains such important matter as the Bible.

There is an extraordinary depth, fullness, and richness in the contents of the Bible. It throws more light on a vast number of most important subjects than all the other books in the world put together. It boldly handles matters which are utterly beyond the reach of man, when left to himself. It treats of things which are mysterious and invisible—the soul, the world to come, and eternity—depths that man has no line to fathom. All who have tried to write on these things, without Bible light, have shown little but their own ignorance.

The Bible alone gives a true and faithful account of man. It does not flatter him as novels and romances do. It does not conceal his faults and exaggerate his goodness

The Bible alone gives us true views of God. By nature man knows nothing of Him. All his conceptions and ideas of Him are low, groveling, and debased.

But time would fail me, if I were to enter fully into all the great things which the Bible reveals. It is not by any sketch or outline that the treasures of the Bible can be displayed. It would be easy to point out many other things, beside those I have mentioned, and yet the half of its riches would be left untold."

From Leviticus, that symbolizes the life and death of Jesus Christ, and the Song of Songs, that pictures the personal relationship of the believer with her Bridegroom, I have been greatly blessed in searching the scriptures for this book. To be honest, this is the first time I have delved into these books, apart from the occasional reference. I am greatly blessed and amazed at the depth and accuracy of God's Word.

"Search from the book of the Lord, and read: Not one of these shall fail . . . For My mouth has commanded it, and His Spirit has gathered them" Isaiah 34:16.

"Oh, how I love Your law! It is my meditation all the day. You, through Your commandments, make me wiser than my enemies; for they are ever with me" Psalm 119:97-98.

"Therefore you shall lay up these words of mine in your heart and in your soul, and bind them as a sign on your hand, and they shall be as frontlets between your eyes. You shall teach them to your children, speaking of them when you sit in your house, when you walk by the way, when you lie down, and when you rise up" Deuteronomy 11:18-19.

FOUNDATION FOR OUR PRAYERS

Reading: Habakkuk 3:17-19
"The LORD God is my strength" Habakkuk 3:19.

At the commencement of this series of thoughts on the prayers of the Bible, I would like to share with you why I feel led to do so.

I have never been satisfied with my prayer life; actually, I have talked with very few believers that are. Many of you who read these TFTWs know my testimony, of how I wanted nothing to do with God for twenty-three years. In retrospect, I am convinced I fell into such a spiritual state because I did not know how to pray.

One of the things that has helped me greatly since God restored me to Himself, is taking note of the prayers offered up by God's people in the Bible—and praying them myself.

David's prayer life is exposed in great detail in the Psalms, and it is a great blessing to pray them personally as just about every aspect of life is addressed.

Prayer is not a mysterious practice reserved only for clergy and the religiously devout. Prayer is simply communicating with God—listening and talking to him. Believers can pray from the heart, freely, spontaneously, and in their own words.

If prayer is considered to be conversing or communication with God, then the first instance of prayer is found in Genesis 3: 8-19, where it is recorded that "God called to Adam and said to him, 'Where are you?'

In this series, I would like to consider some prayers where God's servants "come boldly to the throne of grace, that we may obtain mercy and find grace to help in time of need" (Heb 4:16).

I am very grateful that some of the prayers of the Puritans have been preserved for us. In no way do I place myself on the same par with them spiritually, but, when reading their biographies, I can identify with many of the spiritual battles they faced. This is, of course, because Satan uses the

1

same strategies today as he did in their day. This is also applicable when I read the prayers of both Old and New Testament saints.

It is my prayer that God will use these Thoughts From The Word to His praise and glory as together we may be drawn into a deeper realization of the high honor and privilege that is ours as we communicate with the Almighty God, our Heavenly Father, Jesus, our Redeemer, and the Holy Spirit, who takes our stammering words and "Himself makes intercession for us with groanings which cannot be uttered."

"Now He who searches the hearts knows what the mind of the Spirit is, because He makes intercession for the saints according to the will of God" Romans 8:27.

What is the foundation for our prayers? What gives us the right to pray? Why do we think it is not a waste of time to pray? These are all good questions, and the Bible gives us the answer.

"Remember the word (Your promise—NLT) to Your servant, upon which You have caused me to hope" Psalm 119:49.

"The name of the LORD is a strong tower; the righteous run to it and are safe" Proverbs 18:10.

Our prayers must be based on God's Word to us. When we read the promises He has made, we must believe as did Abraham:

"He did not waver at the promise of God through unbelief, but was strengthened in faith, giving glory to God, and being fully convinced that what He had promised He was also able to perform" Romans 4:20-22.

We must not be like the Chinese worshiper who stood before a temple door and threw a dart at it. He believed his prayer would be answered by his god if the dart stuck, but, if it did not stick and fell off the door, his prayer would not be answered. A true believer must pray with the confidence that God hears our prayer and answers according to His will. Prayer is not a hit-or-miss practice, hoping God will hear and answer.

We must also be convinced that "The name of the Lord is a strong tower"—a source of strength and safety to us. This does not mean that we choose a particular name of God and rely on it (although this is also wonderfully true), but we cast ourselves on who He is; His character, His power, and His sovereignty.

This must be the foundation of our prayers. David knew this well:

"The LORD is my rock and my fortress and my deliverer; the God of my strength, in whom I will trust; my shield and the horn of my salvation, my stronghold and my refuge; my Savior, You save me from violence. I will call upon the LORD, who is worthy to be praised; so shall I be saved from my enemies" 2 Samuel 22:2-4.

"The LORD God is my strength; He will make my feet like deer's feet, and He will make me walk on my high hills" Habakkuk 3:19.

As we will take note over the coming weeks, as we consider the prayers of the Bible, there are many forms of prayer, but there are also fundamental rules that must be taken into consideration, otherwise we will become as the man who threw darts at the door hoping they would stick.

Puritan Quote:

"The one concern of the devil is to keep Christians from praying. He fears nothing from prayerless studies, prayerless work and prayerless religion. He laughs at our toil, mocks at our wisdom, but he trembles when we pray" Samuel Chadwick, 1860—1932.

CHRIST'S EXAMPLE

Reading: Luke 5:12-16 NASU
"He Himself would often slip away to the wilderness and pray" Luke 5:16

These words concerning Jesus are such as set an example for us to follow. Jesus was a very busy Man. Crowds followed Him wherever He went, and His days were filled with preaching to them, healing their sicknesses and teaching His disciples. But, in spite of everything that demanded His time, He would often slip away to the wilderness and pray. Most of our translations say He withdrew into the wilderness or desert to pray.

We may well ask "Why would the incarnate Son of God need to pray?" First of all we must always remember who He was—"Jesus of Nazareth, a Man" Acts 2:22. Yes, He was God, but also a Man,

"Jesus, who, being in the form of God, did not consider it robbery to be equal with God, but made Himself of no reputation, taking the form of a bondservant, and coming in the likeness of men" Philippians 2:5-7.

As a Man Jesus needed the strength that comes from private prayer with God. He became weary as in the boat: "But as they sailed He fell asleep" Luke 8:23. "And when He had sent the multitudes away, He went up on the mountain by Himself to pray. Now when evening came, He was alone there" Matthew 14:23. The stress of His ministry drove Him to prayer. When He engaged in the greatest battle He ever faced He told His disciples to stay where they were, and "He went a little farther, and fell on the ground, and prayed" Mark 14:35. He who does not "slip away" often to pray, will always be weak in his faith.

When Jesus was faced with making a big decision He preceded it with prayer.

"Now it came to pass in those days that He went out to the mountain to pray, and continued all night in prayer to God. And when it was day, He called His disciples to Himself; and from them He chose twelve whom He also named apostles" Luke 6:12-13.

It is a most natural thing to spend time with the one you love. Sweethearts will separate themselves from all others so they may be alone together. Good friends will spend time alone for discussion of personal things, issues they can share with only those they can trust. So with Jesus—He loved His Father and spoke to Him of things only they would understand. The time a Christian spends alone with God is a measure of how much he loves Him. The more any believer loves the Lord Jesus, the more they will delight to be alone with Christ. These are times for tears—tears of repentance, tears of sorrow, and tears of joy. These are also times of bonding, bonding with the One whom you love more than life itself.

Jonathan and David loved each other. and they spent a lot of time together developing their friendship. "The soul of Jonathan was knit to the soul of David, and Jonathan loved him as his own soul' 1 Sam 18:1. 1 Samuel 20 is a wonderful story of two friends who met together in a field so they could be alone. Does your love for God cause you to "slip away to the wilderness and pray"?

When engaged in every day activity, do you feel the need to slip away and pray. Mothers, when your babies are sleeping, take time to slip away from washing their clothes and preparing meals, etc. When at work, slip away and use your lunch hour to be alone with your Lord because you feel the need to do so, or just because you love Him. Withdraw from the busyness to be alone with God.

Oh, to spend time with You, dear Lord,
Alone in the field together;
Alone with the One my soul adores,
Alone with my Friend forever.

"Draw near to God and He will draw near to you" James 4:8.

Puritan Quote:

"The word of God is the food by which prayer is nourished and made strong" E.M. Bounds, 1835-1913.

THE PRAYER OF HABAKKUK

Reading: Habakkuk 3:17-19
"Yet I will rejoice in the LORD" Habakkuk 3:19.

Very little is known of this prophet, although various assumptions have been made by scholars. He probably prophesied in the 12th or 13th year of King Josiah. His name means *Embraced*, probably *one who is embraced by God*.

Habakkuk was a Godly man who lived during the time just prior to God's judgment on Judah. "Plundering and violence are before me; there is strife, and contention arises. Therefore the law is powerless, and justice never goes forth. For the wicked surround the righteous; therefore perverse judgment proceeds" Hab 1:3-4.

God's response to the prophet's complaint was simply to "Watch and be amazed." God told him He was preparing the Chaldeans to attack Judah. It was time for God to fulfill the promised judgment against His rebellious and unrepentant people. He even told Jeremiah not to pray for them, for He would no longer listen (Jer 7:16; 11:14; 14:11-12).

Habakkuk pleads with God on the basis that He is his "Lord, the Holy One, the Rock," and that He is so holy He cannot look upon sin (1:12-14).

Even with the knowledge God was about to bring severe judgment upon His people, the prophet prays one of the most glorious prayers recorded in the Bible. He acknowledges that the words God spoke made him afraid. These were no comforting words from God—they were words of judgment, and they frightened him. Please, the man of God prayed, in Your wrath remember mercy (3:2).

I would like to bring this beautiful hymn with which Habakkuk ends his book to your attention. Perhaps it is unfamiliar to some:

"Though the fig tree may not blossom, nor fruit be on the vines;
Though the labor of the olive may fail, and the fields yield no food;

Though the flock may be cut off from the fold, and there be no herd in the stalls—
Yet I will rejoice in the LORD, I will joy in the God of my salvation. The LORD God is my strength; He will make my feet like deer's feet, and He will make me walk on my high hills" (3:17-19).

This hymn, or psalm, was accompanied by musical instruments, as the final words of the book state. Even though the people (including himself) were about to suffer under the judging hand of God, Habakkuk sings, "Yet will I rejoice in the Lord, I will joy in the God of my salvation." This man of faith knew without a shadow of doubt that his Rock would never desert him, even though the fields would produce no harvest, nor the orchards fruit, though the livestock would be barren and the stables empty, his faith would not waver. *"THE LORD GOD IS MY STRENGTH"* he declares— even in the greatest afflictions he would not cease to rejoice in God. In spite of the devastating events taking place around him, "He will make me walk on my high hills."

From Habakkuk's hymn we can learn that during times of affliction God's people can always rely on His promises, for we are assured of the perpetual favor of our Heavenly Father.

To people worldwide, the deer is a symbol of an animal leaping and bounding effortlessly over every obstacle, springing forward with ease and grace. What a wonderful picture the prophet paints of the child of God who believes and trusts in God's promises.

David expresses this thought in a similar manner:

"For by You I can run against a troop, by my God I can leap over a wall" Psalm 18:29.

And the prophet Isaiah also said:

"Strengthen the weak hands, and make firm the feeble knees. Say to those who are fearful-hearted, 'Be strong, do not fear! . . . Then the eyes of the blind shall be opened, and the ears of the deaf shall be unstopped. Then the lame shall leap like a deer,

and the tongue of the dumb sing. For waters shall burst forth in the wilderness, and streams in the desert" Isaiah 35:3-6.

God does not promise to remove the obstacles we may face, in fact, He may be the One who places them in our path. But He does promise to be our strength, our Rock, and when we cast all our care on Him, he will strengthen our spiritual feet so we can leap like a deer over those obstacles. Those "high hills" will no longer appear impassable. Listen to God's promise to those who love Him and know Him by name:

"To open before him the double doors, so that the gates will not be shut I will go before you and make the crooked places straight; I will break in pieces the gates of bronze and cut the bars of iron. I will give you the treasures of darkness and hidden riches of secret places, that you may know that I, the LORD, who call you by your name, am the God of Israel" Isaiah 45:1-3.

No matter if our fields are non-productive and stables empty, when we trust God as our strength, we will enjoy the ability to "rejoice in the LORD," and to "joy in the God of my salvation."

Puritan Quote:

"We may hence gather a most useful doctrine,—That whenever signs of God's wrath meet us in outward things, this remedy remains to us—to consider what God is to us inwardly; for the inward joy, which faith brings to us, can overcome all fears, terrors, sorrows and anxieties" John Calvin, 1509-1564.

THE PRAYER OF ELIJAH

Reading: 1 Kings 17:17-24
"Then the Lord heard the voice of Elijah" 1 Kings 17:22

When Elijah is introduced to us, there is a great conflict in Israel between Jehovah and Baal. Ahab, the king of Israel "went and served Baal and worshiped him. Then he set up an altar for Baal in the temple of Baal, which he had built in Samaria. And Ahab made a wooden image. Ahab did more to provoke the LORD God of Israel to anger than all the kings of Israel who were before him" 1 Kings 16:31-34.

Israel had given itself over to Baal, but there was one man in particular who knew Jehovah and remained faithful to Him. In spite of the sin and corruption of the people, God withheld rain from the land.

The story of Elijah is a wonderful account of how God provided for His servant. He first guided him to the Brook Cherith where He commanded the ravens to feed him, then to Zarephath where He provided for him through the goodness of a widow.

When the widow's son became ill and died, she blamed the prophet.

But Elijah prayed for him (20) and his life was restored to him "And he stretched himself out on the child three times, and cried out to the LORD and said, 'O LORD my God, I pray, let this child's soul come back to him.' Then the LORD heard the voice of Elijah; and the soul of the child came back to him, and he revived" 1 Kings 17:21-22.

The apostle James used Elijah as an example of prayer—he was a man with a nature just like us, and God heard his prayer and answered (James 5:15). If we look at this prayer and its wonderful answer as an isolated incident, we shall not be able to understand it. We must consider the life of the prophet as a composite picture—Mount Carmel without the Brook Cherith, and the widow's son restored to life without the Ravens feeding the prophet, would leave us with but a series of individual events.

The lesson for us to learn is there is a pathway of life and experiences that prepares a believer to pray a prayer like Elijah's.

1) Elijah's previous familiarity with the Throne of Grace. This was not the first time he had prayed.

These are Elijah's first recorded words: "As the LORD God of Israel lives, before whom I stand" 1 Kings 17:1; 18:15, and Elisha—2 Kings 3:14, 5:16. This was the posture of his life; therefore, it was not unnatural for him to pray fervently and boldly for the life of the child.

He gained familiarity with the Throne of grace from the time (about a year) he spent alone at the Brook Cherith—he learned to commune with God while the Ravens fed him. No man prays like this the first time he prays.

2) His purity of heart and life—"a righteous man" James 5:16.

"For if our heart condemns us, God is greater than our heart, and knows all things. Beloved, if our heart does not condemn us, we have confidence toward God. And whatever we ask we receive from Him, because we keep His commandments and do those things that are pleasing in His sight" 1 John 3:20-21.

"Who may ascend into the hill of the LORD? Or who may stand in His holy place? He who has clean hands and a pure heart" Psalm 24:3-4.

"If we would pray well, we must live well" John Calvin.

If we do not live according to His commands, we cannot expect Him to answer our prayer:

"Now this is the confidence that we have in Him, that if we ask anything according to His will, He hears us. And if we know that He hears us, whatever we ask, we know that we have the petitions that we have asked of Him" 1 John 5:14-15.

Those three words "according to His will" are frequently ignored. It is Christ's will that we keep his commandments (John 1415). How can we expect God to answer our prayer when our lives are governed by our will, and not His?

3) Elijah identified himself with the child—"he stretched himself out on the child three times" 1 Kings 17:21. We must do the same—we must identify our self with the needs of others as if they were our own. Intercessory prayer is when we take another's burden as our own.

Just as we are exhorted to "cast(ing) all your care upon Him, for He cares for you", so we should pray for another—as if his burden (care) is our own. A flippant statement before God that Joe Smith will soon find work, is not intercessory prayer. Place yourself in Joe's position—how would you pray if it was you who desperately needed work?

Intercessory prayer can be likened to the word "comfort", for is it not a great comfort to know others are praying sincerely on your behalf? The word "comfort" (*parakaleo*) carries the thought of "drawing alongside someone and sharing their concern."

"Blessed be the God and Father of our Lord Jesus Christ, the Father of mercies and God of all comfort, who comforts us in all our tribulation, that we may be able to comfort those who are in any trouble, with the comfort with which we ourselves are comforted by God" 2 Cor 1:3-4.

May God teach us what it means to be a man or woman of prayer, and not just one who prays.

Puritan Quote:
"I have benefited by my praying for others; for by making an errand to God for them, I have gotten something for myself" Samuel Rutherford, 1600-1661.

A PRAYER OF DAVID

Reading: Psalm 42:1-8
"A prayer to the God of my life" Psalm 42:8

A volume of books could be written on the prayers of David (and probably has been). Every aspect of prayer covering every circumstance of life is spoken of in the Psalms. David, with all his ups and downs, was a man of prayer. He knew when and how to rejoice, to praise God and to give Him thanks. He often cast himself on God's mercy in repentance and sorrow, pleading with "the God of my life" for forgiveness. He prayed morning and evening, and knew the value of being still and meditating on God's Word during the night (Psalm 4:4).

"When I remember You on my bed, I meditate on You in the night watches. Because You have been my help, therefore in the shadow of Your wings I will rejoice" Psalm 63:6-7.

In Psalm 42 David speaks of "A prayer to the God of my life" (v8). He did not consider Jehovah his God only during the good times or the bad, but of his "life."

This Psalm is an expression of longing after God, like a deer that has been running for its life. The sound of barking hounds, whose sole purpose was to chase it until it could run no more, came closer by the stride. It dare not stop at the river for water but must keep on running. It seems there was no escape from the hounds that relentlessly chased it until it would drop from utter exhaustion.

"As the deer pants for the water brooks, so pants my soul for You, O God. My soul thirsts for God, for the living God" Psalm 42:1-2.

Every believer knows what it is like to be chased mercilessly by the hound of heaven, called elsewhere the "roaring lion" (1 Peter 5:8). The devil and his dogs continually pursue the child of God, but the scriptures tell us our Heavenly Father has provided a source of water, Living Water, that when we stop and drink we will be so refreshed and strengthened we are able to resist the pursuer. The promise of God is He will "restore, support, and strengthen" us (1 Peter 5:10, NLT).

"Oh God," David cries, "my soul is cast down within me." John Bunyan, who spent many years in a dungeon because of his faith, knew from experience what this means, wrote:

"Down, that is deep into the jaws of distrust and fear. And, Lord, my soul in this depth of sorrow, calls for help to thy depth of mercy. For though I am sinking and going down, yet not so low but that thy mercy is yet underneath me. Do, of thy compassions, open those everlasting arms, and catch him that has no help or stay in himself. For so it is with one that is falling into a well or a dungeon."

Even then, David writes:

"The LORD will command His lovingkindness in the daytime, and in the night His song shall be with me" Psalm 42:8.

It is important to note that God does not simply grant or give His lovingkindness, but He commands it. This is no mistranslation, but is the same word used to describe God's sovereignty. Just as He does not hope His people will follow Him but commands them to do so, so He commands His lovingkindness, and all it entails, to be the portion of His people who cry to Him in the time of need.

This is God's promise, and, like Abraham, who under the greatest of trials "did not waver at the promise of God through unbelief," we will be "strengthened in faith, giving glory to God, and be [ing] fully convinced that what He had promised He was also able to perform." Abraham believed God was sovereign and possessed the power, the ability, to keep His promises.

So we who love Him, can call on Him in the day of trouble with full assurance He will command His lovingkindness to flood over us. The principle contained in our text is the need to continue in prayer after God has showered us with His love and grace.

How often we plead with God to deliver us by either removing the obstacle or giving us His strength to endure it, then forget to pray—fail to thank and praise Him for answered prayer. With David it was the reverse. Deliverance from trouble strengthened his confidence in God and emboldened him to continue in prayer.

God's lovingkindness was the subject of his continued prayer:

"Through each day the LORD pours his unfailing love upon me, and through each night I sing his songs, praying to God who gives me life" (NLT).

Whether it be prayer for help, prayer of intercession, prayer of thanks, or prayer of praise, it should be continuous, "praying always with all prayer and supplication in the Spirit" (Eph 6:18).

"Rejoice always, pray without ceasing, in everything give thanks; for this is the will of God in Christ Jesus for you" 1 Thess 5:16-18.

Puritan Quote:

"As the gift bestowed is grace—free favour to the unworthy; so the manner of bestowing it is sovereign. It is given by decree; it is a royal donative. And if he commands the blessing, who shall hinder its reception? Henry March.

A PRAYER OF DAVID

Reading: Exodus 30:1-10
"Let my prayer be set before You as incense" Psalm 141:1:2

Much is said in scripture about incense, unfortunately most references have a negative connotation. The burning of incense was set by God as an important part in His people's worship as described in our reading. The tragedy was that this ceremony was continued when His people rebelled against Him and they worshipped other gods: "Because My people have forgotten Me, they have burned incense to worthless idols" Jeremiah 18:15.

The Bible interprets the meaning of burning incense by associating it with prayer:

"Let my prayer be set before You as incense" Psalm 141:2.
"And the smoke of the incense, with the prayers of the saints, ascended before God" Rev 8:4.

Not any form of incense was acceptable to God—a specific formula was to be followed—Exodus 30:34-36. This incense was considered very sacred: "It shall be most holy to you." So is prayer.

The haphazard and carefree manner in which prayer is frequently offered is an offense to God. This is true in many churches where prayer is nothing but ritualistic repetition of cold words, and also in the way we as individuals approach the Throne of God. When the Bible says to "come boldly to the throne of grace," it does not mean carelessly and without genuine reverence for the Sovereign, Almighty God who occupies that throne.

According to the law, only the priests descended from Aaron could offer incense (Lev 2:2), but today, as appointed priests of God (1 Peter 2:5; Rev 1:6), every believer has the honor of prayer. It is more than an honor, it is our duty as members of His "Holy priesthood."

The altar of incense occupied one of the most conspicuous and honored positions in the tabernacle and temple. It was placed immediately in front of the Holy of Holies where the presence of God dwelt. The symbolism of this position is very important in that the offering of incense prepared the way into the presence of God.

The carefully prepared incense, when offered to God, was to Him a "sweet" fragrance. It was pleasing to Him. So are our prayers. The Lord is pleased when we pray—our prayers bring pleasure to the Almighty, they are as a sweet smelling savor to Him. Think on it, fellow believer, God enjoys communion with His children. The fellowship He had with Adam and Eve was broken when they sinned, but has been restored by the sacrifice of Jesus for our sins. The sacrifice of Jesus is a sweet fragrance to God because it has removed the obstacles that stood in the way of communing with Him:

"And walk in love, as Christ also has loved us and given Himself for us, an offering and a sacrifice to God for a sweet-smelling aroma" Eph 5:2.

But from where does the incense of prayer rise? It is not from a censor swung over the saints by a priest, but from the heart of God's people. But not from any heart—that heart must be a renewed heart, one born again by the Spirit of God, one reconciled to Him by the blood of Jesus Christ. Incense, not made in accordance with God's formula, was rejected as unacceptable to Him.

Just as incense is made by crushing the ingredients into powder, so the heart that is acceptable and pleasing to God is one that is broken and contrite before Him:

"For You do not desire sacrifice, or else I would give it; You do not delight in burnt offering. The sacrifices of God are a broken spirit, a broken and a contrite heart—These, O God, You will not despise" Psalm 51:16-17.

God does not look on the outward appearance of ritual, but on the inward condition of the heart (1 Sam 16:7). An arrogant, unrepentant heart is not acceptable to God.

> *"True prayer is the incense of a heart broken for sin; humbled for its inquiry; mourning over its plague; touched, healed, and comforted with the atoning blood of God's great sacrifice. This is the true censor upon which God looks"* Octavius Winslow.

God Himself tells us, "I will accept you as a sweet aroma when I bring you out from the peoples . . ." Ezek 20:41. When, and only when, God has brought us into the new life which is in Christ Jesus, will our prayers be acceptable to Him as a "sweet aroma."

Incense was faithfully offered to God both morning and evening—a worthy pattern for our perpetual communion with Him:

"Rejoice always, pray without ceasing, in everything give thanks; for this is the will of God in Christ Jesus for you" 1 Thess 5:16-18.

Puritan Quote:

"We are not to look upon prayer as easy work requiring no thought. It needs to be "set forth"; what is more, it must be set forth "before the Lord," by a sense of his presence and a holy reverence for his name: neither may we regard all supplication as certain of divine acceptance, it needs to be set forth before the Lord "as incense", concerning the offering of which there were rules to be observed, otherwise it would be rejected of God" C.H. Spurgeon, 1834-1892.

A PRAYER OF REPENTANCE

Reading: Psalm 51:1-13
"Renew a steadfast spirit within me" Psalm 51:10

Under the guidance and inspiration of the Holy Spirit scripture has recorded a detailed account of David's life—his good times and his bad times. We are blessed when we read of his life because it is a reflection of every believer's life.

We know so little of the lives of many of the kings and prophets, but we can join with David when he praises God for His enduring mercy (Psalm 136), when he thanks Him for delivering him from the hands of his enemies (Psalm 18:46-50), when he acknowledges his sins before God (Psalm 51:3), and when he meditates on the works of God in his life (Psalm 77:6,12).

Here in Psalm 51, the Holy Spirit reaches into the depths of David's heart and restores him from the "guilt of bloodshed" to the "joy of Your salvation" (vss 12,14).

Few will be convicted of murder, but we are all guilty of sin in one form or another—"For all have sinned and fall{en} short of the glory of God" (Rom 3:23). This is sadly true of us all even after we have been born again by the Spirit of God. We are all guilty of backsliding to some degree. Would to God it were not so.

Psalm 51 was written after David had arranged for the death of Uriah so he could have Bathsheba (Uriah's spouse) as his wife. God sent Nathan, the prophet, to David, who confronted him of his sin.

"When the divine message had aroused his dormant conscience and made him see the greatness of his guilt, he wrote this Psalm. He had forgotten his psalmody while he was indulging his flesh, but he returned to his harp when his spiritual nature was awakened, and he poured out his song to the accompaniment of sighs and tears" C.H. Spurgeon.

That is exactly what happened, *"his spiritual nature was awakened."* This was nothing less than the convicting work of the Holy Spirit. To those who have sunk into the swamp of backsliding, when the Spirit of God sets out to restore such a person, it will break their heart. The consciousness that you have sinned against Him who died on the cross for you, who loves you even when you stopped loving Him, will break your heart.

Psalm 51 is not an exaggeration. It is the truth, as anyone will attest who has experienced such a work of God. David's confession, "I have sinned against the LORD" (2 Sam 12:13), resulted in him writing this Psalm. No act of penance could bring him relief or restore him to a close walk with God, but only a broken, contrite heart:

> **"For You do not desire sacrifice, or else I would give it; You do not delight in burnt offering. The sacrifices of God are a broken spirit, a broken and a contrite heart—these, O God, You will not despise" Psalm 51:16-17.**

No matter the depth of sin that caused us to stray from the fold, God will not, neither will He, reject the cry of a broken heart. The prodigal son will always be greeted with his Father's open arms when he returns with a penitent heart:

> **"And he arose and came to his father. But when he was still a great way off, his father saw him and had compassion, and ran and fell on his neck and kissed him. And the son said to him, 'Father, I have sinned against heaven and in your sight, and am no longer worthy to be called your son.' But the father said to his servants, 'Bring out the best robe and put it on him, and put a ring on his hand and sandals on his feet. And bring the fatted calf here and kill it, and let us eat and be merry; for this my son was dead and is alive again; he was lost and is found.' And they began to be merry" Luke 15:20-24.**

Is there a more precious portion of scripture for any prodigal who needs to return to his Heavenly Father?

Behold, I fall before Thy face,
My only refuge is Thy grace.
No outward forms can make me clean;
The leprosy lies deep within.

Listen to the cry of a convicted backslider:

"Have mercy upon me, O God" (vs 1)
"I acknowledge my transgressions, and my sin is always before me" (vs 3)
"Purge me . . . wash me" (vs 7)
"Blot out all my iniquities" (vs 9)
"Create in me a clean heart, and renew a steadfast spirit within me" (vs 10)
"Restore to me the joy of Your salvation" (vs 12)
"Uphold me by Your generous Spirit" (vs 12)
"Deliver me from the guilt" (vs 14).

Such is the cry of any repentant believer. God cannot resist the plea of a broken and contrite heart. He is a God of mercy and is always waiting with open arms for the return of His prodigal son.

The restoration of a backslidden soul cannot be achieved by him who is backslidden. It has to be the work of God, therefore David begins, "Have mercy upon me, O God." It is against You I have sinned, therefore it is to You I plead for mercy.

There is no greater relief or joy than when the Spirit of God leads us from the pig-pen of a backslidden life into the arms of our Heavenly Father.

Puritan Quote:

"This is the holy contrition that the Spirit of God works in the heart of the restored believer. Brought beneath the cross, insight of the crucified Savior, the heart is broken, the spirit is melted, the eye weeps, the tongue confesses, the bones that were broken rejoice, and the contrite child is clasped in his Father's forgiving, reconciled embrace once more" Octavius Winslow, 1808-1878.

DRAW NEAR TO GOD

Reading: Hebrews 4:14-16
"Let us therefore come boldly to the throne of grace" Hebrews 4:16

One of the more astounding statistics is the percentage of Christians who do not pray outside of so called public worship. Even then, much of it is lip service, in other words the pastor or priest prays and the 'worshipper' offers their 'Amen'. Some do not even go that far. We then travel through the statistic chart to those who pray once or twice a week when they think about it or when some need arises, then on to those who love to pray, not out of habit but because they enjoy spending time with their God.

Prayer is not as it used to be when it had to be accompanied with sacrifices, priestly participation, and numerous other rituals. When Jesus met with the woman of Samaria He introduced a new and wonderful manner of prayer. She was arguing that Mount Gerizim was the place ordained by God to worship, not Jerusalem as practiced by the Jews. Jesus changed the entire concept for prayer when He said,

"Woman, believe Me, the hour is coming when you will neither on this mountain, nor in Jerusalem, worship the Father . . . . God is Spirit, and those who worship Him must worship in spirit and truth" John 4:21, 24.

With this one statement Jesus did away with rituals and places (they were, after all, but a shadow of that which was to come), and introduced praying in the Spirit—anywhere and at anytime. God is Spirit and from the conception of Jesus (Matthew 1:18) to the Day of Pentecost (Acts 2:4) everything was and is to be accomplished in, through, and by the Spirit of God.

"All service shall vanish, the veil of the temple shall be rent in twain, and carnal worship give place to one more spiritual. Shadows shall fly

before substance, and the truth advance itself above figures" Stephen Charnock.

Think of it, you may approach the Almighty, all holy God in the privacy of your room, on the river bank, wherever you please, at any time. What a privilege, what an honor, what a joy. Your prayer may be conversational, listening for the voice of God, instantaneous—at the time of immediate need, etc. Why then do so many of us deny ourselves this wonderful privilege? "Draw near to God and He will draw near to you." This is God's promise.

"Three things may cause boldness in prayer; the saints have a Father to pray to, the Spirit to help them to pray, and Jesus Christ as their Advocate to present their prayers" Richard Watson, 1682.

Each member of the Trinity has a part in the prayers of God's people. When a believer approaches the Throne of Grace in prayer, the Father, Son and Holy Spirit become involved with him. Prayer is a joint venture with God. He obviously enjoys it when His children pray, for

"the hour is coming, and now is, when the true worshipers will worship the Father in spirit and truth; for the Father is seeking such to worship Him" John 4:23.

Spurgeon considered prayer to be a state of mind, an attitude of heart whereby the believer is aware of God's presence with him twenty-four hours a day. Daniel prayed three times a day:

"And in his upper room, with his windows open toward Jerusalem, he knelt down on his knees three times that day, and prayed and gave thanks before his God, as was his custom since early days" Daniel 6:10.

Brother Lawrence referred to prayer as "conversing with God." Speaking, listening, meditating, contemplating, requesting, praising, etc., all are a part of conversing with the Almighty. One in love wishes to spend as much time as possible with the one he loves.

How much does our prayer life reflect the level or depth of our faith? The writer to the Hebrews says:

"Let us draw near with a true heart in full assurance of faith" Hebrews 10:22.

Many religions pray out of fear—that is their primary motivation, but for the believer in Jesus Christ our motive is based on faith. When we pray we are responding to God's invitation—we believe He welcomes our prayers and hears us. We pray because we love Him. We pray because we need Him. Prayer is the conduit through which God channels His blessings to His children.

How deep is your faith? Examine your prayer life—that will tell you.

Puritan Quote:

"Oh, what a costly and precious privilege is prayer! Access to God, fellowship with the Most High, communion with the Invisible One, filial relationships with our Heavenly Father—this is a mighty privilege. And yet, vast as it is, it is ours" Octavius Winslow, 1808-1878.

NEHEMIAH'S PRAYER

Reading: Nehemiah 1:1-11
"Please let Your ear be attentive and Your eyes open, that You
may hear the prayer of Your servant" Nehemiah 1:6

Nehemiah held an important position in the King's palace—he was the King's cupbearer (1:11). One day, his brother Hanani came from Judea with news that devastated him—God's people were in "great trouble and shame" (1:3 RSV).

These were God's people who had returned to Judea after seventy years of captivity. Their God-given mission was to build Him "a house at Jerusalem" (Ezra 1:2). They began well, but opposition caused them to stop the work. So the word Nehemiah received was those who started the work with such vigor and determination were now in "great trouble and disgrace" (NLT).

This news had a great effect on Nehemiah who, in spite of working in a foreign king's household, remained a devout servant of Jehovah. The dismal failure of the 'remnant' to carry out the purpose of their return, struck heavily on his heart. When he heard the news, he "sat down and wept, and mourned for many days; [and] was fasting and praying before the God of heaven" (1:4).

The structure and content of Nehemiah's prayer has much to teach us for our own prayer life, however, we would be negligent if we did not first consider his response to the news he received.

Nehemiah's heart was so sensitive to the condition of God's work and those involved in the building of His house, it caused him to stop what he was doing, and weep. What a challenge to us, God's people, when we hear of the condition and plight of our brothers and sisters, and the "building" of God's church.

So many fellow believers throughout the world are suffering persecution because they love God and His Word. I do not mean just opposition, but persecution—imprisonment, beatings, even death. Believers meet in secret because the law of their country forbids Christianity. Yet God is calling out from these countries a people to Himself.

I must ask myself, how do I respond when I hear of the hardships of my brothers and sisters in Christ? I regularly receive the magazine published by *The Voice of Martyrs*, where the plight of persecuted Christians is told. I read their story, I am told their names. How often do I remember them before the Throne of Grace? Distance and conditions are no barrier to prayer.

"No man will do worthy work at rebuilding the walls who has not wept over the ruins" Alexander MacLaren.

How quick we are to complain about the condition of many of the churches in our own country. We see them departing from the basic doctrines taught in the scriptures and replacing them with concepts that "simplify" the gospel, and "make more sense to the unbeliever". Perhaps, if we spent more time praying for our churches instead of criticizing them, we would know the joy of participating with Jesus, who said, "I will build my church, and the gates of Hades will not prevail against it."

Nehemiah was willing to be the answer to his prayer. He left the security and benefits of his employment in the King's palace, and went to Jerusalem.

"The ruins on Zion were more attractive to him than the splendours of Shushan, and he willingly flung away his chances of a great career to take his share of affliction and reproach" Alexander MacLaren.

In this, Nehemiah was like Moses, who chose:

"rather to suffer affliction with the people of God than to enjoy the passing pleasures of sin" Hebrews 11:25.

Nehemiah's response to the conditions in Jerusalem was not a simple prayer, but a deeply felt sorrow, fasting, and prayer. It became a burden to him. He identified himself with the problem:

"Both my father's house and I have sinned. We have acted very corruptly against You, and have not kept the commandments, the statutes, nor the ordinances which You commanded Your servant Moses" Nehemiah 1:6-8.

As someone once observed: When we point, three fingers are pointing back to ourself, one up to God, and only one to the object of blame. How much are we to blame for the condition of our churches? Are we quick to point to others while unwilling to see ourselves as part of the problem?

These are challenging questions, aren't they? I stand convicted in the light of God's Word.

"O Lord, I pray, please let Your ear be attentive to the prayer of Your servant, and to the prayer of Your servants who desire to fear Your name" Nehemiah 1:11.

Puritan Quote:

"Thus prepared for whatever might be the issue of that eventful day, the young cupbearer rose from his knees, drew a long breath, and went to his work. Well for us if we go to ours, whether it be a day of crisis or of commonplace, in like fashion! Then we shall have like defense and like calmness of heart" Alexander MacLaren, 1826-1910.

THE EAR OF GOD

Reading: Psalm 55: 1-23.
"Give ear to my prayer, O God; and hide not
thyself from my supplication" Psalm 55:1

Twelve times in the Psalms, we read the plea of David's heart for God to "Give ear" to what he is asking. Every child of God has wondered at one time or another, if God is listening when we call out to Him. These doubts may arise because we are very conscious of a besetting sin in our life, or maybe Satan causes us to question our salvation, or because we have earnestly prayed for something for many years, perhaps the salvation of a loved one, and our prayer has not been answered.

"Give ear" is the translation of the word *'azan'*, and means more than to *hear*—it is deeper than that. It means to listen, to consider, with the ultimate conclusion of a positive response. "Lord, do not simply hear my prayer, but contemplate my request and answer."

"Give ear to *my words*, O LORD, consider my meditation" Psalm 5:1
"Give ear to *my prayer* which is not from deceitful lips" Psalm 17:1
"Hear my prayer, O LORD, and give ear *to my cry*" Psalm 39:12
"Hear my prayer, O God; give ear *to the words of my mouth*" Psalm 54:2
"Give ear *to my prayer*, O God, and do not hide Yourself from my supplication" Psalm 55:1; 86:6
"Give ear to *my voice* when I cry out to You" Psalm 141:1
"Hear my prayer, O LORD, give ear to *my supplications*! In Your faithfulness answer me" Psalm 143:1.

It does not matter the condition of your heart or the cause of your cry, if you are His child, God will "give ear" to you. That is His promise, and His promises are rock solid—"In Your faithfulness answer me!"

When we pray we can and should have confidence in God's promises:

"Now this is the confidence that we have in Him, that if we ask anything according to His will, He hears us. And if we know that He hears us, whatever we ask, we know that we have the petitions that we have asked of Him" 1 John 5:14-15.

Our confidence does not lie in the premise that whatever we ask of God He will do it. If that were true, God would be at the mercy of our wants and the dictates of our own heart. The four words, "according to His will" are vital to our understanding of true prayer.

But, you ask, how can I know what the will of God is? Perhaps it is easier to know what the will of God is not. If our prayer conflicts with the express mandates of the Word of God, we can be sure it is not "according to His will." If we approach prayer as purely an obligation we feel God requires of us, our requests are probably not "according to His will." If our prayers are a matter of rote (routine; a fixed, habitual, or mechanical course of procedure), they may fall into the category of "vain repetition, casting doubt they are "according to His will."

True prayer is usually the result of the Holy Spirit laying a burden on our heart. God never burdens our heart to plead for things that are not His will.

"As long as you can plead to God with tears, you have every reason to believe that God's Spirit is moving you to pray. The Holy Spirit does not move us to pray in vain ... We can't arbitrarily choose what we want and then force God to include that particular thing in His purposes. This would mean that we control the world and run it with our prayers" John G. Reisinger, *The sovereignty of God in prayer.*

"Beloved, if our heart does not condemn us, we have confidence toward God. And whatever we ask we receive from Him, because we keep His commandments and do those things that are pleasing in His sight" 1 John 3:21-22.

Once again, confidence and answered prayer are coupled together. To coin a phrase used by the Puritans, "They are like twins in the same womb." If, when we go to God in prayer, we are at peace with Him, and are not convicted by the Holy Spirit of unconfessed sin, then we can enjoy this confidence John writes about, then we can have confidence that "whatever we ask we receive from Him." Our confidence is the result of keeping His commandments and doing those things that please Him.

Like all good fathers, God does not reward bad behavior.

In Psalm 5: 1-3, David says, "Give ear to my words, O LORD, Consider my meditation. Give heed to the voice of my cry, my King and my God, for to You I will pray." But he does not leave it there. At the end of verse three, he concludes, "And I will look up."

When we have true confidence in God, we can pray with assurance that He will answer, and we can "*look up*" expectantly for God's answer. May God teach us to pray confidently and expectantly, for this comes not based on our vain repetitions, but on His faithfulness:

"Hear my prayer, O LORD, give ear to my supplications! In Your faithfulness answer me, and in Your righteousness" Psalm 143:1.

Puritan Quote:

"Meditation is the best beginning of prayer, and prayer is the best conclusion of meditation. When the Christian, like Daniel, hath first opened the windows of his soul by contemplation, then he may kneel down to prayer" George Swinnock, 1627-1673.

LOOKING UP

Reading: Zechariah 2:1-13
"Then I raised my eyes and looked" Zechariah 2:1

I am sure most born again believers can look back on times when the Holy Spirit has spoken to them from God's Word with such clarity, that they must continually return to that portion for the continued refreshment of their soul. Such is the second chapter of Zechariah to me.

I am aware of the true historical context of this chapter, however, it is my experience, the Holy Spirit frequently applies God's Word out of context. Maybe it is a single word, or a sentence, or, as in this case, an entire chapter that He uses to encourage and strengthen God's children

The chapter begins with, "Then I raised my eyes and looked." Is this not the first step in communing with our heavenly Father? We cannot expect to commune with God unless we take our eyes off the things of the world and seek His face.

There is a difference between raising our eyes and looking. We can raise our eyes and not see anything. This is a fallacy heathen religions practice, and tragically, even some Christians:

"Hear this now, O foolish people, without understanding, who have eyes and see not, and who have ears and hear not" Jeremiah 5:21.

We must do more than raise our eyes, for that will gain us nothing. The promise of Jesus is: "Seek, and you will find" Luke 11:9.

Let us take the advice of Isaiah, "Search from the book of the LORD, and read" Isaiah 34:16, and follow the example of Solomon:

"I applied my heart to know, to search and seek out wisdom and the reason of things" Ecclesiastes 7:25.

The lazy Christian will raise his eyes, but he that seeks and searches the heart of God will be rewarded, for he will find.

What was it the prophet saw? "Behold, a man with a measuring line in his hand" (2:1). What a blessing to those who love God and have been made new creatures in Christ. One of Satan's often used tactics is to cast doubt in a believer's mind. The more we grow in Christ, the more conscious we become of sin, and the more amazing it becomes that God can still love us. But does He? Oh, the doubts Satan places in our heart.

Believer, lift up your eyes and look! Look to the Throne of Grace, for there you will "behold, a man with a measuring line in his hand" (2:2). That Man is none other than Jesus Christ Himself. When doubt plays havoc with your mind, always look to up to the Man with the measuring line in His hand. If you have trusted Jesus Christ as your Savior, He will meet your inquiry with a smile, for He has measured you and found you to be whole and complete in Him.

He will assure you that you have been justified, and, by His measurement, you have nothing lacking—you *are without fault before the throne of God*" Revelation 14:5. Satan is a "liar and the father of it" John 8:44.

Another lie Satan loves to tell God's children, is that they are worthless, and have nothing to offer God. They are bound by their lack of education; they are limited by their physical disability, or their sins restrict them from being used by God. In other words, Satan builds a wall around us, limiting us from being of service to God. But listen to the words of God:

> **"Run, speak to this young man, saying: 'Jerusalem shall be inhabited as towns without walls, because of the multitude of men and livestock in it. For I,' says the LORD, 'will be a wall of fire all around her, and I will be the glory in her midst'"** (2:4-5).

Just as Jerusalem, so are you, fellow believer: you will be "as towns without walls." No walls! No limits! No restrictions! No boundaries! Has God laid a burden on your heart to serve Him in a particular way? When you look at yourself in your position and determine it cannot be so, remember the words of Paul:

"I can do all things through Christ who strengthens me"
Philippians 4:13.

It did not matter to Paul what his situation was, if God told him to do something, he knew he could do it—in God's strength. God tells us He will be our Wall, not our doubts and weaknesses; He will set our boundaries, not Satan or our perceived limitations, and He will be our strength, not our education or ego.

Not only that, but when His children accept their reality as it is in Jesus Christ, He will be glorified in their lives. What more do we want? What more could we ask for? God does not say we will not face opposition. For we all

"wrestle against principalities, against powers, against the rulers of the darkness of this age, against spiritual hosts of wickedness in the heavenly places. Therefore take up the whole armor of God, that you may be able to withstand in the evil day, and having done all, to stand" Ephesians 6:12-13.

These wonderful truths come to those who raise their eyes and look. Is this not the definition of prayer and communing with our heavenly Father?

Puritan Quote:
"The comfortable sights which by faith we have had of God's goodness made to pass before us should engage us to lift up our eyes again, and to search further into the discoveries made to us of the divine grace; for there is still more to be seen" Matthew Henry, 1662-1714.

FLEE FROM THE NORTH

Reading: Zechariah 2:1-13
"Up, up! Flee from the land of the north" Zechariah 2:6

Last time, we saw the necessity of God's people raising their eyes and looking, and the difference between just raising our eyes and searching God. This practice will undoubtedly lead to the refreshing of our soul, as the Man standing at God's right hand assures us He sees us as "faultless" in God's eyes.

The last seven verses of this chapter challenges us to action. God's children are exhorted to "Up, up! Flee from the land of the north." (2:6)). It was from the north the Chaldean armies swept down on Judea. The Lord asked Jeremiah, "What do you see?" and he answered, "I see a boiling pot, and it is facing away from the north." Then the LORD said to him:

"Out of the north calamity shall break forth on all the inhabitants of the land" Jeremiah 1:13-14.

As God's children, we must always be alert to the dangers to our souls. The Chaldeans, or Babylonians, are a constant threat to us. The Babylonians typify the world, the flesh, and the devil—anything that attacks us, and causes us to take our eyes off God. It makes no sense to bury our heads in the sand and pretend the enemy does not exist. It does. One of Satan's acts of deceit is to lull Christians into a condition of apathy, to embrace the world and expose them to its temptations and sins.

A Christian magazine article recently quoted a pastor as saying, "We try to be as close to the world as possible in order to attract unbelievers into our church. Then, when they attend regularly, we preach the gospel to them." Whatever happened to,

"Come out from among them and be separate, says the Lord. Do not touch what is unclean, and I will receive you. I will be a

Father to you, and you shall be My sons and daughters, says the LORD Almighty" 2 Corinthians 6:17-18.

You cannot play with fire without getting scorched. The Holy Spirit does not need the world's help to draw people to Christ. The gospel *is* the power that accomplishes that (Romans 1:16).

God's children must strive to keep from being entangled by the world:

"Stand fast therefore in the liberty by which Christ has made us free, and do not be entangled again with a yoke of bondage" Galatians 5:1.

"For if, after they have escaped the pollutions of the world through the knowledge of the Lord and Savior Jesus Christ, they are again entangled in them and overcome, the latter end is worse for them than the beginning" 2 Peter 2:20.

This was the message to the Jews: "Up, Zion! Escape, you who dwell with the daughter of Babylon" (2:7). Paul states it this way: "Do not be unequally yoked together with unbelievers. For what fellowship has righteousness with lawlessness? And what communion has light with darkness? And what accord has Christ with Belial? Or what part has a believer with an unbeliever?" 2 Corinthians 6:14-15.

God's anger is against the world (2:8-9), so why do so many of us embrace it? When we raise our eyes and look to God; when we see the Man with the measuring line, and hear Him tell us, "You stand faultless before the Throne of Grace," and hear Him say, "he who touches you touches the apple of [My] eye" (2:8), then surely our heart should "Sing and rejoice" (2:10).

God is not pleased when we embrace that which nailed His Son to a cross. The world must be "Anathema" to the redeemed child of God.

When we understand we are accepted by God because we have been made one with His Son, our hearts will "sing and rejoice." When our eyes are truly fixed on Him, the world will lose its attraction. When we "submit to God", then we can "resist the devil and he will flee from you." Then we can "draw near to God, and He will draw near to us [you]" James 4:7-8.

What wonderful promises God gives His people, promises that were true then, now, and in the future: "*I am coming and I will dwell in your midst,*" *says the LORD.* "Many nations shall be joined to the LORD in that day, and they shall become My people. And I will dwell in your midst. Then you will know that the LORD of hosts has sent Me to you. And the LORD will take possession of Judah (His people, you and I) as His inheritance" (2:10-12).

While these marvelous truths cause us to "sing and rejoice," we are also exhorted to "Be silent, before the LORD" (2:13). Scripture tells us to:

"Know that the LORD has set apart for Himself him who is godly; The LORD will hear when I call to Him . . . Meditate within your heart on your bed, and be still."

"Be still, and know that I am God; I will be exalted among the nations, I will be exalted in the earth! The LORD of hosts is with us; the God of Jacob is our refuge" Psalm 4:3-4; 46:10-11.

All this because we take the time to *raise* our eyes and look—to pray, to contemplate on the things of God, and to commune with Him.

Puritan Quote:

"*Prayer will make a man cease from sin, or sin will entice a man to cease from prayer.*" *John Bunyan, 1628-1688.*

A BETTER HOPE

Reading: Hebrews 7:11-19

"The law made nothing perfect; on the other hand, there is the bringing in of a better hope, through which we draw near to God" Hebrews 7:19

On this the 12th anniversary of Thoughts From The Word, I am breaking protocol by quoting in length another's thoughts. This was a great blessing and encouragement when I first read it, and feel led to share it with you:

Puritan Quote:

"The Holy Spirit teaches the believer to plead the atoning blood of Christ. He puts this great and prevailing argument in his mouth, and when sin seems a mountain, when unbelief would suppress the aspiration, and when a deep consciousness of unworthiness causes his soul to "stand afar off," the Spirit reveals this precious and encouraging truth of the prevailing power of the blood of Jesus with God on behalf of His people. In a moment the mountain is leveled; unbelief is checked and the soul, unfettered and unrestrained draws near to God, even to the bosom of its Father.

What a view of the love of the Spirit as the Author of prayer, Who, having experienced it, is yet a stranger to the blessed exercise of communion with God? How often guilt causes the head to hang down, the sense of utter vileness and worthlessness covers the soul with shame, and even the very destination keeps the believer back just as the wretched covering of the poor beggar kept him from the door. Then the blessed Spirit, in the plentitude of His grace and tenderness, unfolds Jesus to the soul as being all that the soul needs for full, free, and near access to God.

He moves our eyes from ourselves and fastens them on the blood that pleads for mercy louder than all his sins can plead for condemnation. He also brings the righteousness near that clothes and covers the soul as is befitting for appearance in the presence of the King of kings—not merely with acceptance but with delight. **Beholding him thus washed and clothed, God rests in His love, and rejoices over him with singing.**

We must not overlook the understanding between God the Father and the Spirit. The Father, the searcher of hearts, knows the mind of the Spirit. He understands the desire and the meaning of the Spirit in the souls of His saints. He understands the "groanings which cannot be uttered." He can interpret their sighs: He can read the meaning of their very desires. And when feeling is too deep for utterance and thought too intense for expression—when the soul can only groan out its wants and requests—then God understands the mind of the Spirit.

Oh, the inconceivable preciousness of a throne of grace! To have a God to go to who knows the mind of the Spirit, a God who can interpret the groan and read our wants; to have promise upon promise bidding the soul to come close! When our mouths cannot express our thoughts because of the fullness of the heart and the poverty of language, then God, who searches the hearts and knows the mind of the Spirit says, "You never prayed to me, my child, as you did then; your voice was never as sweet, as powerful, as persuasive; never were you so eloquent as when my Spirit made intercession for you with "groanings you could not utter."

Perhaps it was your last resource; refuge failed you and no man cared for your soul; friends failed you, and your heart failed you; everyone forsook you and fled; and, in your extreme need, you took yourself to God—and He failed you not. You found the throne of grace accessible; you saw a God of grace upon it, and the sweet incense of the Redeemer's precious merits going up; you drew near and sighed, groaned, and whispered your wants, and said, "It is good for me to draw near to God" Psalm 78:23.

Yes, He "knoweth what is the mind of the Spirit" Romans 8:27. The secret desire for Jesus, the longing for divine conformity, the hidden mourning over the existence and power of indwelling sin, the feeblest rising of the heart to God, the first sigh of the humble and contrite spirit—all are known to God. Let this encourage you, dear reader, when you feel you cannot pray because of the weakness of the flesh or the depth of your feeling; if the Spirit is interceding for you, your heavenly Father "Knows the mind of the Spirit, and not a sigh or a groan can escape His notice."

Quoted from "Evening Thoughts" by Octavius Winslow, 1808-1878.

"It is good for me to draw near to God" Psalm 78:23.

THE THRONE OF GRACE

Reading: Hebrews 4:14-16
"Let us therefore come boldly to the throne of grace, that we may obtain
mercy and find grace to help in time of need" Hebrews 4:16.

I am returning again to this verse (Biblical Prayer #8, Feb 15, 2012)
because the Holy Spirit has laid it heavily on my heart. The more I
contemplate these words, the more astounding they become.

To know you and I, sinners once at enmity with Almighty God, can
approach His throne with no fear of condemnation, is, to say the least,
marvelous beyond all comprehension.

Part of the punishment on Adam and Eve when they sinned was to be
expelled from God's presence. To keep them from returning to the Garden
of Eden, the place where God communed with them, God placed two
cherubim with flaming swords (Gen 3:23-24). There is a divine principle
for God's action:

**"You are of purer eyes than to behold evil, and cannot look on
wickedness" Habakkuk 1:13.**

Why then does God's Word invite us to "come boldly to the throne
of grace" the very place where God resides? Why is God's presence not
protected by sword-waving Cherubim?

To many it still is. However, for a select few, it is not.

The throne of grace is typified by the Mercy Seat which sat on the
Ark of the Covenant in the Holy of Holies, At each end were Cherubim
reminding us of those guarding the entrance into God's presence at the
entrance of Eden. Here the Cherubim were not holding flaming swords
because they protected the Mercy Seat. Now it was possible for man to
approach God's presence, even though it was one man—the High Priest,
and that only one time a year.

As the Book of Hebrews so clearly shows, the High Priest foreshadowed Jesus Christ, who died and entered the presence of God. Because Jesus is seated in the presence of God, we may come with boldness and without hesitancy or fear and ask for all the mercy we need. We come, not depending on our own merits, but on the merits of Jesus who died for our sins, thereby procuring unchallenged entrance into God's presence.

Forgive the simplicity of my thought, for when I approach God in prayer, I see the Cherubim guarding entrance to God's throne, but when they see me clothed in the righteousness of Jesus, they recognize me as an adopted son of God and step aside, permitting me to enter my heavenly Father's presence.

Entrance into God's presence is a privilege granted only to those who have been born again and made one with Jesus Christ. The cherubim continue to guard the entrance to God to all who have not been washed in the blood of Christ, for they are still in their sins, and are still at enmity with Him:

> **"For to be carnally minded is death, but to be spiritually minded is life and peace. Because the carnal mind is enmity against God; for it is not subject to the law of God, nor indeed can be. So then, those who are in the flesh cannot please God" Romans 8:6-8.**

> *"Only a child of God can truly pray to God. Only a son can enter his presence. It is gloriously true that anyone can cry to Him for help—for pardon and mercy. But that is scarcely prayer. Prayer is much more than that. Prayer is going into 'the secret place of the Most High,' and abiding under the shadow of the Almighty (Psalm 41.1). Prayer is making known to God our wants and desires, and holding the hand of faith to take His gifts, Prayer is communion with God" The Kneeling Christian.*

We sin every day, therefore we need God's mercy every day. The place where mercy is to be found is the throne of God. "Let us therefore come boldly to the throne of grace, that we may obtain mercy."

Every day we have needs. Where will we find "grace to help in the time of need?" Nowhere but at "the throne of grace."

When, as Paul writes in Ephesians 1:6, God makes us acceptable to Himself in Christ, then we find "grace" or "favor" with Him. Our text is speaking of the special assistance or "help" we receive when we approach God boldly.

When Paul asked God for relief from his "thorn in the flesh," he received this answer:

"My <u>grace</u> is sufficient for you, for My strength is made perfect in weakness" 2 Corinthians 12:9.

Paul received an assurance of God's care and good-will toward him, and that powerful assistance with which God would supply him against his specific temptation. Hebrews 4:16 does not promise the removal of our temptation or problem, but God's grace "to help in the time of need."

As sons of God, may we with boldness and without fear, take every opportunity to commune with our heavenly Father, for He sits on His throne of mercy and grace—both of which He has promised to give us.

Puritan Quote:

"It appears that there is with God in Christ, God on His throne of grace, a spring of suitable and seasonable help for all times and occasions of difficulty. He is 'the God of all grace,' and a fountain of living waters is with Him for the refreshment of every weary and thirsty soul" John Owen, 1616-1683.

OUR GREAT INTERCESSOR

Reading: Romans 8:31-39
"... who is even at the right hand of God, who also
makes intercession for us" Romans 8:34

Last week we centered our thoughts on the Throne of Grace where God's children can go to "find help in the time of need" (Heb 4:16). Today, I would like us to return there and meditate a little further as to why we are so welcome and why we can find and receive grace? The simple answer is because Jesus is seated there. Instead of being faced with the guarding cherubim, we are welcomed by Jesus.

Jesus is not merely sitting there in his role as Victor over sin and Satan, but as our intercessor. After His resurrection, Jesus ascended to heaven where He was declared successful in His work of Salvation (Dan 7:13-24). But He did not forget His brothers and sisters still on earth facing the onslaughts of the world and the devil.

The intercessory work of Jesus is typified in the Old Testament:

"Then he shall take a censer full of burning coals of fire from the altar before the LORD, with his hands full of sweet incense beaten fine, and bring it inside the veil. And he shall put the incense on the fire before the LORD, that the cloud of incense may cover the mercy seat that is on the Testimony" Lev 16:12-13.

When Aaron entered the Holy of Holies, he foreshadowed our Lord's entrance into heaven. The blood sprinkled at the mercy-seat was the presentation of the Atonement within the veil. And the incense overshadowing the mercy-seat with its fragrant cloud, pictured the ceaseless intercession of our Great High Priest in the Holiest Place.

The intercession of Jesus on behalf of His people is more than an obligation He feels He must undertake as part of the mission of salvation. The salvation that Jesus acquired by His life, death, resurrection, and ascension, is a personal one. Jesus does not intercede on behalf of His church as a single entity, but for each of His brothers and sisters individually. His intercession is personal—for us as individuals.

> *"It (Christ's intercession) embraces all the personal needs of each believer, it precedes each temptation and trial, and, at the moment that the sympathy and the prayers of Jesus are the most needed and the most soothing, it bears the saint and his sorrow before the throne. At a crisis of his history, at a juncture, or perhaps at the most critical moment in his life when a believer's heart is oppressed with emotion and cannot breathe a prayer—Jesus is remembering him, sympathizes with him, and interceding for him. Oh, who can fully describe the blessings that flow through the intercession of the Son of God? The love, the sympathy, the care, the complete interest in all our concerns are blessings beyond description"* Octavius Winslow, Evening Thoughts.

As our Intercessor, Jesus stands between God and man. He is our Advocate. He is the only medium of access to God. No sinner can approach God with any other acceptance but in and through Him. Without Jesus as our Mediator, God cannot have fellowship with us. Jesus unites God and those for whom He died. So close and personal is this unity that every groan touches Him, every sigh touches Him, every pain touches Him, and in all our afflictions—He is afflicted (Isaiah 63:9).

Can there be a more wonderful comfort and encouragement to the child of God that he has been united to God? The rebel and the Sovereign—one! The vile sinner and the Holiest—one! He, by whom this unity is established, is not only our Mediator, but is our great and faithful Intercessor. There is not a moment that passes, not a trial or temptation that challenges us, not an enemy that attacks us, but that our Intercessor is unaware and prays for us. Indeed, Christ's intercessory work is personal. He does not see us as a part of a whole, but as an individual for whom He died.

We often revel in the words of Romans 8:35-39 where it asks, "Who shall separate us from the love of Christ? Shall tribulation, or distress, or persecution, or famine, or nakedness, or peril, or sword?" The answer, of course, is nothing. However, the answer is based on vs 34—nothing can separate us from God because Jesus is seated at the right hand of God interceding for us! Our salvation is a complete salvation because of the intercessory work of Jesus:

"Therefore He is also able to save to the uttermost those who come to God through Him, since He always lives to make intercession for them" Hebrews 7:25.

Puritan Quote:

"He [Jesus] is there, not unconcerned about us, not forgetful of us, but making intercession. He is agent for us there, an advocate for us, to answer all accusations, to put in our plea, and to prosecute it with effect, to appear for us and to present our petitions. And is not this abundant matter for comfort? What shall we say to these things? Is this the manner of men, O Lord God? What room is left for doubting and disquietment? Why art thou cast down, O my soul?" Matthew Henry, 1662-1714.

EXPECTANT PRAYER

Reading: 1 Kings 18:41-46
"There is a cloud, as small as a man's hand, rising out of the sea"
1 Kings 18:44

Previously, in this account of Elijah, God answered his prayer with a great display of power—He sent fire from heaven which burned his saturated sacrifice:

"Then the fire of the LORD fell and consumed the burnt sacrifice, and the wood and the stones and the dust, and it licked up the water that was in the trench" 1 Kings 18:38.

There was a severe famine in the land because it had not rained for a long time (1 Kings 17:7), even the Brook Cherith had dried up. In our reading, we find Elijah in prayer, seeking God's face and praying for rain. How encouraged he must have been when God sent fire to consume the sacrifice. Now he prayed for water. But his prayers were not mere words, he prayed with his ears open, listening for the expected rain, and with his eyes watching for it.

Herein lies the difference between Elijah's prayer and so many of ours. He prayed expectantly. His ears and eyes were tuned in to God, looking for any sign that God's answer was on its way.

What is our attitude when we pray? Do we pray that maybe God will see fit to answer? Do we pray hoping what we asked for is His will and perhaps He will answer?

Twenty-one times in the Old Testament we are told to "wait on" or "wait upon" the Lord. The Hebrew word translated "wait upon" is *qavah*, which means to wait expectantly:

"Are there any among the idols of the nations that can cause rain? Or can the heavens give showers? Are You not He, O

LORD our God? Therefore we will wait for You, since You have made all these" Jer 14:22.

It is the same word that is used to describe a servant's attitude toward his master (Psalm 123:2).

After pouring out his soul to God for rain, Elijah tells his servant to "Go up now, look toward the sea." He was expecting God to answer his prayer, and was looking for any sign to that effect.

Seven times the servant looked to the sky, and there wasn't a cloud in sight, but Elijah was not discouraged. On the seventh time he returned and reported, "There is a cloud, as small as a man's hand, rising out of the sea!" (1 Kings 18:44). That is all Elijah needed. That is what he expected. That is what he based his next action upon.

Remember the Canaanite woman who persistently pleaded with Jesus to heal her daughter from evil spirits—she did not give up even though her persistency aggravated the disciples (Matt 15:21-28). Her persistency was coupled with expectancy. That is how the scriptures teach us to pray.

Expectant prayer overcomes discouragement. There are times when we pray and do not see an answer; there is not a single cloud in the sky, there is no trace of an answer. We begin to doubt. Our expectancy weakens. Expectant prayer, however, looks beyond the cloudless skies. Expectant prayer goes again to pray and to look—seven times or more if necessary.

God does not always answer our prayer on the first time of asking. What a thrill when He does, but do not give up if He asks you to wait. It might be several or many years before a specific prayer is answered. Friends prayed diligently and expectantly for my restoration to the Lord. Twenty-three years later their prayers were answered.

"Wait on the LORD; be of good courage, and He shall strengthen your heart; Wait, I say, on the LORD!" Psalm 27:14.

Puritan Quote:
"Wait on the Lord. Wait at his door with prayer; wait at his foot with humility; wait at his table with service; wait at his window with expectancy" C.H. Spurgeon, 1834-1892.

WATCH AND PRAY

Reading: Matthew 26:36-46
"Watch and pray, lest you enter into temptation" Matthew 26:41

Scripture often presents us with combinations of words—mercy and truth (Psalm 85:10); righteousness and justice (Psalm 97:2; Hosea 2:19), and Paul frequently opened his letters with grace and peace (1 Cor 1:3). On more than one occasion, Jesus told His disciples to "watch and pray," an exhortation it behooves every child of God to take to heart.

A practical illustration of this is found when the Jews returned to Jerusalem following their 70 years of captivity in Babylon:

"Those who built on the wall, and those who carried burdens, loaded themselves so that with one hand they worked at construction, and with the other held a weapon. Every one of the builders had his sword girded at his side as he built" Nehemiah 4:17-18.

Prayer is a vital part of a believer's life. While the Holy Spirit works to conform (build) us into the image of Jesus, so we must watch and pray lest we fall into temptation. As we grow in Christ, we can be sure that our enemy will continually assault us with one goal in mind—to make us "fall into temptation." Peter speaks of Satan as a "roaring Lion":

"Be sober, be vigilant; because your adversary the devil walks about like a roaring lion, seeking whom he may devour. Resist him, steadfast in the faith" 1 Peter 5:8-9.

How do we resist the enemy? Peter says, "Be sober, be vigilant"; James says, "Submit yourselves to God, resist the devil, and he will flee from you. Draw near to God and He will draw near to you" (James 4:7-8), Jesus says, "Watch and pray, lest you fall into temptation."

We must be like the Jews of old when they built the walls of Jerusalem, we must have a trowel in one hand and a sword in the other. Our trowel is prayer, and our sword is the Word of God. With this combination alive and well in our lives, Satan faces a wall he cannot weaken or demolish.

The watchman spoken of in the Old Testament refers to one who stands guard in a tower built specifically on the city wall. His eyes were trained to look for anything unusual that might be the enemy (2 Kings 9:17-20). Watchmen were also employed by orchardists and ranchers to look for intruders that could steal the crop or livestock, whether it be man or animal.

The word used for "watch" is *greygoreo*, which means to be alert and vigilant, to guard. A soldier on guard is said to be "on watch."

This is true regarding our prayer life. As we pray, we must be on watch, we must watch against distractions, wandering, self-centered thoughts, and all types of imaginations. How often, while in prayer, do we find ourselves thinking of other non-sensical things? Have you ever fallen asleep while praying? We must be on guard for these devil initiated intrusions into our prayers. Some people find that praying aloud helps them to concentrate, while others find help by preparing a list of personal concerns and those for whom to pray. Whatever helps us to watch over our times of prayer is of value. If possible, we should pray when we are alert, not when we are tired.

Prayer is a critical part in a believer's life. Prayer is where spiritual life flourishes, but also where it decays—backsliding usually begins when we fail to pray or only pray when we can cram it into our busy schedule, for then we are usually tired. Our prayer life can serve as a barometer of our spiritual life.

Wandering thoughts, tiredness, and distracting cares invade our prayers like the vultures that continually came down to feast on Abraham's sacrifice, but "Abram drove them away" (Genesis 15:11).

There is another sense in which we should watch and pray—as we pray, watch for God's answer. Be on the lookout for circumstances that happen that may be God answering our prayer. Is God speaking to you from His Word? Is he using the advice of a friend? Is the Holy Spirit speaking directly to your heart?

The story is told of a man who climbed onto the roof of his house during a massive flood. He could not swim, so he prayed to God that

He would save him from drowning. Before too long a row boat, already carrying several people, pulled alongside the roof. "Climb in," the boatman said. "No thanks, the man replied, God will save me." The floods continued to rise until the man on the roof drowned. When he got to heaven, Peter met him at the pearly gates. The man asked, "I prayed that God would save me from drowning. Why didn't He?" Peter looked at him and said, "Do you remember the boat?"

A lighthearted story, but one that brings home a lesson. Sometimes God answers our prayers in a very simple and obvious way, and, if we are not watching for it, we may miss it. God does not always answer in a spectacular way. Sometimes He does not move mountains to answer our prayers—it could be as simple as a verse of scripture or a telephone call from a friend.

Puritan Quote:

"*The battle of prayer is against two things in the earthlies: wandering thoughts, and lack of intimacy with God's character as revealed in His word. Neither can be cured at once, but they can be cured by discipline*" Oswald Chambers, 1874-1917.

PRAY SINCERELY

Reading: Luke 18:9-14
"God, be merciful to me a sinner" Luke 18:13

This story told by Jesus is well known and its message clear—God is not impressed with our vain repetitions and religious rites. God is not interested in the expressiveness of our voice, the multitude of our words, or the eloquence of our expressions. Rather, He takes note of the sincerity of our heart. To pray sincerely is to be honest and frank with God, and to pray without pretense or deceit.

"The LORD is near to all who call upon Him, to all who call upon Him in truth" Psalm 145:18.

Sincerity and truth go hand in hand—they are like two oxen yoked together. Paul's prayer for the Philippian believers was

". . . that you may approve the things that are excellent, that you may be sincere and without offense till the day of Christ" Philippians 1:10.

The Greek word for sincere is *eilikrines* which means judged by sunlight. When a scribe sought to purchase a piece of high quality parchment, he would hold it up to the sun. If it had been repaired with wax, the light of the sun would show the repair. If it was pure and no wax seen, he would declare it to be "without wax," or *sincera* in Latin. When we pray, God knows if our prayers are *sincera*, without wax.

The cry of the tax collector caught Jesus' ear. It was short, to the point, and sincere, whereas the prayer of the Pharisee was wordy and self-aggrandizing.

Hezekiah understood this principle of prayer when he said:

"Remember now, O LORD, I pray, how I have walked before You in truth and with a loyal heart, and have done what was good in Your sight" 2 Kings 20:3.

Truth is very precious to God. Anything, including prayer, that is not sincere and true, is unacceptable to Him.

The reason sincerity and truth are combined is because it is possible to be sincerely wrong. There are many caught up in so called Christian denominations, sects, and cults, that are very sincere in what they believe, yet, we believe, are sincerely wrong in their understanding of God and His Word. Consider the Mormons who do not believe that Jesus is God, and Roman Catholics who look to their priests for forgiveness of sins, and who pray to Mary and various saints—none can deny that many of them are sincere in their beliefs, yet, we believe, are sincerely wrong.

At the end of his life, Joshua exhorted the Israelites to serve the Lord in sincerity and in truth (Joshua 24:14). The Hebrew word here translated sincerity is *tamiym,* and is elsewhere translated without blemish, complete, full, perfect, sound, without spot, undefiled, and upright. This word carries the same concept as the Latin word *sincera*—without wax.

True effective prayer carries no pretense. James puts it this way:

"The effective, fervent prayer of a righteous man avails much" James 5:16.

Prayer is not a complicated thing. All God asks is sincerity and truth from His children. He is not impressed with our rites and rituals, for they can be practiced by pretenders, by those who have not been made righteous by the blood of Jesus Christ. The Pharisee trusted in his own righteousness: *"I thank You that I am not like other men—extortioners, unjust, adulterers, or even as this tax collector. I fast twice a week; I give tithes of all that I possess" Luke 18:11-12.* Jesus was not impressed.

The only righteousness acceptable to God is that of His Son Jesus. We are acceptable to God only because we have been clothed in the righteousness of Jesus:

"I will greatly rejoice in the LORD, my soul shall be joyful in my God; for He has clothed me with the garments of salvation, He has covered me with the robe of righteousness" Isaiah 61:10.

Prayer is not a means of forcing our will upon God. It is, however, a means of enforcing His will into our lives. We must, therefore, offer our prayers in all sincerity and truth, for anything else is unacceptable to Him, and is a stench in His nostrils.

"LORD, who may abide in Your tabernacle? Who may dwell in Your holy hill? He who walks uprightly, and works righteousness, and speaks the truth in his heart" Psalm 15:5.

Puritan Quote:
"When the eye is single, when we are inward with God in what we do, are really what we appear to be, and mean honestly, then we are sincere" Matthew Henry, 1662-1714.

PRAY EARNESTLY

Reading: James 5:13-18
"Elijah . . . prayed earnestly" James 5:17

The Bible says Elijah prayed earnestly or "fervently" (ASV). In the Greek, most commentators agree, the words literally mean "he prayed with prayer." This is what is called a Hebraism. Jesus used this form of speech when He said, "With fervent desire I have desired to eat this Passover with you before I suffer" *Luke 22:15*. In other words, Elijah's prayer was more than a formal exercise, but he poured himself into his praying.

> *"A man may pray with his lips and yet not pray with an intense desire of the soul" Alexander Ross.*

Unless we fall into the trap of thinking such men of God had an exceptional walk with God, therefore their prayers were heard and answered, James explicitly states that "Elijah was a man with a nature like ours." In other words, he faced the same temptations and fought the same spiritual battles as we do. This is written so we might be encouraged by his example. In fact, this same introduction can be said of Moses, Samuel, David, Ezekiel, and every man and woman who saw their prayers answered.

One man who was greatly used by God was Martin Luther (1483-1546). Before we study the great things such men accomplished in the name of God, it is important to learn of their prayer life. No great work for God is accomplished before it is first bathed in prayer—earnest, fervent prayer.

It is recorded of Martin Luther that he set aside "the best two hours of every day alone with God." When he was facing a day that was particularly challenging, Luther told his friends, "*If I fail to spend two hours in prayer each morning, the devil gets the victory through the day. When I have so much business, I cannot get on without spending three hours daily in prayer.*"

This is not to say we must spend at least two hours a day in prayer, but that to Martin Luther, prayer was so essential to his everyday life, he felt the need to do so. Not everyone is called to take on such huge tasks for God as was Luther.

Phillip Melanchthon (1497-1560), Luther's most able and trusted assistant, overheard him praying aloud, as was his custom, for Luther said he wanted even the devil to hear what he was praying. Melanchthon said, *"Gracious God. What faith! What spirit! What reverence, and yet with what holy familiarity did Master Martin pray."*

To most of us, earnest prayer does not come easy—the devil makes sure of that. Satan's knees buckle when God's children pray earnestly. Satan fears the prayers of dedicated, sincere believers. It is the promise of Scripture:

"Therefore submit to God. Resist the devil and he will flee from you" James 4:7.

Prayer is hard work. Luther also wrote:

"There is no work like prayer. Mumbling with the mouth is easy . . . but with earnestness of heart to follow the words in deep devotion, that is, with desire and faith, so that one earnestly desires what the words say, and not to doubt that it will be heard: that is a great deed in God's eyes." Also, *"Prayer is a difficult matter and hard work. It is far more difficult than preaching the Word or performing other official duties in the church . . . this is the reason why it is so rare."*

One of Satan's masterful successes is to blind many Christians to the potential of prayer, and to the multitude of blessings available to us, and through us to others.

"Ah! How often, Christians, hath God kissed you at the beginning of prayer, and spoke peace to you in the midst of prayer, and filled you with joy and assurance upon the close of prayer" Thomas Brooks, 1608-1680).

We must ask ourselves, "How much importance do we place on prayer?" The answer lies in how much time we devote to prayer and meditation in God's Word? To those of us who have retired from our occupation, we should examine our days. What are our days now occupied with? What percentage of time is given to watching television, or working in the garden, compared to prayer and meditation? There is nothing wrong with watching some television programs (although quality programs are becoming fewer and fewer), or working in the garden, or other forms of exercise, but what percentage of time is given to prayer? It is a challenging question, isn't it?

"Be sober, be vigilant; because your adversary the devil walks about like a roaring lion, seeking whom he may devour. Resist him, steadfast in the faith, knowing that the same sufferings are experienced by your brotherhood in the world. But may the God of all grace, who called us to His eternal glory by Christ Jesus, after you have suffered a while, perfect, establish, strengthen, and settle you. To Him be the glory and the dominion forever and ever. Amen" 1 Peter 5:8-11.

Puritan Quote:

"Prayer itself must be a fervent, in-wrought, well-wrought prayer. It must be a pouring out of the heart to God; and it must proceed from a faith unfeigned" *Matthew Henry, 1662-1714.*

PRAY BELIEVING

Reading: Psalm 4:1-8
"Hear me when I call, O God of my righteousness!" Psalm 4:1

Has this not been the cry of each one of us at one time or another? Circumstances have so clouded our spiritual eyes that we question whether God hears our prayers or if He really cares. On such occasions, we forget the numerous times when He has heard and answered our prayers.

The name by which David addresses God is unique to this occasion—"O God of my righteousness." This is the only time this name is ascribed to God, and is very meaningful when see it in this context. One of the greatest strengths and encouragements to me is to remember and think on my justification, to remember that the righteousness of Jesus Christ has been imputed to me:

"Now it was not written for his (Abraham's) sake alone that it (righteousness) was imputed to him, but also for us. It shall be imputed to us who believe in Him who raised up Jesus our Lord from the dead" Romans 4:23-25, Parenthesis added).

When I remember, that when God sees and hears me, He sees the righteousness of His Son in me, then I can be sure He does hear my prayers. It is not always easy to believe the promises of scripture. One of Satan's most effective weapons is doubt, even to the point of doubting our salvation. It is imperative that we stay in God's Word whether we feel like it or not. It is also imperative that we pray whether we feel like it or not.

David reminded himself that he belonged to God. God was his righteousness, therefore he was counted among those whom God had "set apart" for Himself. Based on this truth, David boldly declared:

"The LORD will hear when I call to Him" Psalm 4:3.

Just because God does not answer us immediately, does not mean He is ignoring us or did not hear us. Patience is an important attribute in prayer. Another time, David said:

"I waited patiently for the LORD; and He inclined to me, and heard my cry" Psa. 40:1.

Scripture gives several examples where God delayed to answer prayer. The Lord promised Abraham that his seed would be innumerable, yet Isaac was not born until he was 100 years old, many years later. God promised David he would be king of Israel, yet for years he fled from Saul. He became so discouraged that he cried; "Now I shall perish someday by the hand of Saul. There is nothing better for me than that I should speedily escape to the land of the Philistines" 1 Samuel 27:1. Mary, the brother of Lazarus, even chided Jesus in her grief, "Lord, if You had been here, my brother would not have died" John 11:32. All their grief would have been avoided if Jesus had come as soon as He was called. But if He had not delayed, God would not have been glorified in the miraculous resurrection of her brother. Mary and Martha glorified God even more when they understood that Jesus did not delay, but came at the appropriate time according to God's plan. A greater miracle than healing was seen—Lazarus was raised from the dead.

We must believe that God's timing is perfect. He does not delay. His timing is perfect, it transcends ours. We must beware not to use "our time" as the standard by which God fulfills His purpose.

Not only does God delay in answering our prayers, but sometimes He denies it. Paul asked God three times to remove his *"thorn in the flesh,"* but God did not, instead He told him, "My grace is sufficient for you, for My strength is made perfect in weakness" 2 Cor 7-10. When God says "No" and makes it clear He will not answer your prayer, we must learn to accept it graciously:

"Therefore most gladly I will rather boast in my infirmities, that the power of Christ may rest upon me. Therefore I take pleasure in infirmities, in reproaches, in needs, in persecutions,

in distresses, for Christ's sake. For when I am weak, then I am strong" 2 Cor 12:9-10.

Moses asked God to allow him to "see the good land beyond the Jordan, those pleasant mountains, and Lebanon," but God denied his request because of his act of anger and unbelief. Although God forgave him, He said, "Enough of that! Speak no more to Me of this matter" Deut 3:25-27. When God declines our request, we are wasting our breath and dishonoring Him if we continue with the same prayer.

To those who love God and truly seek to honor Him in their life, the Holy Spirit will convince them of God's answer—immediate, delayed, or "No."

Puritan Quote:

"If God defers or prolongs to grant our petitions, even so long that He seems apparently to reject us, yet let us not cease to call; prescribing Him either time, neither manner of deliverance, as it is written, 'Let not the faithful be too hasty, for God sometimes defers and will not hastily grant, to the probation of our continuance' as the words of Jesus Christ testify" John Knox—1514-1572.

PRAYER AND THE SOVEREIGNTY OF GOD

Reading: James 4:13-16
". . . if we ask anything according to His will, He hears us" 1 John 5:14

The debate concerning prayer and Sovereignty of God has been ongoing for centuries, and continues today. The question is asked: If God has ordained all things that come to pass, then why should we bother to pray?

A plaque that hangs on walls in many believer's homes and churches, states that "Prayer changes things." But does it? Is this a true statement, or is it based on an over emphasis of the free-will of man?

The statement "Prayer changes things" is a half-truth.

"A half-truth that represents a whole truth is a no truth that soon becomes an anti-truth" John Reisinger, *The Sovereignty of God in Prayer.*

If prayer changes things, in the way many Christians believe, then we are conceding that we can change God's mind from that which He originally purposed. If this is true, it dethrones God and places us there instead.

If we can by prayer change the mind of God, it must be a change for the better or a change for the worse. If He could be changed for the better, then He was not perfect before He changed. If He could change for the worse, then He would be less than perfect after He changed. God is very dogmatic when He says, "I am the LORD, I do not change" Malachi 3:6.

The reason the phrase "Prayer changes things" is a half-truth, is based on our understanding of the word "things". If we think we can change God's mind about His planned purpose for our lives, or convince Him to give us things we want, then we are misguided as to the power of prayer. However, if by "things" we mean our growth in, and understanding of, Jesus Christ, then our prayers are according to the will of God:

"Now this is the confidence that we have in Him, that if we ask anything according to His will, He hears us. And if we know that He hears us, whatever we ask, we know that we have the petitions that we have asked of Him" 1 John 5:14-15.

Prayer is not meant to change what we have or give us what we want, but to change us. Prayer will change us, not God. We are encouraged to pray for others, that God will comfort the downtrodden, encourage the depressed, and give strength to the persecuted. God has already promised to provide us with food and clothing and our daily needs:

"Therefore do not worry, saying, 'What shall we eat?' or 'What shall we drink?' or 'What shall we wear?' For after all these things the Gentiles seek. For your heavenly Father knows that you need all these things. But seek first the kingdom of God and His righteousness, and all these things shall be added to you" Matthew 6:31-34

Those who propagate the "name it and claim it" doctrine misguide their congregations and ignore the Sovereignty of God. If we ask God for something He does not want us to have, will He lay aside His will and submit to ours? For our prayers to be answered, they must be in accordance with *His* will.

James addressed this when he wrote:

"And even when you do ask, you don't get it because your whole motive is wrong—you want only what will give you pleasure" James 4:3, NLT.

John G. Reisinger, in his little book The Sovereignty of God in Prayer (which I highly recommend), suggests we must ask ourselves three questions before we use 1 John 5:14-15:

1) *Is my earnest desire to do **the will of God** (John17:7)?* To pray for anything without this desire in our hearts is a waste of time.

2) *Am I seeking God's wisdom in His Word in order to* **discover His will for me** *in all of my life?* Again, prayer for what I want with willful ignorance of what God wants cannot be called prayer.

3) *Can I honestly pray in the same attitude as my blessed Lord when He said, "Nevertheless,* **not My will, but Thy will** *be done"?* Am I greater than my Master when I pray?

It is so vitally important that we do not neglect the reading of God's Word—not just reading, but meditating on what we read. Just as Mary pondered the words of the shepherds (Luke 2:19), so should we ponder the words, principles, and directives of scripture. God sometimes shows us His will directly by the Holy Spirit, but more frequently in the reading of His Word.

Puritan Quote:

"I take my stand on the declaration of Paul, that no prayer is genuine which springs not from faith, and that faith cometh by the Word of God. In these words he has, if I mistake not, distinctly intimated that the Word of God is the only sure foundation for prayer. It is, however, still more conclusive of the point, when he declares that prayer depends on the Word of God" John Calvin. 1509-1564.

PRAY WITHOUT CEASING

Reading: 1 Thessalonians 5:12-19
"Pray without ceasing" 1 Thessalonians 5:17

Our text for this week's meditation is difficult to understand when taken as a stand-alone exhortation. For us to "Pray without ceasing" is impossible, so, as with all scripture, it must be considered in its context. Immediately preceding it is another short, direct, exhortation, "Rejoice always," followed by yet another, "In everything give thanks".

The reader is told "Rejoice always"; but what does that mean? Although a strong body of believers, the Thessalonians suffered opposition from the Greek Jews, including defamatory lies about Paul and Silas. It was not easy to be a Christian in the early church, so, among other things, Paul exhorts them to "Rejoice always." Now, as then, we might ask, "How can I rejoice always? How can I be joyful when I am faced with opposition and persecution?" Paul answers, "Pray without ceasing," or "fight opposition with prayer."

Prayer is not a resource we fall back on or practice for fifteen minutes a day, but is an attitude we as believers should develop and carry with us twenty-four hours a day. Charles Spurgeon was thought to be mentally handicapped by one man who approached him on the street. It appeared he was talking to himself, but he was actually praying as he walked. Eli thought Hannah was drunk when he observed her lips moving but she was silent. When challenged, she replied:

"No, my lord, I am a woman of sorrowful spirit. I have drunk neither wine nor intoxicating drink, but have poured out my soul before the LORD" 1 Samuel 1:15.

When we have an attitude of prayer, we can pray at any time and anywhere. Has your heart responded in praise to God when standing before a magnificent view? Have you felt the leading of the Holy Spirit to pray while driving? Do you find yourself unexpectedly thinking of a friend in need during the day? Have you awakened in the middle of the night with a specific burden on your heart? These things do not just happen—if you are walking with the Lord, these occasions are prompted by the Holy Spirit, and, because you have the attitude of prayer, you pray.

Albert Barnes wrote about this attitude: "when alone, to improve any moment of leisure which we may have when we feel ourselves strongly inclined to pray."

The exhortation that follows our text "Pray without ceasing" is "In everything give thanks."

"When joy and prayer are married their first born child is gratitude" C.H. Spurgeon.

These three texts present the life of a true Christian, and the link that connects them is prayer. Rejoicing is the result of prayer, and prayer leads to thanksgiving when we see answers to our prayers and feel it an unbelievable honor and privilege to spend time with God at His throne of grace. Yes, even though we are invited to *"come boldly to the throne of grace,"* we should not take it lightly, for it is indeed a privilege reserved for those who love God, and are the called according to His purpose.

Under the Old Covenant, access to the Mercy Seat was restricted to one man once a year:

> **"and the LORD said to Moses: 'Tell Aaron your brother not to come at just any time into the Holy Place inside the veil, before the mercy seat which is on the ark, lest he die; for I will appear in the cloud above the mercy seat'" Leviticus 16:2.**
> **"But into the second part the high priest went alone once a year" Hebrews 9:7.**

How different for you and I. The veil that hung before the Holy Place has been torn in two (Matthew 27:51), so that the mercy seat, God's throne of grace, is accessible to every child of God, to every one who is born again by His Spirit.

"The dead of night is not too late for God; the breaking of the morning, when the first grey light is seen, is not too early for the Most High; at

midday he is not too busy; and when the evening gathers he is not weary with his children's prayers" C.H. Spurgeon.

One thing implied in our text is that we should never be in a place where we cannot continue to pray. This applies to books we read, television programs we watch, friends with whom we keep company—anything in which you would feel embarrassed to include Jesus. Consider Jesus sitting, walking, and watching with you. He is, in fact, closer than that—He lives in you—"Christ in you, the hope of glory" Colossians 1:27. In other words, have nothing to do with that upon which you cannot invoke God's blessing.

Prayer—an honor.

Prayer—a privilege.

Prayer—an invitation to every child of God.

Prayer—communion with our Creator at any time.

Prayer—the source of joy and thanksgiving.

Puritan Quotes:

"There has been evil done to the soul if it is not prepared for communion with God at all times, and if it would not find pleasure in approaching his holy throne" Albert Barnes, 1798-1870.

"Anything that is right for you to do you may consecrate with prayer, and let this be a sure gauge and test to you, if you feel that it would be an insult to the majesty of heaven for you to ask the Lord's blessing upon what is proposed to you, then stand clear of the unholy thing. If God doth not approve, neither must you have fellowship therewith" C.H. Spurgeon, 1834-1892.

NEW CREATION

Reading: 2 Corinthians 5:12-19

"... old things have passed away; behold, all things have become new"
2 Corinthians 5:17

Today I would like to begin a series of meditations on the phrase "all things" as found in scripture. This little two word phrase carries such a large and important concept, and has been on my heart for some time.

The gospel of salvation is not a partial redemption, but a full and complete one. When we are saved, the blood of Jesus Christ saves us from God's condemnation by cleansing us from sin—every sin is forgiven.—past, present and future. Satan may try to convince us that some sins are just too bad that even God cannot forgive them. That is not the gospel of Jesus Christ. Salvation encompasses every sin, if it did not do so, God would still have ground to condemn us, but

"there is therefore now no condemnation to those who are in Christ Jesus, who do not walk according to the flesh, but according to the Spirit" Romans 8:1.

There is no hidden or secret sin that the Holy Spirit overlooked when He transacted our new birth, therefore, the "all things" in our text—"old things have passed away; behold, all things have become new." These words are the explanation of the previous statement, *"if anyone is in Christ, he is a new creation."* Salvation is defined as a "new creation."

When sin entered the world, Adam and Eve did not receive a different body, but their souls were affected. Their souls came under the curse of death—the condemnation of God. So, when the Bible says "all things are made new," it is speaking of our soul. Sin caused communion with God to be impossible, but salvation brings about reconciliation to Him.

Salvation is a new birth for the soul. If a person claims to have been saved, and there is no change in their character—their morals, ethics, attitude, etc.—then they are not saved. If they continue to participate in a way of life that the Bible says is displeasing to God, and there is no evident change, they have not been born again.

"That a change is produced so great as to make it proper to say that he is a new man. He has new views, new motives, new principles, new objects and plans of life. He seeks new purposes, and he lives for new ends . . . There is such a change as to make the language proper. And so in the conversion of a sinner. There is a change so deep, so clear, so entire, and so abiding, that it is proper to say, here is a new creation of God, a work of the divine power as decided and as glorious as when God created all things out of nothing" Albert Barnes.

Out text is a declaration of God's power and of the effectiveness of the blood of Christ. Elsewhere, Paul tells us to put off the "old man" and put on the "new man":

"put off, concerning your former conduct, the old man which grows corrupt according to the deceitful lusts, and be renewed in the spirit of your mind, and that you put on the new man which was created according to God, in true righteousness and holiness" Ephesians 4:22-24.

To the Colossian believers, Paul names some of the "old things": "anger, wrath, malice, blasphemy, filthy language. lies", then goes on to list some characteristics of the "new man": "tender mercies, kindness, humility, meekness, longsuffering; bearing with one another, and forgiving one another, love, and peace". And how is this to be done? "Let the word of Christ dwell in you richly" Colossians 3:8-16.

There is a distinct difference between the one who remains under God's condemnation, and the born again child of God:

+   The one is said to be *"dead in his trespasses and sins"*, while the other is *"made alive"* Eph 2:1;
+   The one *"walks in darkness"*, and the other in *"light"* John 8:12; Eph 5:8; 1 Peter 2:9;

+ The one is in *"bondage"*, while the other enjoys the *"liberty by which Christ has made us free"* Gal 5:1;
+ The one is at *"enmity"* with God, while the other has been *"reconciled"* to Him; compare Rom 8:7 with 2 Cor 5:18.
+ The one will *"perish"* while the other has *"eternal life"* John 3:16;

Many others could be listed, but suffice it to say that these "old things" have passed away, and to the one who is truly born again, "all things have become new."

Therefore,

"Just as Christ was raised from the dead by the glory of the Father, even so we also should walk in newness of life" Romans 6:4;
"But now we have been delivered from the law, having died to what we were held by, so that we should serve in the newness of the Spirit and not in the oldness of the letter" Romans 7:6.

Puritan Quote:

". . . very man by his own natural will hates God; but when he is turned unto the Lord, by evangelical repentance, then his will is changed; then your consciences, now hardened and benumbed, shall be quickened and awakened; then your hard hearts shall be melted, and your unruly affections shall be crucified. Thus, by that repentance, the whole soul will be changed, you will have new inclinations, new desires, and new habits" George Whitfield, 1714-1770.

RECONCILIATION

Reading: 2 Corinthians 5:12-19
"Now all things are of God" 2 Corinthians 5:18

In our previous meditation we considered that conversion is equivalent to a new creation (2 Cor 5:17). When we are born again, we are given a new heart, a new nature. The following verse tells us that all these things come from God.

The Greek word *pas* is a common word (used over 1200 times) and denotes "all," "each," and "every".

> "Every (*pas*) good gift and every (*pas*) perfect gift is from above, and comes down from the Father of lights, with whom there is no variation or shadow of turning" James 1:17.

The immediate result of God's new creation is reconciliation with Him. Man, who, because of sin, lost all communication and relationship with God, has now been brought together with Him. Everything that brought about our separation from God has been dealt with by the blood and sacrifice of Jesus Christ. This is such a complete work that Paul can say:

> "Who shall separate us from the love of Christ? Shall tribulation, or distress, or persecution, or famine, or nakedness, or peril, or sword? . . . For I am persuaded that neither death nor life, nor angels nor principalities nor powers, nor things present nor things to come, nor height nor depth, nor any other created thing, shall be able to separate us from the love of God which is in Christ Jesus our Lord" Romans 8:35-39.

The word reconciliation carries the thought that there was, at one time, a relationship between the two parties. When we are born again by

the Spirit of God, that relationship has been restored. The two parties—
He who was "dead in trespasses and sins," and He who is so Holy that
He cannot look upon sin (Habakkuk 1:13), have been reconciled. He
who was an enemy of God is now a child of God. He, who was under the
condemnation of God, has now been made one with Him. He, who was
bound for hell, is now the possessor of everlasting life.

While the majority of Christians readily agree that God is the Source
and Provider of all things in general, our text is referring specifically to
everything involved in our new nature. The creation of our new nature is
the fulfillment of God's promise through Ezekiel:

**"I will give you a new heart and put a new spirit within you; I
will take the heart of stone out of your flesh and give you a heart
of flesh. I will put My Spirit within you and cause you to walk
in My statutes, and you will keep My judgments and do them"
Ezekiel 36:26-27.**

Only those who are reconciled to God will have the desire and ability
to walk in His statutes. "If anyone loves Me," said Jesus, "he will keep My
word; and My Father will love him, and We will come to him and make
Our home with him" (John 14:23). That is reconciliation.

The hugs and kisses of the father welcoming his prodigal son is a
glorious picture of reconciliation (Luke 15:20). When Jacob travelled to
Egypt to be with Joseph, his son, also depicts the doctrine of reconciliation
(Gen 46:29). But none is greater than when God and man meet at the cross
where the bleeding Son of God died for our reconciliation with God.

In what way are "all things" of God? First: Directly based on the
context, everything to do with the new nature God gives His children is of
Him. Man has nothing to do with his or her salvation. Remember, every
person is a sinner, from birth to death, unless they are reconciled to God.
Before our new birth, we were all "dead in our trespasses and sins" (Eph
2:1), and dead men can do nothing of themselves. Therefore, any change to
the one who is dead, has to come from someone else, someone who is alive.
God is Life, Eternal Life, and this is what He gives to those who, by the
grace of God, believe.

How helpless guilty nature lies,
Unconscious of her load,
The heart unchanged can never rise
To happiness and God.

Second: "All things", period, are of God. He is the Creator, and "all things" are the result of His creative power:

"Thus says the LORD, your Redeemer, and He who formed you from the womb: "I am the LORD, who makes all things, who stretches out the heavens all alone, who spreads abroad the earth by Myself; who frustrates the signs of the babblers, and drives diviners mad . . ." Isaiah 44:24-25.

Puritan Quote:

"Everything moreover with regard to the new nature is of God, not merely as to its first implanting, but as to its subsequent outworking and full development. Has the believer strength—it is of God. Does he stand, and is he kept from falling—his standing is of God. Is he preserved in the midst of temptation true to his covenant, and does he stand in the day of trial firm to his Master—his integrity is of God" C.H. Spurgeon, 1834-1892.

THE SOURCE

Reading: 1 Chronicles 29:6-20
"For all things come from you" 1 Chronicles 29:14

When I read these words of David I feel so inadequate before God. We recently concluded a series of thoughts on Biblical prayer, well, here is another one. This is a magnificent prayer, one that speaks of a close and confident relationship with God, one that speaks to the total dependence of David upon God.

When I think of my prayers to the same Almighty God, I am aware of my lack of appreciation of who God is—of His greatness, power, and majesty. Yet, at the same time, I thank God He hears the simple heartfelt cry of the sinner, "Jesus, Son of David, have mercy on me!" Mark 10:47. God is not impressed by our eloquence, but by the sincerity in our heart.

It is interesting to note the number of times David uses the word *kol* in his prayer. *Kol* is the Hebrew equivalent to the Greek *pas* (all) we considered last week in 2 Corinthians 5:18—it means "all," "each," and "every".

Consider this word in David's prayer:

+ "all that is in heaven and in earth is Yours" vs 11
+ "You are exalted as head over all" vs 11
+ "You reign over all" vs 12
+ "In Your hand it is to make great and to give strength to all" vs 12
+ All things come from You" vs 14
+ "All [is] Your own" vs 16.

It is clear that God is both Sovereign and the Source of all things. All that exists belongs to Him, and He is the Head over these things and rules over them. He owns everything as is His right as the Creator, and He is the Source of everything we are and receive. Is there anything more conclusive than this?

The context of David's prayer is the construction of God's house. He wanted to build a temple for God, but God told him that honor was to go to Solomon, his son. This must have been a great disappointment to David, yet he went ahead and made provision for the construction. He gave Solomon the plans he had received "by the Spirit" of God" (28:11-12), along with the necessary gold and silver required for "all articles used in every kind of service" (28:14). He not only collected from others the necessary gold, silver, etc., but he gave from his personal wealth (29:3-4). After setting this example of giving, David challenges the people,

"Who then is willing to consecrate himself this day to the LORD?" 1 Chronicles 29:5.

David did not consider his contribution a sacrifice, for he acknowledged that all he had came from the hand of God:

"But who am I, and who are my people, that we should be able to offer so willingly as this? For all things come from You, and of Your own we have given You" 1 Chronicles 29:14.
"O LORD our God, all this abundance that we have prepared to build You a house for Your holy name is from Your hand, and is all Your own" 1 Chronicles 29:16-17.

When we give to the Lord, whether it is in the form of money, time, or service, we are returning to Him that which He has already given to us. God is glorified when we give to Him, not by the amount, but by our obedience to what He asks of us. It is impossible to give to God anything that did not originate from His hand.

"For all things originate with Him and come from Him; all things live through Him, and all things center in and tend to consummate and to end in Him" Romans11:36, AMP.

The first thing David mentions after making the statement "all that is in heaven and in earth is Yours" is "Yours is the kingdom, O LORD" vs11.

David, appointed by God as king over His chosen people, acknowledges before the people that the kingdom belongs to God.

"Yours, O LORD, is the greatness, the power and the glory, the victory and the majesty" vs 11.

Similar words were said by Jesus when He taught His disciples to pray: "Yours is the kingdom and the power and the glory forever" Matthew 6:13. God, the Creator of all things, is the Supreme Sovereign over all He has made. He is the Monarch over the Kingdom He created.

"You reign over all" declares David, and when compared to You, O God, "Who am I, and who are my people?" vs14. The greatest servants of God acknowledge their insignificance and unworthiness before Him. Men like Jacob (Gen 32:10), Job (Job 42:5-6), Isaiah (Isaiah 6:5), Ezekiel (Ezek 1:28), and John (Rev 1:17). The only response possible when God begins to open our eyes to a fraction of His glory and greatness, is to confess our unworthiness.

That which is ascribed to God—greatness, power, glory, victory, majesty, and might—is the source of the strength He gives us:

"In Your hand is power and might; in Your hand it is to make great and to give strength to all" vs 12.

Is there any wonder that Paul could say, "I can do all things through Christ who strengthens me"? Phil 4:13. Jesus said, "With God all things are possible" Matt 19:26. This is truth we can depend on, because "all things come from God [You]."

Puritan Quote:

"All things are of God, for He is the Author of all; His will is the origin of all existence. All things are through Him, for all things are created by Him as the grand agent. All things are likewise to Him for all things tend to his <u>glory</u> as their final end" John Gill, 1697-1771.

GOD IS ABLE

Reading: Matthew 19:23-30
"With God all things are possible" Matthew 19:26

Paul defines the gospel as "the power of God to salvation" (Romans 1:16). No person can be saved from the penalty of their sins apart from the power of God. The unregenerate man is so held in the grip (power) of Satan, that nothing but the power of Almighty God can release him. Worldly riches and wealth is one of those things that requires the power (*dunamis—dynamite*) of God to break the chain that imprisons a man in his sin.

It is not impossible for a rich person to be saved, but their wealth so often has a stranglehold on them that it is an obstacle most of them have. The disciples, to whom Jesus was speaking, were not wealthy; they were of the working class. There are two things we must be careful not to assume, 1) It is sinful to be rich, and 2) Rich people cannot be saved. That is not what the Bible teaches.

An abundance of wealth can be, however, a great deterrent that stands in the way of salvation, one that the majority of us do not have.

> "[Jesus] said this to his disciples, who were poor, and had but little in the world, to reconcile them to their condition with this, that the less they had of worldly wealth, the less hindrance they had in the way to heaven" *Matthew Henry*.

It is very unusual for a rich man to not be absorbed by his wealth; and it is impossible for a man that sets his heart upon his riches, to get to heaven:

> **"Do not love the world or the things in the world. If anyone loves the world, the love of the Father is not in him. For all that is in the world—the lust of the flesh, the lust of the eyes, and**

the pride of life—is not of the Father but is of the world" 1 John 2:15-16.

James tells us that "friendship with the world is enmity with God? Whoever therefore wants to be a friend of the world makes himself an enemy of God" James 4:4. An abundance of wealth has such a hold on a person, it appears that an extra portion of grace is needed to break them free from its hold. Again, it is James who says, "He gives more grace" James 4:6.

The illustration Jesus gives that it is "easier for a camel to go through the eye of a needle" has been given several meanings over the years. One popular theory is that the eye of a needle refers to a small gate in Jerusalem which opened after the main gate was closed at night. A camel could only pass through this smaller gate if it was stooped and had its baggage removed. This thought has been expounded since at least the 15th century, and possibly as far back as the 9th century. However, there is no evidence for the existence of such a gate.

Variations on this story include that of ancient inns having small entrances to deter thieves, or a story of an old mountain pass known as the "eye of the needle", so narrow that merchants would have to dismount from their camels and were therefore more vulnerable to waiting bandits. There is no historical evidence for any of these, either.

Another possible solution comes from the possibility of a Greek misprint. The suggestion is that the Greek word *kamelos* ('camel') should really be *kamêlos*, meaning 'cable, rope', as some late New Testament manuscripts say. It is therefore easier to thread a needle with a rope rather than a strand of cotton than for a rich man to enter the kingdom. Calvin suggests the word *camel* denotes a rope used by sailors, rather than the animal so named.

However you look at it, the meaning is the important thing here. That which is impossible for man is possible with God. In fact, "all things" are possible with God—no exceptions. If God wanted to create a universe out of nothing, He could do it. If God wanted to teach His prophet a lesson by having a "big fish" swallow him and three days later vomit him onto a beach, that would be no problem. If God wanted to redeem His elect from the clutches of Satan, He could do it. If God wanted to save a rich man, He can do it. If God wanted to take a poor fisherman and turn him into a miracle-working preacher of the gospel, He could do it. If God wants to preserve His children from the clutches of Satan, He will do it. If God wants to create a new heaven and new earth, and place His redeemed people on it, He can do it. There are no exceptions to what God can do, therefore the words "all things."

The words of Jesus to His disciples should bring comfort and encouragement to everyone who knows Him and loves Him: "With God all things are possible." Read the numerous promises of God to His children—God is able to keep them. Jesus said, "I will build My church"—He is able. As far as salvation is concerned:

"He is also able to save to the uttermost those who come to God through Him" Hebrews 7:25.

"Now to Him who is able to keep you from stumbling, and to present you faultless before the presence of His glory with exceeding joy, to God our Savior, Who alone is wise, be glory and majesty, dominion and power, both now and forever. Amen" Jude 24-25.

Puritan Quote:

"God is able to do more than man can understand" Thomas À Kempis, Imitation of Christ

GOD'S PROVIDENCE

Reading: Romans 8:26-30
"All things work together for good!" Romans 8:28

The above text might well be the most well known and most often quoted of the "all things" statements in scripture. Whenever something goes wrong or some adverse circumstance arises, our well-meaning friends remind us of this verse.

While this statement is true, I question whether or not I really believe it. Shall all my severe trials, troubles, and afflictions work together for my good? The answer is a resounding "Yes", but they are not necessarily good when they stand alone—they usually must be seen and accepted in the context of other things.

An unexpected circumstance might happen which, at the time, may be devastating. For the child of God who is walking in close communion with Him, the Holy Spirit will often bring that circumstance into line with what God has been teaching him, or it will bring enlightenment as to the direction or next step He wants him to take. Never does anything happen "just because"!

James Smith suggests that things outward are often coupled with things inward; things painful with things pleasant; joyous and grievous; gains and losses, victories and defeats, all work together!

God oversees the working, so as to secure our good and fulfill His purpose in our life. God aims at our real and lasting good in all that He does, and in all that He permits. He does nothing, nor allows anything to be done, which affects us but what we shall bless and praise Him for, when we see the entire whole in the light of providence.

Remember, these words do not stand alone—they are qualified by the preceding words and those that follow, "to those who love God, to those who are the called according to His purpose."

From verse 18, Paul speaks of sufferings, futility, groans and labors, weaknesses—things the children of God will face in their lifetime. He then draws this conclusion from what has just been said, that, so far are the troubles of this life from hindering our salvation, that, on the contrary, they are helps to it.

Immediately before the "all things work together for good" statement, Paul reminds us that the Spirit of God "makes intercession for the saints according to the will of God."

Nothing comes into the life of a child of God that is neither sent nor permitted by God's divine providence, or, as scripture states, "according to the will of God." All things are governed by God's will. Events may take us by surprise, but never is God surprised.

Let us also take note of the words, "work together." The things that shape our life, especially our Christian life, work together in opposition to their apparent confliction. There is no opposition in God's providence.

"The raven wing of war is co-worker with the dove of peace. The tempest strives not with the peaceful calm—they are linked together and work together, although they seem to be in opposition" Charles Spurgeon.

To the human mind, some events seem to be in conflict, but, by faith, we accept that, under God's governing hand, they work together in unison.

Not only do all things work together, but they do so for our "good." Well may we wonder, "What good is coming because I am laid up sick?" or "What good can possibly come by me losing my job?" Jesus, hanging on a cross, wounded, bleeding, and dying,

"cried out with a loud voice, saying, 'Eli, Eli, lama sabachthani?' that is, 'My God, My God, why have You forsaken Me?'" Matthew 27:46.

Jesus took our sin upon Himself, He actually became sin, and the Bible tells us that God is "of purer eyes than to behold evil, and cannot look on wickedness" (Habakkuk 1:13), therefore He turned away from His Son. What good could possibly come of this? John 3:16 gives us the answer:

"God so loved the world that He gave His only begotten Son, that whoever believes in Him should not perish but have everlasting life."

The greatest good that God has ever bestowed on man came from the greatest act of injustice the world has ever known.

Every day we are faced with circumstances where we have to make decisions, decisions as to how we respond—with irritability and anger or with calm and peace. In other words, which nature comes to the forefront, the old man or the new man? Just when we think the old man is dead and buried, he raises his ugly head and shows us he is still alive and active. The good that comes from these instances is that they often lead to our spiritual growth—if we respond with the old man, the Spirit will convict us until we ask for forgiveness, and hopefully will respond differently the next time we face such a temptation.

Another important word in our text is "will." This is not a maybe or a perhaps, it is a definite. Faith will grasp this as fact even though its reality may not be immediately evident.

Puritan Quote:

"Your being sick very probably might not be for your good only, God has something to follow your sickness, some blessed deliverance to follow your poverty, and he knows that when he has mixed the different experiences of your life together, they shall produce good for your soul, and eternal good for your spirit" C.H. Spurgeon.

INCOMPARABLE GOD

Reading: Mark 7:31-37
"He has done all things well" Mark 7:37

In the Book of Isaiah we read, "To whom then will you liken God? Or what likeness will you compare to Him?" (Isaiah 40:18). Indeed, the God whom we love and worship is incomparable. Throughout history man has tried to find fault with God. They think their intelligence is superior to that of their Creator, and they will be elevated in their own mind, as well as that of others, if they can cast doubt on the incomparableness of God.

When Israel turned from God and made idols to worship, He reminded them of how He had cared for them, and said:

"To whom will you liken Me, and make Me equal and compare Me, that we should be alike" Isaiah 46:5.

Not only is God perfect in who He is—His glorious attributes and character—but He is perfect in all that He has done, is doing, and will do. How can He that is perfect in His Being perform and produce anything that is imperfect? If we could but see God through the eyes of angels and our departed brothers and sisters, we would proclaim, without any doubt and with full assurance, that "He has done all things well."

As we are today, surrounded by evil and wickedness at every turn, we "live by faith" Galatians 2:20. By faith, we believe our salvation guarantees us eternal live and deliverance from the condemning wrath of God. By faith, we believe we have been reconciled to God, and we have a personal relationship with Him, and that God is with us and in us. By faith, we believe Jesus Christ sits at the right hand of His Father interceding on our behalf. By faith we believe Jesus will soon return in glory and triumph to gather His completed church to Himself so we can live for ever with Him on His new earth and heavens. By faith, therefore, we believe "He has done all things well."

No matter what we read in the newspapers or see on television, we believe "He has done all things well."

No matter our personal circumstance with its trials and challenges, we believe "He has done all things well."

No matter the seemingly perpetual bombardment of temptations and failures, we believe "He has done all things well."

No matter what, by faith in Him, we believe "He is able to aid those who are tempted" Hebrews 2:18.

No matter what, by faith, we believe "He is able to keep what I have committed to Him until that Day" 2 Timothy 1:12.

No matter what, by faith, we believe "He is also able to save to the uttermost those who come to God through Him" Hebrews 7:25.

No matter what, by faith, we believe "He has done all things well" Mark 7:37.

I was once told that my "so called faith" is nothing but a "crutch" upon which I lean to avoid the realities of life. That same person told me Jesus Christ is my "imaginary friend." Another said I am like an Ostrich that buries its head in the sand. In these things I am not alone. Christians throughout the centuries have been ridiculed because of their undying faith.

Jesus is declared to be "the Wisdom of God" 1Cor 1:24. Study the universe and you will see the "Wisdom of God" at work. Look through the microscope and discover the "Wisdom of God" in the world of irreducible minimums. In the book of beginnings (Genesis), this fact is stated as the truth of the ages:

"Then God looked over all he had made, and he saw that it was excellent in every way" Genesis 1:31, NLT.

Jesus is the Creator and Preserver of all things:

"For by Him all things were created that are in heaven and that are on earth, visible and invisible, whether thrones or dominions or principalities or powers. All things were created through Him and for Him. And He is before all things, and in Him all things consist. And He is the head of the body, the church, who

is the beginning, the firstborn from the dead, that in all things He may have the preeminence" Colossians 1:16-18.

Consider Jesus as our Redeemer; our Intercessor and mediator; the Good Shepherd and Preserver of our soul; our Rock and Refuge in the time of trouble; consider Him in every possible way, and you will find "He has done all things well."

Pilate spoke for all mankind when three times he told the Jews, "I find no fault in Him" John 18:38; 19:4, 6. Jesus was accused of blasphemy because He said He was the Son of God (John 10:36; 19:27). The Jews did not point to the miracles Jesus performed, or any other aspect of His life, other than when He claimed to be the Son of God, for all that He did while on this earth, He did well.

The entire existence of the Son of God can be summarized by the words, "He has done all things well."

Puritan Quote:

"*It is a consolation to know that Jesus reigns, and that all things, all creatures, and all events are in His hands, and beneath His control. Oh, what a privilege for such worms of the earth to have fellowship with the great and mighty God of the universe, and such nearness of access to the very heart of a precious Jesus!*" *Mary Winslow, 1774-1854, Mother of Octavius Winslow.*

ABOVE ALL THINGS

Reading: Ephesians 1:3-23
"He put all things under His feet" Ephesians 1:22

Our reading today is one of those gems of scripture that shines brighter each time it is read. Marvelous truths of each member of the Trinity are disclosed as the works of our heavenly Father are revealed from before the foundation of the world to the end of time itself.

Jesus Christ is the center and all-encompassing subject of the Father's work. As Paul wrote elsewhere:

"All things were created through Him and for Him. And He is before all things, and in Him all things consist" Colossians 1:16-18.

This glorious declaration of the work of the Father is summarized in the words,

"And He put all things under His feet" Ephesians 1:22.

This reality was not only true at the time of Paul's writing, but for all time and eternity. Three days after His Son was executed on a cross, His Father raised Him from the dead, then, forty days later, that same power that raised Jesus from the dead, took Him from this earth, seated Him at His right hand, and "put all things under His feet."

When we look around us, it is sometimes difficult to accept this truth as fact. Everywhere we turn man is fighting against God and appears to be winning. Prayers can no longer be said in our schools, teachers cannot mention the name of Jesus for fear they will lose their jobs, plaques containing the Ten Commandments have been stripped from court houses, and depictions of the nativity cannot be placed in public areas. A young boy was sent home from school to change his shirt because it had the words "Jesus Lives" on it,—the list can go on.

Scripture often presents that which is ordained of God as current fact. By faith, we believe God's Word that "all things are under His feet." By faith, we believe Jesus is building His church—of this there is ample proof. Even in countries where to name the name of Jesus is certain death, the church is growing—sometimes faster than in many of our local churches.

Paul broadens the stroke when he wrote:

"Then comes the end, when He delivers the kingdom to God the Father, when He puts an end to all rule and all authority and power. For He must reign till He has put all enemies under His feet. The last enemy that will be destroyed is death. For 'He has put all things under His feet.' But when He says 'all things are put under Him,' it is evident that He who put all things under Him is excepted. Now when all things are made subject to Him, then the Son Himself will also be subject to Him who put all things under Him, that God may be all in all" 1 Corinthians 15:24-28.

There we have it. Jesus **is** currently reigning. He **is** on the throne. He **is** the King of kings and Lord of lords. All things **are** under His feet—with one exception—His Father. When Jesus has laid the last stone in place, when He has saved the last son of Adam according to His purpose, then, and not before, His kingdom will be fully populated, and He will present it to His Father, Himself included, so the Father may be "all in all."

In one sense we, born again believers, are under His feet, and willingly so, but it is also true that the Father has "made us sit together in the heavenly places in Christ Jesus" Ephesians 2:6. We readily acknowledge Him to be our Sovereign. We trust He has our good at heart, for He willingly shed His blood for us.

When the Bible says "all things are under His feet," it includes "all principality and power and might and dominion, and every name that is named, not only in this age but also in that which is to come" Ephesians 1:21. Satan and his host are under Jesus' feet; that which to us is powerful and mighty, every false religion and doctrine, indeed, "all things are under His feet."

This means Jesus is Sovereign of the universe. Not only do we love Him as our Savior and Friend, but we stand in awe of who He is, and bow in submission before Him, as we acknowledge Him as our Sovereign King.

These classifications also refer to the angels and to their various ranks. Jesus is not only Sovereign over His earthly church, but over the faithful angels who serve Him without question in the heavenly realms.

Puritan Quotes:

"Go up and down, then, in the world, and be not troubled by many things that now disquiet you. Say, 'I do not know how this will glorify Christ, but I am persuaded that, in some mysterious way which I cannot yet fully comprehend, his eternal purposes are being accomplished.' See Christ in everything, and see everything in the light of Christ" C.H. Spurgeon, 1834-1892.

"Therefore the kingdom cannot be given up until all rule and government be cast down. So that while the world lasts, Jesus, as the Messiah and Mediator, must reign; and all human beings are properly his subjects, are under his government, and are accountable to him" Adam Clarke, 1762-1832.

PREEMINENCE

Reading: Colossians 1:15-18
"that in all things He may have the preeminence" Colossians 1:18

When it comes to considering the phrase "all things", we could spend several weeks in this passage of scripture. We are told:

For by Him all things were created

All things were created through Him and for Him.

He is before all things,

In Him all things consist.

In all things He may have the preeminence.

Our text is the summary phrase; it is the natural conclusion of what has just been said. Because Jesus Christ created all things, etc. He must have the preeminence in all things. Or, as some translations put it, "so he is first in everything" (NLT; TLB).

Some commentators consider our text to apply strictly to the preceding statement, "He is the firstborn of the dead," therefore "He is first in everything."

No matter the reason, for the believer who has been born again by the Spirit of God, Jesus must be given the preeminence in their life. This is one of the more difficult "all things" for the believer to grasp and practice. This is why the fully dedicated believer is often called a fanatic.

But surely, some may ask, isn't this is one occasion when exceptions can be made when the Bible says "all things"? If these words are taken literally, we must learn what the will of God is, and what His demands are on our life, and constantly yield to those demands—without exception.

Just because very few of us live this life of complete commitment to Christ and His teachings, does not make them invalid. When Paul introduces this subject to the Colossian believers, he tells them that he prays

"that you may be filled with the knowledge of His will in all wisdom and spiritual understanding; that you may walk worthy of the Lord, fully pleasing Him, being fruitful in every good work and increasing in the knowledge of God; strengthened with all might, according to His glorious power, for all patience and longsuffering with joy; giving thanks to the Father who has qualified us to be partakers of the inheritance of the saints in the light" Colossians 1:9-13.

In order that we may "walk worthy of the Lord," and be "fully pleasing [to] Him," we need to be "filled with the knowledge of His will." When we willfully and willingly participate in that which we know is displeasing to God, it cannot be said we are walking worthy of Him.

Life is a process of choices, and, as believers in Jesus Christ, we have to make decisions every day. A necessary part of our sanctification, our growing in Christ, is making wise decisions we know are pleasing to Him.

This goes for the company we choose to keep, the music we choose to listen to, the T.V. programs and movies we choose to watch, the books we choose to read, etc. In other words, everything we do must be governed by that which we know is pleasing to the Lord.

We learn these Godly principles in two ways. First, by reading and meditating in God's Word. The Scriptures are God's revelation of Himself to us. The more we learn of Him, the more we learn what pleases Him. Second, by the Holy Spirit's direct communication to our spirit. Part of His work is to convict us of sin in our life, and to guide us along the path of righteousness. When we are sensitive to His leading, we will respond to His guidance:

"When He, the Spirit of truth, has come, He will guide you into all truth; for He will not speak on His own authority, but whatever He hears He will speak; and He will tell you things to come. He will glorify Me, for He will take of what is Mine and declare it to you" John 16:13-14.

In the broader sense, Jesus has the preeminence in sustaining His creation. All things consist by Him. He upholds all things by the Word of His power (Hebrews 1:3).

Greater still is the preeminence of Jesus in redemption. Redemption would be an eternal impossibility without Him. He is the Central Figure in our redemption. It is He who left heaven's glory and became man. It is He who died on the cross bearing our sin and its judgment. It is He who rose from the dead, victorious over death. It is He who sits at the right hand of His Father making intercession for us.

As the glorified Man He is the Heir of God, and, as such, He holds the preeminence in heaven. He has been made so much better than the angels, as He has by inheritance obtained a more excellent name than they. Far above all the angelic beings, higher than the archangel is the Lord Jesus Christ, the Man in Glory.

Puritan Quote:

"Our hearts too can never fully know the blessed peace of God and rest of faith till we give our Lord the first place. Anything less than that will mean dishonor to Him. 'Not I—but Christ' must be the constant cry of our hearts. Not I—but Christ in our daily walk; Not I—but Christ in our service. Oh! that we might realize our great and holy calling, our wonderful privilege, a privilege which is ours for but a little while longer to live for Him, who has in all things the preeminence" A. C. Gaebelein, 1861-1945.

Note: While some of the Puritan Quotes used in these Bible meditations are not directly from those men of God known as the Puritans, they do reflect the thoughts and principles taught by them. Today's quote is an example of this.

CHRIST'S STRENGTH IS OUR ABILITY

Reading: Philippians 4:10-13
"I can do all things through Christ who strengthens me" Philippians 4:13

How many times have we seen these words reproduced on plaques, pictures, and religious articles? Throughout the centuries they have been the source of comfort and encouragement to God's children. The more our relationship with Jesus Christ develops, the more conscious we become of our own weaknesses and inadequacies, and the more we have to lean on Him and His strength.

No matter what God asks of us, we can do. He will never call us to do anything apart from our ability to do it. The truth is, however, we know if we rely on our own ability, we will fail. The secret of our success is the same as that of Paul: "I can do all things through Christ who strengthens me." Whether it is the Apostles, or the men and women who face[d] persecution and death if they profess Jesus as their Savior, or those called by God to take His Word to the uttermost parts of the world, or the student who seeks to maintain his testimony among the rampant Godlessness found in most campuses today, there is only one source of strength—Jesus Christ.

The strength, with which Jesus defeated Satan when He was a man, is the same strength He makes available to us today:

"Finally, my brethren, be strong in the Lord and in the power of His might" Ephesians 6:10.

His strength is our strength; His power is our power, and His might is our might. The power with which God created the heavens and earth is the same power He makes available to us as we seek to serve Him. David knew this truth:

"God is my strength and power, and He makes my way perfect. He makes my feet like the feet of deer, and sets me on my high

places. He teaches my hands to make war, so that my arms can bend a bow of bronze" 2 Sam 22:33-35.

When Jesus was teaching His disciples the principle of abiding in Him, and how important it is that they bare "much fruit", He told them:

"Without Me you can do nothing" John 15:5.

One of the biggest challenges in my spiritual life is knowing how to appropriate Christ's strength to myself. I know His strength and power is there, and that God has made it available to me as part of the inheritance He has given me as His adopted Son. I see it as ripe fruit on a tree, waiting for me to reach up and pick it. That is the key to this practice. Have you ever tried eating an apple while it is still hanging on the tree? To make it mine I must reach out and pluck it. So it is with Christ's strength, power and might. Indeed, if we need any of the attributes God has given us in in His Son, we must reach out and grasp it. We cannot be refreshed and fed by an apple when it is still hanging on the tree—we must reach out and grasp it and make it ours.

But, how do we do this? Thanking God for blessing us with every spiritual blessing in Christ Jesus is not enough. The orchardist can look at his maturing crop and thank God for it, but if it is not harvested, he cannot enjoy it.

When Jesus ate with His disciples, He "took bread, blessed and broke it, and gave it to the disciples and said, 'Take, eat; this is My body.' Then He took the cup, and gave thanks, and gave it to them, saying, 'Drink from it, all of you'" Matthew 26:26-27. Jesus wanted them to participate with Him: "Take, eat ... Drink from it."

We cannot stand on the sidelines and watch God fight our battle. We are told to

"Fight the good fight of faith, lay hold on eternal life, to which you were also called and have confessed the good confession in the presence of many witnesses. I urge you in the sight of God who gives life to all things, and before Christ Jesus who witnessed the good confession before Pontius Pilate, that you

keep this commandment without spot, blameless until our Lord Jesus Christ's appearing" 1 Timothy 6:12-14.

We are told to "walk worthy of the calling with which you are called" (Ephesians 4:1; Colossians 1:10, 1 Thessalonians 2:12). One of the major principles in scripture is that we are to participate with God—Moses had to raise his staff over the Red Sea, David had to place a stone in his sling and throw it, elders are to anoint the sick with oil and lay their hands on them, but what is the secret of success?

"Run with endurance the race that is set before us, looking unto Jesus, the author and finisher of our faith" Hebrews 12:1-2.

There is the key to success in the Christian life—"Looking unto Jesus." When I look back on my life and take note of my failures, it always boils down to this one thing, I did not look to Jesus. I tried to do God's will in my own strength. Is there any wonder I failed? Prayer played such a minor part in my life, and I have to continually remind myself of this truth. May our prayer, along with David, constantly be:

"Turn away my eyes from looking at worthless things, and revive me in Your way" Psalm 119:37.

Anything can be classified as "worthless things" when we look to them for strength to help in the time of need instead of "looking unto Jesus."

Puritan Quote:

"'I can do all things,' says he, 'but it is in Christ, not by my own power, for it is Christ that supplies me with strength.' Hence we infer, that Christ will not be less strong and invincible in us also, if, conscious of our own weakness, we place reliance upon his power alone. When he says all things, he means those things which belong to his calling" John Calvin, 1509—1564.

THE TRUE CONDITION OF OUR HEART

Reading: Jeremiah 17:9-13
"The heart is deceitful above all things, and desperately wicked"
Jeremiah 17:9

During the course of our thoughts on the "All Things" of scripture, we have considered some wonderful, indeed magnificent, blessings that belong to those who love God and are His children by a divine act of grace.

As grand as man considers himself to be, His Creator has a different opinion. The creature mandates that Jesus cannot be discussed or even referenced in our centers of education. Yes, God and Jesus are on the lips of countless numbers throughout the day, but not in the form of worship and adoration, but as an expression of frustration and cursing. Along with the commands to not steal or commit murder, is the command to "not take the name of the LORD your God in vain" Exodus 20:7. The law of the land punishes thieves and murderers, but the world turns a deaf ear to the sin against God's name.

When the name of Jesus passes through the lips of a true believer, its source is a heart redeemed by the precious blood of the Son of God, but for all others, it comes from a heart that is "deceitful above all things, and desperately wicked."

A heart that is in such a woeful condition can do nothing but produce that which is deceitful and wicked in the eyes of God. The very best an unsaved man can produce can do nothing to correct the condition of an unsaved heart:

"For the LORD does not see as man sees; for man looks at the outward appearance, but the LORD looks at the heart" 1 Samuel 16:7.

It is the obvious progression that a heart that is deceitful above all things deceives the person it governs. A deceitful heart convinces its owner that God does not exist, or that the god they acknowledge is the true god. Many religions create their own gods out of wood, stone, gold, etc., and are deceived into believing they hear them when they cry out to them. In today's world, idols are made of plastic and porcelain, and are even found in places that profess to worship the God who commanded against their use. This, indeed, is the height of deception.

Satan himself is the master of deception:

"But I fear, lest somehow, as the serpent deceived Eve by his craftiness, so your minds may be corrupted from the simplicity that is in Christ ... For Satan himself transforms himself into an angel of light" 2 Corinthians 11:3,14.

Darkness is seen as light; wickedness is perceived as righteousness; false teachers are accepted as ministers of the gospel; the thief is accepted as the Good Shepherd—these are all the results of deception.

God has set a principle in nature: like produces like: "Can a fig tree, my brethren, bear olives, or a grapevine bear figs?" James 3:12.

A deceitful heart cannot produce that which is pleasing to God. The only fruit acceptable to Almighty God is that which is produced from a heart redeemed by the blood of Jesus Christ.

"For a good tree does not bear bad fruit, nor does a bad tree bear good fruit. For every tree is known by its own fruit. For men do not gather figs from thorns, nor do they gather grapes from a bramble bush. A good man out of the good treasure of his heart brings forth good; and an evil man out of the evil treasure of his heart brings forth evil. For out of the abundance of the heart his mouth speaks" Luke 6:43-45.

Jesus Christ supported the words of Jeremiah when He named that which comes from an unregenerate heart (Mark 7:21-23). The most hideous, degenerate actions a man can conjure up comes "from within, out of the heart."

This divine principle is expounded by Paul in his letter to the Galatian believers:

> "Do not be deceived, God is not mocked; for whatever a man sows, that he will also reap. For he who sows to his flesh will of the flesh reap corruption, but he who sows to the Spirit will of the Spirit reap everlasting life" Galatians 6:7-8).

Paul expands this principle by taking it into eternity. He who sows spiritual seed by living a Christ-like life will reap "everlasting life," but the unregenerate heart can produce nothing that is acceptable to God, therefore he reaps "corruption," the reward for which is to face God's judgment and be condemned to an eternity where nothing but the wrath of God is their portion.

Man may mock God in this life and think he is getting away with it, but "God is not mocked." The tongue that curses God, and the unrepentant heart that sows corruption, will one day "confess that Jesus Christ is Lord, to the glory of God the Father" Philippians 2:11. God "knows the heart" (Acts 15:8), and no man has the ability to hide its condition from Him.

Even as believers, it is well for us to remember the truth of our text, that the "heart is deceitful above all things, and desperately wicked." How much we have to thank God for. Those men and women who have been saved by His grace are the fulfillment of Ezekiel's prophecy:

> "I will give you a new heart and put a new spirit within you; I will take the heart of stone out of your flesh and give you a heart of flesh. I will put My Spirit within you and cause you to walk in My statutes, and you will keep My judgments and do them. Then you shall dwell in the land that I gave to your fathers; you shall be My people, and I will be your God. I will deliver you from all your uncleannesses" Ezekiel 36:26-29.

Puritan Quote:

"Desires are the spiritual pulse of the soul, always beating to and fro and showing the temper of it; they are therefore the characters of a Christian and show more truly what he is than his actions do" Richard Sibbes,1577-1635.

GOD'S PROVIDENCE

Reading: Romans 8:26-30
"All things work together for good!" Romans 8:28

This is the second time in this series we have considered Romans 8:28 see #5, 6/27/12. Previously we concentrated on those things that happen to us and affect us negatively, and it is hard to understand why. However, by necessity of the words "all things" we must include those elements of our Christian life that are positive—things that encourage, embolden, and comfort us.

Included in this category are God's attributes, those characteristics of Almighty God that He applies to the fulfillment of His purposes, including the construction, maintenance, and welfare of His Kingdom.

1. The power of God. Paul speaks of God's power as "His glorious power" (Col 1:11). It is glorious because it enables us to [be]:

(a) "Filled with the knowledge of His will"
(b) "walk worthy of the Lord"
(c) "fully pleasing to Him"
(d) "fruitful in every good work,"
(e) "increasing in the knowledge of God" and
(f) "strengthened with all might" Colossians 1:10-11.

God's power works for good in supporting us in times of trouble:

"The eternal God is your refuge, and underneath are the everlasting arms; He will thrust out the enemy from before you, and will say, 'Destroy!'" Deut 33:27.

What delivered Moses and over two million Israelites from the Egyptian army? What sustained Jonah in the stomach of the whale for three days? What upheld Daniel in the Lion's den? The three Hebrews in the furnace heated seven times more than normal? One thing only—the "glorious power" of God.

What keeps Satan from robbing us of the salvation God has given us? Only the power of El Shaddai keeps us from the jaws of our "adversary the devil [who] walks about like a roaring lion, seeking whom he may devour" 1 Peter 5:8.

It is the power of God that works for us in supplying our needs. God provided food for Elijah in the beaks of Ravens, and maintained the flour and oil for the widow (1 Kings 17:6, 14). It is with confidence in the power of God that Paul says, "And my God shall supply all your need according to His riches in glory by Christ Jesus" Philippians 4:19.

2. The Wisdom of God. When one considers the wisdom of God who created the heavens and earth and devised the plan of redemption, then realize that same wisdom governs and controls "all things" for good to those who love God, and who are the called according to His purpose, why is it so difficult to accept the absoluteness of His Word?

"O LORD, how manifold are Your works! In wisdom You have made them all" Psalm 104:24.

"Oh, the depth of the riches both of the wisdom and knowledge of God! How unsearchable are His judgments and His ways past finding out! . . . For of Him and through Him and to Him are all things, to whom be glory forever. Amen" Romans 11:33, 36.

3. The Promises of God. Peter speaks of God's promises as "exceedingly great and precious promises" 2 Peter 1:4. No matter the circumstance we are in, there is a promise we can claim to comfort, strengthen, and encourage us.

Are we under the guilt of sin? There is a promise: "The LORD, the LORD God, [is] merciful and gracious, longsuffering, and abounding in goodness and truth" Exodus 34:6. Are we walking apart from God? Are we like the prodigal son, feeding on husks thrown to the hogs? There is a promise: "I will heal their backsliding, I will love them freely, for My anger has turned away from him" Hosea 14:4.

Are we in some form of trouble? There is a promise that works for our good: "He shall call upon Me, and I will answer him; I will be with him in trouble; I will deliver him and honor him" Psalm 91:15.

Let us not be afraid to claim God's promises and trust them, they are for our good.

Put yourself in the place of Hagar when the angel of God said to her, "What ails you, Hagar? Fear not, for God has heard" Genesis 21:17.

"Let your conduct be without covetousness; be content with such things as you have. For He Himself has said, 'I will never leave you nor forsake you.' So we may boldly say: 'The LORD is my helper; I will not fear. What can man do to me?'" Hebrews 13:5-6.

Puritan Quote:

"God's promises are notes from His hand; is it not good to have security? The promises are the milk of the gospel; and is not milk for the good of the infant? They are cordial to the soul that is ready to faint" Thomas Watson,

REST FOR OUR SOUL

Reading: Matthew 11:25-30
"All things have been delivered to Me by My Father" Matthew 11:27

One of the texts I remember learning as a child is "Come to Me, all you who labor and are heavy laden, and I will give you rest. Take My yoke upon you and learn from Me," but I have never heard it spoken of in the context of our reading.

Jesus is telling His disciples they can find rest to their souls because He is in control of "all things."

Jesus was rebuking the people because of their lack of repentance in the light of God's warning. To the Jews He said, "John came neither eating nor drinking, and they say, 'He has a demon.' The Son of Man came eating and drinking, and they say, 'Look, a glutton and a winebibber.'" In other words, "God has sent two messengers calling on you to repent, instead, you criticize and point the finger at them."

Then He began to rebuke the cities in which He had performed many miracles—Chorazin and Bethsaida. Chorazin is thought to be Kerazeh, a city near the Sea of Galilee, which, within a short time, was destroyed. He then speaks to Capernaum where He spent much time during His early ministry. It was there Jesus took up the ministry of John the Baptist, "From that time Jesus began to preach and to say, 'Repent, for the kingdom of heaven is at hand'" Matthew 4:17.

The door to salvation is repentance,

"Repent therefore and be converted, that your sins may be blotted out" Acts 3:19.

The contrast is made between the power and authority of man (prosperous and influential cities), and Jesus Christ, to whom "all things have been delivered" Matthew 11:27. This same thought is repeated several times in the New Testament, cp John 3:35; Col 1:16-17. These "all things" are specifically defined by Paul in Ephesians 1:21-23:

> "**all principality and power and might and dominion, and every name that is named, not only in this age but also in that which is to come. And He put all things under His feet, and gave Him to be head over all things to the church, which is His body, the fullness of Him who fills all in all."**

There is nothing in heaven, His Father excluded, or on earth, that possesses greater power and authority than Jesus. Therefore, Jesus says,

> "**Come to Me, all you who labor and are heavy laden, and I will give you rest. Take My yoke upon you and learn from Me, for I am gentle and lowly in heart, and you will find rest for your souls. For My yoke is easy and My burden is light"** Matthew **11:28-30.**

You who live under the influence of sin, repent, "turn from your sins and turn to God, so you can be cleansed of your sins" Acts 3:19, NLT. "Come to Me," Jesus says, "for it is only in Me you can find relief from the turmoil sin is causing you." Break away from the evil influences that cause you grief and unrest, and turn to Me, "and I will give you rest."

He then uses an illustration with which the people were familiar: "Take My yoke upon you and learn from Me . . . For My yoke is easy and My burden is light." When a young oxen needed to be trained, he was yoked with a mature, experienced one, whose strength and understanding taught him.

Repentance means turning away from the evil and wickedness that influences your life, and yield to Him who possesses all power and authority over all things that would keep you from God. This is true not only for the unbeliever, but for every child of God. How readily we are influenced by sin because we fail to yield to the strength and authority of Jesus. We need to heed the advice of Paul:

"Be strong in the Lord and in the power of His might. Put on the whole armor of God, that you may be able to stand against the Wiles of the devil. For we do not wrestle against flesh and blood, but against principalities, against powers, against the rulers of the darkness of this age, against spiritual hosts of wickedness in the heavenly places" Ephesians 6:10-12.

Puritan Quote:

"There was no place for the foot to rest on in the miry slough of that which had departed from God. In the midst of a world of evil Jesus remained the sole revealer of the Father, the source of all good. Whom does He call? What does He bestow on those who come? Only source of blessing and revealer of the Father, He calls all those who are weary and heavy laden. Perhaps they did not know the spring of all misery, namely, separation from God, sin" J.N. Darby, 1800-1882.

PRECIOUS PROPHECIES

Reading: Luke 24:44-53
"All things must be fulfilled" Luke 24:44

How reassuring it was for Jesus' closest friends to see Him in their company (once they got over the shock), whole, healthy, and in complete soundness of mind. The last time they had seen Him His flesh was shredded to pieces and His body covered with His blood. They watched as His crucified body was hauled away to be buried in a stranger's tomb. We should never be critical of Thomas when He doubted the report of Jesus' resurrection. Put yourself in his sandals and ask if you would be any different.

It is now, the day of His resurrection, that Jesus "opened their understanding, that they might comprehend the Scriptures" vs.45. If they had understood the Old Testament scriptures, they would have been looking for His resurrection, not surprised by it. Now, He wanted His disciples to understand them, to see from the three divisions of their scriptures, the "the Law of Moses and the Prophets and the Psalms" things concerning Him. Their scriptures prophesied of His birth, ministry, death, resurrection, and ascension, and Jesus wanted them to know that not one "jot and tittle" would remain unfulfilled:

"Do not think that I came to destroy the Law or the Prophets. I did not come to destroy but to fulfill. For assuredly, I say to you, till heaven and earth pass away, one jot or one tittle will by no means pass from the law till all is fulfilled" Matthew 5:17-18.

As current day disciples of Jesus, we too must understand that Old Testament scriptures, including the "Law of Moses" have been fulfilled. How? In the resurrection of Jesus Christ. The reason He "took the humble position of a slave and appeared in human form" (Phil 2:7, NLT), was to fulfill the "Law and the Prophets."

While the passage we are reviewing concerns primarily the resurrection of Jesus, the words of Matthew 5:17-18 broadens the concept to the "Law and the Prophets" period.

I have often wondered why Christians do not offer sheep, cattle, and doves as sacrifices to God, yet continue to tithe ten percent of their income to the church? Tithing was a part of the O.T. law. The early church did not tithe ten percent of everything they had, instead

"Now all who believed were together, and had all things in common, and sold their possessions and goods, and divided them among all, as anyone had need" Acts 2:44-45.

"Nor was there anyone among them who lacked; for all who were possessors of lands or houses sold them, and brought the proceeds of the things that were sold, and laid them at the apostles' feet; and they distributed to each as anyone had need" Acts 4:34-35.

This was the reason why Deacons were first appointed in the church— seven men were appointed to oversee the fair distribution of money, food, etc. (Acts 6:1-4). The two appointed offices in the church are elders and deacons: elders for the spiritual oversight of the local assembly, and deacons for the administrative needs.

One very important lesson we can learn from these words of Jesus is His attention to and acceptance of the scriptures. He knew of what and whom they spoke. He understood they were God's revelation to man. They were so important to Him that every "jot and tittle" were there for a reason. To put it in current day vernacular, every period, comma, indeed, every grammatical stroke was important.

There are those who would lessen the authority of holy Scripture, even to the extreme of some church leaders denying the resurrection and ascension of Jesus. The validity of scripture is challenged. Some consider the accounts of Moses, David, etc. as nothing more than campfire stories, enhanced at every telling.

May we always be submissive to and accepting of the ministry of the Holy Spirit in our lives who "will teach you all things, and bring to your remembrance all things that I said to you" John 14:26.

Puritan Quote:

"'It is written' is his [Jesus'] weapon against Satan, his argument against wicked men. The learned at this hour scoff at the Book, and accuse of Bibliolatry those of us who reverence the divine word; but in this they derive no assistance from the teaching or example of Jesus" C.H. Spurgeon, 1834-1892.

ALL THINGS RIGHT

Reading: Psalm 119:128

"All Your precepts concerning all things I consider to be right"
Psalm 119:128

This is one of those texts, if we really were honest, many of us wish was not included in the Word of God. After all, it is very inclusive, and leaves no room for any exclusions.

First of all, it refers to "All Your precepts"—those we might consider small and insignificant as well as those that characterize true believers in Jesus Christ. The law of the land will designate certain behavior as unacceptable, but by omission designate other things as acceptable. Christians are governed by a different law—the Law of God. Often, when a Christian stands up for that which God designates as unlawful, but is accepted by others, they are ridiculed, slandered, and verbally and sometimes physically abused.

Two things that come immediately to mind are gay marriage and abortion. The born again believer is not in a position to pick and choose those precepts of God when it suits them. Any disobedience of God's Law in dishonoring to Him.

Those who honor God's Word and try to live according to its precepts are usually personally troubled by one or more of what the Bible calls "besetting sins."

"Let us lay aside every weight, and the sin which doth so easily beset us, and let us run with patience the race that is set before us" Hebrews 12:1.

This is as individual as it gets:

"In one it may be pride; in another vanity; in another worldliness; in another a violent and almost ungovernable temper; in another a corrupt

imagination; in another a heavy, leaden, insensible heart; in another some improper and unholy attachment. Whatever it may be, we are exhorted to lay it aside, and this general direction may be applied to anything which prevents our making the highest possible attainment in the divine life" Albert Barnes (1798-1870).

Such individual sins are personal and usually between the believer and God. They can be hidden from other believers, but not from God.

The first step in "laying aside" these "sin[s] which doth so easily beset us", is to acknowledge that all God's precepts are right. If we don't, we have an escape clause.

The Holy Spirit is God's Teacher and is faithful to convict the people of God of their sins (John 14:26). It is so important for us to read and study God's Word, for He uses it to teach us what the precepts of God are.

"Many could be content with God's law, so far as it doth not cross their carnal interest, or hinder their corrupt desires; but we must esteem all the laws of God: they are all holy, just, and good, not one excepted" Thomas Manton.

There is a Godless trend afoot in many our churches today, and that is to dissect the Word of God into that which we are willing to accept without question, and that which we choose to set aside as not applicable to today's way of thinking. The trend includes interpreting scripture based on today's economy, rather than interpreting today's economy by the Word of God. One wonderful thing about God is that He never changes—that which was sin to Him two thousand years ago is still sin today. His precepts are eternal, and because they were established by God, they are still appropriate today.

Just because man seeks to expunge God's Law, does not mean he has convinced God to do the same. Manton suggests that two things go together: a hearty embracing of God's Law and the diligent practice of it.

Is it possible to live a blameless life this side of heaven? Not according to scripture, for, says Paul, "For what I am doing, I do not understand. For what I will to do, that I do not practice; but what I hate, that I do" Romans 7:15. But this is not an excuse, it is a reason.

It is the desire of every believer to live a Godly life, one that is pleasing to God, and this is only possible when we know what it is He wants us to do.

Puritan Quotes:

"It is not enough to be right in commands in general, or the lump, but in this and that in particular; not in some, but in all" Thomas Manton, 1620-1677.

"It is no compromising testimony to the integrity and value of the Lord's precepts with which the Psalmist concludes, 'I esteem all thy precepts concerning all things to be right'—every command, however hard; every injunction, however distasteful; every precept, however severe . . . What a blessed truth to arrive at, and find comfort in" Barton Bouchier, 1794-1865.

THE SEARCHING SPIRIT

Reading: 1 Corinthians 2:6-12
"The Spirit searches all things, yes, the deep things of God"
1 Corinthians 2:10

The ministry of the Holy Spirit is both varied and extensive, and is vital to the maintenance and fulfillment of our salvation. He is our "Counselor, Helper, Intercessor, Advocate, Strengthener, Standby" (all translations of the same word) John 14:26, AMP. He is our "Teacher" (NKJV).

When man sinned, he was blinded to the things of God. It is impossible for any man to discover, by his own effort, the things of God, let alone the "deep things" of God. Throughout time man has attempted to do this, and the result is the foundation of false doctrines and false religions.

In His grace, God has established a way, the only way, by which man can know God. The means by which this is accomplished is the death of His Son, Jesus Christ. However, it is by His Spirit alone that man can come into this knowledge.

We are not saved by any effort on our part, by the the Spirit of God:

"Jesus answered, 'Most assuredly, I say to you, unless one is born of water and the Spirit, he cannot enter the kingdom of God'" John 3:5 (6-8).

The vehicle through which the knowledge of God is revealed is the Bible, the Word of God. It contains everything God wishes to reveal of Himself at this time, but to the unregenerate person they are a black hole of mysteries, they are blind to its truths—they are incapable of deciphering the secrets contained within it:

"But the natural man does not receive the things of the Spirit of God, for they are foolishness to him; nor can he know them, because they are spiritually discerned" 1 Corinthians 2:14.

Jesus said the Holy Spirit would guide His own into all truth—that which God has revealed, the Holy Spirit will teach. But, what qualifies Him to do this? "He will not speak on His own authority, but whatever He hears He will speak" John 16:13.

Paul illustrates the Holy Spirit's qualification to teach God's people the "deep things" of God by comparing the Spirit's knowledge of God's mind to a person's knowledge of his own mind. No person can know another person as well as he knows himself. Even husbands and wives who have lived together for many years, and who have shared their hopes, dreams, and problems with each other, never come to know their spouse as intimately as they know themselves. Our innermost thoughts in the deep recesses of our hearts and minds are known only to ourselves.

Therefore, because the Holy Spirit is a member of the Divine Trinity, He knows the depths of God and the thoughts of God intimately. He alone is qualified to teach the secret things of God because to Him they are not a mystery. He chooses what and to whom to teach the hidden things of God.

The truth is:

"Eye has not seen, nor ear heard, nor have entered into the heart of man the things which God has prepared for those who love Him" 1 Corinthians 2:9.

Man's knowledge, let alone his imagination, cannot come close to comprehending the plan and purpose of Almighty God, but the Holy Spirit knows, and His commission is, to teach these things to those who love God.

God's truth cannot be discovered by man no matter how technologically advanced he becomes, but he can receive it. Before he can receive it, something has to take place—he must be "born again," he must be adopted into God's family; he must be clothed with the righteousness of Jesus Christ. In short, he must be saved, for only then is he able to "receive the things of the Spirit of God" 1 Cor 2:14.

Through the ministry of the Holy Spirit, the impossible becomes possible, the unteachable become teachable, secrets are opened, mysteries are revealed, and the blind are made to see.

May the prayer of David always be on our lips:

"Open my eyes, that I may see wondrous things from Your law" Psalm 119:18.

Then our testimony will be:

"Your servant meditates on Your statutes. Your testimonies also are my delight and my counselors" Psalm 119:23-24.

Puritan Quote:

"There is this difference, however, between God's thoughts and those of men, that men mutually understand each other; but the word of God is a kind of hidden wisdom, the loftiness of which is not reached by the weakness of the human intellect.

"Let it suffice us to have the Spirit of God as a witness, for there is nothing in God that is too profound for him to reach. For such is the import here of the word searcheth. By the deep things you must understand—not secret judgments, which we are forbidden to search into, but the entire doctrine of salvation, which would have been to no purpose set before us in the Scriptures, were it not that God elevates our minds to it by his Spirit" John Calvin, 1509-1564.

LOVE BEARS ALL THINGS

Reading: 1 Corinthians 13:1-13
"Love . . . bears all things" 1 Corinthians 13:7

The chapter we have just read is often called, and rightfully so, "The Love Chapter." It also contains words that align themselves with our "All things" series. Over the course of the next four weeks, I would like to spend time thinking about how Paul combines Love with "all things."

When Paul writes "Love . . . bears all things," he uses the word "stego" which means to "cover." True love protects others from exposure, ridicule, or harm—to put it another way, from gossip. One of the traits of human nature is to spread the faults and weaknesses of another. This is something the world thrives on. Go to any newsstand and you will find publications, such as the Enquirer, and True Confessions, that make millions of dollars by exposing the actions of celebrities, politicians, and other well-known persons. More than one television program is dedicated to exposing the failures of others. Tragically, this practice is alive and well in our churches, among those who claim to be disciples of the King of Love, Jesus Christ.

True love has no part in that—it does not expose or exploit, gloat or condemn.

"Hatred stirs up strife, but love covers all sins" Proverbs 10:12.

The Bible has laid out the procedure the church should follow when a brother or sister is known to have sinned (Matthew 18:15-20). Love does not gossip. Love protects.

The mercy seat is a perfect example of our thought—it was where the blood of atonement was sprinkled (Leviticus 16:14)—it was a covering, not only for the ark itself but for the sins of the people. The mercy-seat prefigured the perfect and final covering of sin by Jesus on the cross (Romans 3:25-26).

"In the cross, God threw the great mantle of His love over sin, forever covering it for those who trust in His Son" John F. MacArthur.

Another example from the Old Testament is found in sons of Noah. His younger son discovered and declared the shame of his father, but his other sons took a garment and covered the nakedness of their father (Genesis 9:20-23). This pictures how we should deal with the sins of our fellow believer. Love covers; that is, it never broadcasts the errors of good men. There are busybodies who never see a fault in a brother but they must talk about it.

During Oliver Cromwell's reign as lord protector of England, a young soldier was sentenced to die. The girl to whom he was engaged pleaded with Cromwell to spare his life, but to no avail. Her fiancée was to be executed when the curfew bell sounded, but when the bell-rope was pulled there was no sound. After several attempts the sexton stopped trying. The girl had climbed into the belfry and curled herself around the clapper so it could not strike the bell. Her body was smashed and bruised, but she did not let go until the clapper stopped swinging. She managed to climb down, severely bruised and bleeding. When she explained what she had done, Cromwell commuted her fiancée's sentence. A poet beautifully recorded this incident as follows:

At his feet she told her story,
showed her hands all bruised and torn.
And her sweet young face still haggard
With the anguish it had worn.
Touched his heart with sudden pity,
lit his eyes with misty light.
'Go, your lover lives,' said Cromwell:
'Curfew will not ring tonight.'

This does not mean we are to ignore the sins of each other or to give sanction to them, but that we must refrain from using the knowledge as fodder to feed the gossip animal that dwells in many of us.

This also applies to the incident when we feel we have been unjustly hurt or slighted by a fellow brother or sister in Christ. How readily we are to share our hurt with anyone who will lend us their ear. It might be true, but should be handled within Biblical procedures. How ready we are to justify our own position and shed the shadow of blame and injustice on others.

In retrospect, how much Love have we exhibited throughout our Christian life?

As one who stands justified before the bar of God, how precious is the blood of Christ who willingly shouldered the blame for my guilt? As Jesus hung on the cross, dying for no fault of His own, do we hear Him declare His innocence? If anyone had cause to cry out, "I am innocent! This is a big mistake!," it was He. Instead of pointing His finger at me, the guilty one, He prayed for his executioners.

LOVE! There is no greater example.

"And above all things have fervent love for one another, for "love will cover a multitude of sins"' 1 Peter 4:8.

Puritan Quote:

"Love stands in the presence of a fault, with a finger on her lip. If anyone is to smite a child of God, let it not be a brother. Even if a professor be a hypocrite, love prefers that he should fall by any hand rather than her own. She sitteth alone, and keepeth silence. To speak and publish her wrong is too painful for her, for she fears to offend against the Lord's people" C.H. Spurgeon, 1834-1892.

LOVE BELIEVES ALL THINGS

Reading: 1 Corinthians 13:1-13
"Love . . . believes all things" 1 Corinthians 13:7

To believe everything a person (primarily a fellow Believer) says or does is both ignorant and foolish. What these words tell us is that true love for our brother or sister in Christ will always believe them unless there are litigating circumstances that prove otherwise. We should always give them the benefit of the doubt, and never rush to judgment. If his reputation is one of Christlikeness, we must be slow to accept any rumor or gossip that says otherwise. Such a rumor or gossip can destroy a person's life, his reputation, his marriage, his business, to say nothing of his faith.

It can be devastating to have fellow Believers accept and spread false accusations against you, especially against one who is new in the faith or not firmly grounded in it. Even under the Old Testament Law, the punishment for falsely accusing a brother Israelite, was severe (Deuteronomy 19:15-21).

Love for a brother in Christ will always assume him innocent until proven guilty. If the charge is proven to be true, love will always seek the best way to restore him into true fellowship through forgiveness and friendship. Tragically, this is where the test of our love for a "guilty" brother so often fails. The easier road is to "gossip" about it, and before we know it, we have convicted him in the court of public opinion. Then we join the ranks of those who need forgiveness, because we are now guilty of the sin of hypocrisy.

Jesus had strong words about this:

"Judge not, that you be not judged. For with what judgment you judge, you will be judged; and with the measure you use, it will be measured back to you. And why do you look at the speck in your brother's eye, but do not consider the plank in your own eye? Or how can you say to your brother, 'Let me remove

the speck from your eye'; and look, a plank is in your own eye?
Hypocrite! First remove the plank from your own eye, and then
you will see clearly to remove the speck from your brother's eye"
Matthew 7:1-5.

While Jesus is addressing the problem of judging another, the principle
is the same. If we choose to gossip about a brother's failure instead of
drawing alongside him in the attitude of love, we are guilty of hypocrisy,
and we hope others treat us better than how we did our failing brother.

Jobs friends showed few signs of love. They were quick to believe the
worst about him. They were convinced his problems were the result of his
sins even though he lived an exemplary life. He had the reputation as one
who "was blameless and upright, and one who feared God and shunned
evil" Job 1:1. Job himself did not understand why he was suffering so
terribly, but he knew it was not because of his sins.

Job's "friends" are a perfect example of "rushing into judgment. They
chose to point the finger of blame rather than draw alongside him and love
him. Paul exhorted the Roman believers:

"Now may the God of patience and comfort grant you to be
like-minded toward one another" Romans 15:5.

It was the command of Jesus to "Love one another" John 12:34-35), not
to gossip about each other. This is not to say we should ignore each other's
sins, but believe the best of each other's motive until the truth is determined
one way or the other. To do so is an act of love.

"Finally, all of you be of one mind, having compassion for one
another; love as brothers, be tenderhearted, be courteous; not
returning evil for evil or reviling for reviling, but on the contrary
blessing, knowing that you were called to this, that you may
inherit a blessing" 1 Peter 3:8-9.

Puritan Quote:

"*Love trusts on—ever hopes and expects better things, and this, a trust springing from itself and out of its own depths alone*" Frederick W. Robertson, 1816-1853.

LOVE HOPES ALL THINGS

Reading: 1 Corinthians 13:1-13
"Love . . . hopes all things" 1 Corinthians 13:7

One of the great comforts and enduring strengths of the believer in Jesus Christ is his hope of eternal life and the complete fulfillment of God's promises to him. Hope for the believer is not something based on wishful thinking, but on a sure and certain outcome of everything accomplished in the redemptive work of Jesus Christ.

Unlike today, when the word "hope" is based on uncertainty, the believer's hope speaks to that which is firm and unshakable:

"This hope we have as an anchor of the soul, both sure and steadfast, and which enters the Presence behind the veil, where the forerunner has entered for us, even Jesus" Hebrews 6:19-20.

The word 'elpis', translated "hope" in Hebrews 6:19, is the same root word found in our text: "Love . . . hopes all things." When considered in the light of this context, The Living Bible paraphrases it as "always expect the best of him." When a fellow believer says or does something that discredits his faith, before we rush to judgment against him, we are called upon to hope his motive was pure and sincere. The Amplified Version translates these words as "its hopes are fadeless under all circumstances."

Love is not naïve, or like an Ostrich that buries its head in the sand in an attempt to avoid an oncoming problem, but gives the conduct of others the benefit that all will turn out well. Hope always looks at the situation and delays a final decision until the facts are known. Even if the brother or sister are in error in their behavior, the solution is not in gossiping about it, but continuing in the firm hope that the offending brother will respond positively to wise counsel, and claim the forgiveness that is always there in his relationship with Jesus Christ.

God, our heavenly Father, is always protective of His children. When we sin, does He cast us aside and dismiss us from His family? Jesus did not take Peter's failure as final; neither did Paul take the Corinthian's failure as final. The Bible is rampant with promises that makes God's love hopeful—something upon which we can depend; something upon which we stand and take comfort. If this is the mind of God, then, as imitators of Jesus Christ, should we not show the same love and hope in our fellow brothers and sisters in Christ?

"Love will hold on to this hope until all possibility of such a result has vanished and it is compelled to believe that the conduct is not susceptible of a fair explanation. This hope will extend to "all things"—to words and actions, and plans; to public and to private contact; to what is said and done in our own presence, and to what is said and done in our absence. Love will do this, because it delights in the virtue and happiness of others, and will not credit anything to the contrary unless compelled to do so" C.H. Spurgeon.

There is a story of a dog who stayed at an airport of a large city for over five years waiting for his master to return. Employees and others fed the dog and took care of him, but he would not leave the spot where he last saw his master. He would not give up hope that someday they would be reunited. Five years, almost to the day, his hope was rewarded. When his master disembarked, he was met by an excited, tail wagging dog who had never given up hope. If a dog's love for his master can produce that kind of hope, how much larger should our love make hope last?

As many of you know, my mother and father, along with some of you, never gave up hope for me, and for twenty-three years prayed for my restoration to God. In November 1999, their diligent hope and prayers were rewarded.

Gossip, in so many cases, is an attempt to gain self-gratification. By speaking randomly of another's failure, we are in essence saying, "Look at me, I am so much better than him."

"As the love of God shed abroad in the hearts of the redeemed does not seek its own good (1 Corinthians 13:5), so self-love does nothing but that" Arthur W. Pink.

So, what is our motive for gossiping about the failure of others?

"They all look to their own way, every one for his own gain" Isaiah 56:11.

"The rope of love's hope has no end. As long as there is life, love does not lose hope" John MacArthur.

Puritan Quote:

"Hope fills the afflicted soul with such inward joy and consolation, that it can laugh while tears are in the eye, sigh and sing all in a breath; it is called "the rejoicing of hope" (Hebrews 3:6) William Gurnall, 1617-1679.

LOVE ENDURES ALL THINGS

Reading: 1 Corinthians 13:1-13
"Love . . . endures all things" 1 Corinthians 13:7

One of the major teachings found in Paul's writings is that of endurance. He constantly exhorts those to whom he ministers to "hold fast":

"Let us hold fast our confession" Heb 4:14.
"Let us hold fast the confession of our hope without wavering" Heb 10:23.

The word translated "endure" is a military term used of an army's holding a vital position at all costs. Applied here spiritually, it can speak to the love we have for Christ—no matter what opposition comes our way, we will endure it and not turn aside. *"Endureth—persecutions in a patient and loving spirit" (from Jamieson, Fausset, and Brown Commentary).* "Endures through every circumstance" NLT.

The words that follow those quoted above from Hebrews 4:14 are important in that we are encouraged to look to Christ as our Example:

"For we do not have a High Priest who cannot sympathize with our weaknesses, but was in all points tempted as we are, yet without sin" v15. We are not asked to endure anything that our Savior has not suffered. We are encouraged to look to Jesus:

"the author and finisher of our faith, who for the joy that was set before Him endured the cross, despising the shame" Heb 12:2.

It is said of Abraham: "And so, after he had patiently endured, he obtained the promise" (Heb 6:15-16), and of Moses: "he endured as seeing Him who is invisible" (Heb 11:27).

In each of these examples the one that endured was rewarded:

Jesus "sat down at the right hand of the throne of God" Hebrews 12:2.

Abraham "obtained the promise" Hebrews 6:15.

Moses "passed through the Red Sea as by dry land" Hebrews 11:29.

The immediate reward for us who believe in Jesus as our Savior is that we can "come boldly to the throne of grace, that we may obtain mercy and find grace to help in time of need" Hebrews 4:16. This is the very same throne upon which Jesus is seated as the reward for His endurance.

The Greek word 'hupomeno', translated "endure" in our text, is frequently used in the context of suffering: "And you will be hated by all for My name's sake. But he who endures to the end will be saved" Matthew 10:22; "rejoicing in hope, patient in tribulation, continuing steadfastly in prayer" Romans 12:12—here translated "patient".

This venue does not allow a full study of this word, but suffice it to say it is used in the context of physical and spiritual afflictions, such as persecutions and temptations.

As believers in Jesus Christ, we are called upon to endure anything that challenges our faith or causes us to question the validity of our standing in Christ, which, as every believer knows, is a favorite ploy of Satan to throw us off the tracks.

Physical suffering may cause us to ask, "Why me? What have I done to deserve this?" Paul learned the answer to this question when God answered his prayer to have his "thorn in the flesh" removed. God answered by saying:

"My grace is sufficient for you, for My strength is made perfect in weakness" 2 Corinthians 12:9.

Once Paul understood God had a purpose for his suffering, he accepted it and yielded to it:

"Therefore most gladly I will rather boast in my infirmities, that the power of Christ may rest upon me. Therefore I take pleasure in infirmities, in reproaches, in needs, in persecutions, in distresses, for Christ's sake" 2 Corinthians 12:9-10.

And his conclusion was:

"For when I am weak, then I am strong."

"Lord Jesus Christ, Thou hast opened a new and living way by which a fallen creature can approach Thee with acceptance.
I can come to Thee in my need and feel peace beyond understanding!
The grace that restores is necessary to preserve, lead, guard, supply, help me.
To Thee I repair for grace upon grace, until every void made by sin be replenished and I am filled with all Thy fullness.
Do Thou be with me, and prepare me for all the smiles of prosperity, the frowns of adversity, the losses of substance, the death of friends, the days of darkness, the changes of life, and the last great change of all.
May I find Thy grace sufficient for all my needs" Puritan prayer— Valley of Vision.

Puritan Quote:

"endureth all things; that are disagreeable to the flesh; all afflictions, tribulations, temptations, persecutions, and death itself, for the elect's sake, for the sake of the Gospel, and especially for the sake of Christ Jesus" John Gill, 1697-1771.

JUSTIFIED FROM ALL THINGS

Reading: Acts 13:26-41

"By Him everyone who believes is justified from all things" Acts 13:39

Of all the previous meditations in this "All Things" series, I would venture to say today's scripture carries the most important and eternal ramifications of all. The heart of every born again believer will be changed forever as the depths of this truth becomes a reality to them.

The Bible tells us: "For all have sinned and fall short of the glory of God" (Romans 3:23), and "the wages of sin is death" (Romans 6:23), and "the wrath of God is revealed from heaven against all ungodliness and unrighteousness of men, who suppress the truth in unrighteousness" Romans 1:18.

Now, this does not paint a very pleasant picture, does it? The bottom line is that all mankind is tainted with sin, therefore no one is exempt from facing the wrath of God. That is until he or she believes in Jesus as their Savior.

"He who believes in the Son has everlasting life; and he who does not believe the Son shall not see life, but the wrath of God abides on him" John 3:36.

Jesus is the one and only Way through whom we can receive the forgiveness of our sins and be "justified from all things." The words preceding our text is very explicit:

"Therefore let it be known to you, brethren, that through this Man is preached to you the forgiveness of sins" Acts 13:38.

To be justified in the eyes of Almighty God means not only to be pardoned of our sins of the past, but also those we will commit in the future. The reason for this is because justification is more than being pardoned of our sins, but being freed from the guilt of our actions.

Even if a person is pardoned of his crime by the President, he remains guilty. No President, Judge, King or Queen has the power or ability to remove a person's guilt. Once the crime is committed, the guilt remains forever. Man can forgive and pardon, but only God can remove the guilt.

The marvelous truth of our text is that our justification is inclusive of "all things." There is not one sin that remains uncovered by the justifying grace of God. If there were, we would remain under the wrath of God.

The phrase "all things" includes sins of action, thought, and intent.

However, this does not mean a believer can willingly continue in sin. Even though we have been forgiven and justified, and made "new creatures in Christ," we will still sin—even though we do not wish to. Paul admits to this when he wrote:

> "For I know that in me (that is, in my flesh) nothing good dwells; for to will is present with me, but how to perform what is good I do not find. For the good that I will to do, I do not do; but the evil I will not to do, that I practice" Romans 7:18-19.

Our sinful nature is not eradicated when are born again, but the desire to sin has been removed. As a believer, when I sin, I am convicted by the Holy Spirit. Thankfully, God is still willing to forgive my sins:

> "If we confess our sins, He is faithful and just to forgive us our sins and to cleanse us from all unrighteousness" 1 John 1:9.

As we continue to walk with God we will grow in Christ. This growth means that the Holy Spirit will not only convict us of sin after we have committed it, but will convict us before we do. We then learn to call on God's strength and power to keep us from committing that sin.

> "Finally, my brethren, be strong in the Lord and in the power of His might" Ephesians 6:10.

"To the Lord our God belong mercy and forgiveness, though we have rebelled against Him" Daniel 9:9.

Puritan Quote:

"Therefore, let this remain sure and certain that the righteousness which we have in Christ is not for one day or a moment, but it is everlasting, as the sacrifice of his death doth daily reconcile us to God" John Calvin, 1509-1564.

ALL THINGS MADE NEW

Reading: Revelation 21:1-8
"Behold, I make all things new" Revelation 21:5

How wonderful that the last time the phrase "all things" is mentioned in the Bible is in the last chapter of the last book. Not only that, but they speak of the consummation of the divine purpose of Almighty God for His people.

This is the grand conclusion of the redemptive plan, the process of which included the birth, life, death, resurrection, and reign of the King of kings and Lord of lords.

Last week we considered the endurance of Jesus as He fulfilled the will of His Father, and for which He was rewarded to sit on the throne at His right hand (Hebrews 12:2). It is from this position on this throne that Jesus makes the royal proclamation:

"Behold, I make all things new" Revelation 21:5.

The beginning of this process is not to be found in the future— it began with the resurrection of Jesus. Jesus is the Forerunner of the resurrection body. Once again, Jesus is the Example of what is planned for those who have been made new creatures in Him (2 Corinthians 5:17). Regarding the resurrection and our body, Paul writes:

"So also is the resurrection of the dead. The body is sown in corruption, it is raised in incorruption. It is sown in dishonor, it is raised in glory. It is sown in weakness, it is raised in power. It is sown a natural body, it is raised a spiritual body" 1 Corinthians 15:42-44.

This is not a description of our human body only, but also that of Jesus. The new creation began with Jesus, is continued by the new spiritual creation when a person is born again by the Spirit of God, and is continued when Jesus makes the New Heaven and New Earth when He returns to gather His elect to Himself (Matthew 24:31).

It is important to note that creation is a continual process. The word translated "make" is *poioó*, which is more correctly translated as "making."

"And the one sitting on the throne said, "Look, I am making everything new!" see New Living Translation, The Living Bible.

Just as the sanctification of the new creature in Christ Jesus is a process (we grow in Christ), so is the New Earth and New Heaven.

"This suggests an ongoing process of renovation. Christ is a creator, and His creativity is never exhausted. He will go right on making new things. Heaven is not the end of innovation; it is a new beginning, an eternal break from the stagnancy and inertia of sin" Randy Alcorn, Heaven.

The inclusion of the words "all things" is very significant because, guess what, it means "all things!" Nothing of the old earth and heaven will remain—that includes the spiritual realm where Satan and his angels currently abide—they are destined for another location the Bible calls "the Lake of fire and brimstone."

As for God:

"Behold, the tabernacle of God is with men, and He will dwell with them, and they shall be His people. God Himself will be with them and be their God" Revelation 21:3.

This new earth where God will dwell with His people will have none of the fruits of wickedness and unrighteousness. Sin will be a thing of the past, and the fight against principalities and powers will be over.

"And God will wipe away every tear from their eyes; there shall be no more death, nor sorrow, nor crying. There shall be no more pain, for the former things have passed away" Revelation 21:4.

There will be a total absence of "the cowardly, unbelieving, abominable, murderers, sexually immoral, sorcerers, idolaters, and all liars [because they] shall have their part in the lake which burns with fire and brimstone, which is the second death" Revelation 21:8.

God will reign supreme, and His sovereignty will be unquestioned. As glorious as these things will be, surely the greatest blessing of all will be:

"They shall see His face" Revelation 22:4.

What a contrast from when Moses asked to see God's glory:

"So it shall be, while My glory passes by, that I will put you in the cleft of the rock, and will cover you with My hand while I pass by. Then I will take away My hand, and you shall see My back; but My face shall not be seen" Exodus 33:22-23.

This is the hope and great expectation of every true believer. This is the future God is preparing for His children, and for which He is preparing us. Take comfort and encouragement in this, the greatest of all Biblical "all things."

"For now we see in a mirror, dimly, but then face to face" 1 Cor 13:12.

Puritan Quote:

"Your comforts are now a taste, but then they shall be a feast. How soon do our conquered fears return, and what inconsistency and unevenness is there in our peace! Then, our peace will be perfect and permanent. We then shall enjoy Him continually" Richard Baxter, 1615-1691.

THE LORD SPEAKS

Reading: Leviticus 1:2-17
"Now the Lord called to Moses, and spoke to him" Leviticus 1:1

"There is no book, in the compass of that inspired volume which the Holy Ghost has given us, that contains more of the very words of God than Leviticus. It is God that is the direct speaker in almost every page; His gracious words are recorded in the form wherein they were uttered. This consideration cannot fail to send us to the study of it with singular interest and attention" Andrew Bonar.

Yet, when it comes to the most read and thought upon books of the Bible, Leviticus is one of the least considered by believers. Over the next several weeks, I would like to delve into this wonderful, yet neglected, part of God's Word—for it is surely that.

From the moment when God dismissed Adam and Eve from His presence and guarded the Garden of Eden with "cherubim at the east of the garden of Eden, and a flaming sword which turned every way, to guard the way to the tree of life" (Genesis 3:24), He has communicated with His people, but they could not freely communicate with Him.

The opening words of Leviticus stipulate this, "Now the Lord called to Moses, and spoke to him from the tabernacle of meeting." Previously, God had spoken to His people from Mount Sinai—from the fiery mount "came a fiery law" Deuteronomy 33:2. This was a totally different position.

From the place where God announced to Moses:

"I have seen this people, and indeed it is a stiff-necked people! Now therefore, let Me alone, that My wrath may burn hot against them and I may consume them" Exodus 32:9-10

128

to that which speaks of mercy and grace, to the place where He would take up His earthly residence, the Holy of Holies in the Tabernacle of Meeting. Holiness is the major theme found in Leviticus.

God is Holy, no matter from where He speaks. He was holy on Mount Sinai, and holy above the mercy-seat; but on Sinai, His holiness stood connected with a "devouring fire," but now, in the Tabernacle of Meeting, it was connected with mercy and grace.

In the holy laws presented from this place of mercy, God provides a way whereby these "stiff-necked" and rebellious people can have their sins forgiven through the offerings and sacrifices of certain animals:

"the burnt offering . . . will be accepted on his behalf to make atonement for him" Leviticus 1:4.

The fact that "the Lord called to Moses, and spoke to him" speaks to the heart of God. There is always joy in heaven where God is surrounded by beings that worship Him day and night, yet, in the midst of all that joy, He longs to pour out His love to man.

It was not until His beloved Son, Jesus Christ, came to earth and offered Himself as the perfect sacrifice, that free communication with God was made possible:

"Let us therefore come boldly to the throne of grace, that we may obtain mercy and find grace to help in time of need" Hebrews 4:16.

God chose the Tabernacle as the place where He would reside on earth. Previously, He was "in a pillar of cloud by day and in a pillar of fire by night" (Exodus 13:22; Numbers 14:14). Wherever His people went, so God went with them. This is why when God gave Moses the instructions for the construction of the Tabernacle, He made it portable, so when the people moved locations as they travelled to the Promised Land, so the Tabernacle (ohel—Tent) of meeting was broken down and reconstructed wherever they stopped (Exodus 40:36-38; Numbers 9:15-23).

John, in his gospel, wrote "And the Word became flesh and dwelt among us" John 1:14. The word translated "dwelt" is 'skenoo', and means to "tent or tabernacle." In the person of Jesus Christ, God now tabernacled among us. After His ascension, God tabernacles in His people, those born again by His Spirit:

> **"Do you not know that your body is the temple of the Holy Spirit who is in you" (1 Corinthians 6:19); "For the temple of God is holy, which temple you are" 1 Corinthians 3:17; "You are the temple of the living God" 2 Corinthians 6:16.**

In the new creation, heaven and earth are one, and it will be loudly proclaimed:

> **"Behold, the tabernacle of God is with men, and He will dwell with them, and they shall be His people. God Himself will be with them and be their God" Revelation 21:3.**

It has been from the very beginning, in the eternal counsel of God, that He desires to tabernacle with His people, and neither the devil nor any of God's foes, can derail this wonderful plan that "God will dwell with His people."

Puritan Quote:

"Sinai and its law a few weeks before, with the dark apostasy in the matter of the golden calf, had lately taught Israel the necessity of reconciliation, and made their conscious thirst for that living water. And it is given here. The first clause of this book [Leviticus] declares a reconciled God—"The Lord called to Moses," as a man to his friend" Andrew Bonar, 1810-1892.

AN OFFERING TO THE LORD

Reading: Leviticus 1:1-2
"When any one of you brings an offering to the Lord" Leviticus 1:2

From the day Adam and Eve sinned, Man was banned from the presence of God, even to the point where God placed cherubim with flaming swords at the gate of Eden to keep them from returning (Genesis 3:24).

Because God is Merciful and Gracious, He made a way for man to approach Him in the establishing of the priesthood and the sacrificial system.

The word translated "offering" is 'qorban', and comes from the root word 'qrb' meaning "draw near." The custom of the east was (and still is) that no man was permitted to approach the presence of a superior without a present or gift; this gift, or offering, was called "korban," which properly means the introduction-offering, or offering of access.

A man brought something to prepare him to enter the presence of God. What these offerings were (five in number) is given in chapters 1 through 7.

The offering required by God was in the form of sacrifice. This is important, for the work of Jesus can be summed up in the word "Sacrifice."

As with everything man is involved in, he found a way to corrupt the system. The rule of sacrifice was that the animal be unblemished, if it was not, it would be rejected by God. And man, exhibiting his corrupt nature, began offering blemished stock to God:

> "You bring the stolen, the lame, and the sick; thus you bring an offering! Should I accept this from your hand?" Says the Lord. "But cursed be the deceiver who has in his flock a male, and takes a vow, but sacrifices to the Lord what is blemished—for I am a great King" Malachi 1:13-14.

"I have no pleasure in you," says the Lord of hosts, "Nor will I accept an offering from your hands" Malachi 1:10.

God considered the offering of inferior stock to Him as dishonoring His name, and as an act of irreverence (Malachi 1:6). Therefore, when Jesus came to offer Himself the eternal Sacrifice for sin, it is said of Him that He was "without sin" Hebrews 4:15. We are redeemed "with the precious blood of Christ, as of a lamb without blemish and without spot" (1 Peter 1:19); also "And walk in love, as Christ also has loved us and given Himself for us, an offering and a sacrifice to God for a sweet-smelling aroma" Ephesians 5:2.

Because the Laws of the Old Covenant served as types and symbols of that which was to be fulfilled in Jesus (Matthew 5:17), and were corrupted by sinful acts of man, the writer to the Hebrews said:

"Sacrifice and offering, burnt offerings, and offerings for sin You did not desire, nor had pleasure in them"(which are offered according to the law), then He said, 'Behold, I have come to do Your will, O God.' He takes away the first that He may establish the second" Hebrews 10:8-9.

The only sacrifice acceptable to God for the redemption of His people was in the Person of His only Son. Satan tried to taint Jesus with sin, but he failed. When Jesus hung on the cross, having been made sin for us, yet never having sinned personally, Satan could not point his finger at him and accuse Him of being a sinner. This is a favorite ploy of Satan (Revelation 12:10), but he totally failed when it came to the spotless Son of God.

Satan also fails when he accuses God's elect of sin. Although we have sinned and are deserving of God's wrath and punishment, when our redemption became a reality at our new birth, we were, and are, clothed with that same robe of righteousness worn by Christ Himself. Therefore, Satan's accusations are again null and void because Jesus offered Himself as the perfect Sacrifice for the atonement of our sins.

"He has appeared to put away sin by the sacrifice of Himself" Hebrews 9:26.

"Be silent in the presence of the Lord God; for the day of the Lord is at hand, for the Lord has prepared a sacrifice; He has invited His guests. And it shall be, in the day of the Lord's sacrifice, that I will punish the princes and the king's children, and all such as are clothed with foreign apparel" Zephaniah 1:7-8.

"By that will we have been sanctified through the offering of the body of Jesus Christ once for all" Hebrews 10:10.

Puritan Quote:

"Jesus Christ has opened the way to God the Father, by the sacrifice He made for us upon the cross. The holiness and justice of God need not frighten sinners and keep them back. Only let them cry to God in the name of Jesus, only let them plead the atoning blood of Jesus, and they shall find God upon a throne of grace, willing and ready to hear. The name of Jesus is a never-failing passport to our prayers. In that name a man may draw near to God with boldness, and ask with confidence. God has engaged to hear him. Reader, think of this; is not this encouragement?" J. C. Ryle, 1816-1900.

THE HEAVY HAND

Reading: Leviticus 1:3-9
"Then he shall put his hand on the head of the burnt offering"
Leviticus 1:4.

The act of laying on of hands was expressive of full identification. By that significant act, the offerer and the offering became one. The burnt offering, offered in the right way, shadowed the transference of a believer's sins to Christ, and by so doing, the believer acquires complete atonement.

The words of prophecy puts it this way:

"He has borne our griefs . . . He carried our sorrows . . . He was stricken . . . smitten . . . afflicted . . . He was wounded for our transgressions . . . bruised for our iniquities . . . chastised . . . the Lord has laid on Him the iniquity of us all" Isaiah 53:4-6.

The heavy hand of a just and righteous God transferred our sins to His only Beloved Son. Indeed, it was a very heavy hand. When the Ark of the Covenant was removed from its rightful place, everywhere it was taken suffered from the "heavy hand of God" 1 Samuel 5:6-12. The word "put" is a translation of the Hebrew 'camak', which carries a more forcible meaning of "to lean". The same word is used In Psalm 88:7 "Your wrath lies heavy upon me, and You have afflicted me with all Your waves."

When we consider the immense weight of our sin that was laid on Christ, it was no easy thing for Him to absorb. Andrew Bonar wrote: "We lean our soul on the same person on whom Jehovah leant His wrath."

"To the Jew it was a sacrifice to be slain, to you it is a sacrifice already offered; and this you are to accept and recognize as your own" C.H. Spurgeon.

"My faith doth lay her hand
On that dear head of thine;
While like a penitent I stand,
And there confess my sin"
Isaac Watts, 1674-1748

Peter expressed it well when he said, "who Himself bore our sins in His own body on the tree, that we, having died to sins, might live for righteousness—by whose stripes you were healed" 1 Peter 2:24.

In the case of the offering of the scapegoat goat (Lev 16:21), the same word is used, and translated:

"Aaron shall lay both his hands on the head of the live goat, confess over it all the iniquities of the children of Israel, and all their transgressions, concerning all their sins, putting them on the head of the goat, and shall send it away into the wilderness."

The laying of our sins on Jesus is the only way provided by God whereby we can have our sins forgiven and atoned for. It is also the only way whereby we can be identified with God: "we are in Him who is true" 1 John 5:20. The person who is not in Christ is still in his sins. There is no middle ground. Just as all the iniquities and all their transgressions and all their sins were transferred to the scapegoat, so all the sins of the redeemed are laid on Jesus. There is no such thing as being partly in Christ, or slipping in and out of Him. The sins of a believer do not nullify his identification with his Savior. Truly, believers do sin, and even those sins were born by Christ when He died on the cross. Thank God for 1 John 1:9:

"If we confess our sins, He is faithful and just to forgive us our sins and to cleanse us from all unrighteousness. If we say that we have not sinned, we make Him a liar, and His word is not in us."

On Christ's own authority, a believer "is completely clean" John 13:10. Can a believer backslide? Certainly, but he never ceases to be his Father's son:

"This my son was dead and is alive again; he was lost and is found" Luke 15:24.

Puritan Quote:

"The moment he, by the power of the Holy Ghost, believed the gospel, he passed from a positive state of unrighteousness and condemnation into a positive state of righteousness and acceptance" C.H. Mackintosh, 1820-1896.

A SWEET AROMA

Reading: Leviticus 1:3-9
". . . a sweet aroma to the Lord" Leviticus 1:9.

Of the 37 times "a sweet aroma to the Lord" is mentioned in scripture, 34 times it is found in Leviticus and Numbers, and every time it is speaking of the sacrifices the people were to make to God for atonement of their sins. The sacrifice was a sweet aroma to the Lord because it was unblemished, perfect, and without spot. These sacrifices were a picture of Jesus Christ, who Himself was "without sin" Hebrews 4:15.

Jesus was the perfect man on earth accomplishing the will of God, even in death. If Jesus came to accomplish the glorious work of atonement, His highest object in so doing was the glory of God:

"Behold, I have come to do Your will, O God" Hebrews 10:9.

Although we have benefitted from Christ's obedience to the will of God, the primary aspect of His work was Godward.

"It was an ineffable delight to Him to accomplish the will of God on this earth. No one had ever done this before. Some had, through grace, done "that which was right in the sight of the Lord;" but no one had ever perfectly, invariably, from first to last, without hesitation, and without divergence, done the will of God." C. H. Mackintosh.

The life and death of Jesus Christ was, to His Father in heaven, a "sweet aroma."

In the light of this, Paul wrote:

"Therefore be imitators of God as dear children. And walk in love, as Christ also has loved us and given Himself for us,

an offering and a sacrifice to God for a sweet-smelling aroma"
Ephesians 5:1-2.

The question begs to be asked of each of us who call ourselves
Christians: Are we imitators of God? Do we seek to walk as He walked?
Are we willing to walk in love as Christ loved us? When held up to this
standard, I find myself falling far short. Is my life a "sweet smelling aroma"
in the nostrils of my heavenly Father? I know, and rejoice, that I am fully
justified in His sight, but what about my daily walk? It is easy to ask, "What
would Jesus do?" but are we willing to do it?

The unblemished male of the first year was a type of the Lord Jesus
offering Himself for the perfect accomplishment of the will of God.

The important aspect in studying the doctrine of the burnt-offering,
is not the meeting of the sinner's need, but the presentation to God of
that which was infinitely acceptable to Him. No person has ever had
any asset that would be acceptable to God, other than Jesus Christ. Our
righteousness is like filthy rags:

"But we are all like an unclean thing, and all our righteousnesses
are like filthy rags; we all fade as a leaf, and our iniquities, like
the wind, have taken us away. And there is no one who calls on
Your name, who stirs himself up to take hold of You; for You
have hidden Your face from us, and have consumed us because
of our iniquities" Isaiah 64:6-7.

God, however, does not expect His children to be perfect. If we say
we don't sin, we deceive ourselves (1 John 1:8), so He offers us a means
to confess our sins (1 John 1:9), and the wonderful thing is that it is all
premised on His faithfulness. Instead of punishing us for our sins, as
in Isaiah 64 above, He forgives us and cleanses us. What a wonderful,
forgiving, and faithful Father we have.

All of this is pre-pictured in the sacrifices of Leviticus.

"Father, if it is Your will, take this cup away from Me; nevertheless
not My will, but Yours, be done" Luke 22:42.

May this be our attitude and commitment as we walk this earth with God as our Father, and Jesus as our Savior and Example.

Puritan Quote:

"It is sweet to Jehovah to behold this sight in a fallen world. This 'sweet savour' is literally 'savour of rest; as if the Savior stayed His wrath and calmed His soul" Andrew Bonar, 1810-1892.

INWARD MOTIVE FOR OUTWARD CONDUCT

Reading: Leviticus 1:3-9
"He shall wash its entrails and its legs with water"" Leviticus 1:9.

Previously, we considered the ascending smoke of the sacrifice as a "sweet aroma" to God, speaking of how the sacrifice of Jesus was received by His Father. The words for consideration today presents Jesus' sacrifice as "pure"—both inwardly and outwardly.

On no occasion was there any conflict between these two aspects of Christ's life. He didn't believe one thing and do another—in other words, He was not a hypocrite. One man commenting on this concept wrote: "The latter was the index of the former."

The priests partook of some sacrifices, but the burnt-offering was completely consumed by fire, and was exclusively for God. The priests might arrange the wood and the fire, and see the flame ascend, but they did not eat any of the sacrifice. We must never lose sight of the fact that Christ's sacrifice of Himself on the cross, as typified in the burnt-offering, was solely for the satisfaction and glory of His Father.

No created being can ever fully appreciate the pure and holy relationship between the Father and His Only-begotten Son. The Father's glory was the motive and driving force in the life and death of Jesus. The fact that our salvation and eternal welfare is achieved through the same life and death of Jesus is a matter for further study.

To whom was the sacrifice made? To whom was the debt paid? It was the Father who had been offended by sin. It is the Father's wrath that must be assuaged. It is the Father to whom we must be reconciled. In 1964, I wrote the following words in the front of my Bible: *"I owed a debt I could not pay; Jesus paid a debt He did not owe."* That which we sinners deserved, Jesus experienced.

"Christ also has loved us and given Himself for us, an offering and a sacrifice to God for a sweet-smelling aroma" Ephesians 5:2.

"Those who trust in Christ, who is their substitute burnt-offering, are free from the coming wrath of God in hell. They died in Christ's death and they live by faith in the Son of God who loved them and gave himself for them" Philip H. Eveson.

As Jesus is an Example of how we should commit ourselves fully to God, so Paul writes:

"I beseech you therefore, brethren, by the mercies of God, that you present your bodies a living sacrifice, holy, acceptable to God, which is your reasonable service" Romans 12:1.

Not that we can ever duplicate the sacrifice of Jesus, we are called upon to present to God all that we have and are. As was the Levitical sacrifice, so the presentation of our sacrifice must be both "holy" and "acceptable" to Him. Although we might, and often do, think this is asking too much, the apostle tells us it "is [y]our reasonable service."

Puritan Quote:

"We now also find what sacrifices Paul recommends to the Christian Church: for being reconciled to God through the one only true sacrifice of Christ, we are all through his grace made priests, in order that we may dedicate ourselves and all we have to the glory of God" John Calvin, 1509—1564.

NO PARTIALITY WITH GOD

Reading: Leviticus 1:10-17

"If his offering is of the flocks—of the sheep or of the goats . . ."
Leviticus 1:10.

It appears that a wealthier man usually selected oxen as their offering, and less able men sacrificed sheep or goats, while the poorer laboring class could offer doves. There is a definite principle shown here, in that no person was excluded because of his social standing—the rich, the middle class, and the poor, were included in the opportunity to offer their best to God.

This is a principle often addressed in the New Testament, and Paul sums it up with his words to the Roman church: "there is no partiality with God" Romans 2:11. He is more specific when he wrote to the Colossian saints about the Creator:

"where there is neither Greek nor Jew, circumcised nor uncircumcised, barbarian, Scythian, slave nor free, but Christ is all and in all" Colossians 3:11.

The gospel message is summarized by Jesus when He said, "All that the Father gives Me will come to Me, and the one who comes to Me I will by no means cast out" John 6:37. There is no distinction of race, religious background, philosophy, or social class. All classifications of persons are included in the "whosoever" of Acts 2:21.

Above all things, the "whosoever" is referring to the gentiles, not only the Jews. This was huge, as the gentiles were looked upon as heathen, people to be avoided, but it was prophesied that God's message would be preached to the gentiles, of which Paul was proclaimed as the "light to the gentiles" Isaiah 42:6; Acts 13:47. Jesus declared that Paul was His "chosen vessel . . . to bear My name before Gentiles" Acts 9:15.

You and I of the western world are the benefactors of this, in fact, any non-Jew are characterized as "gentile." Thanks be to God that in Jesus Christ there is neither Jew nor gentile [Greek]" Romans 10:12; Galatians 3:28; Colossians 3:11.

According to Jewish rabbis, 'It matters not whether one gives much or little, so long as he directs his heart to heaven' Mishnah tractate Menaloth 110a. I respectfully disagree, as this gives the opportunity for one to offer a dove when he could afford an ox. God expects His people to give their best to Him, to "seek first the kingdom of God and His righteousness, and all these things shall be added to you" Matthew 6:33. Jesus demands we give Him our all, not a dove when we can afford an ox:

"You still lack one thing. Sell all that you have and distribute to the poor, and you will have treasure in heaven; and come, follow Me" Luke 18:22.

When He asks us to give Him that which is precious to us, we must be willing to do so. It is not that the rich ruler didn't give all to Jesus, but that he was not willing to do so—it all has to do with our attitude.

Do we give less when we could give more? Finances are not the only issue here, but our time, our effort, our commitment, etc. God does not ask for an ox when all we have are sheep or goats. Each child of God is accountable to God as an individual. He does not ask the same thing from all, except the best of what He has given us. He does not ask us all to be Charles Spurgeon or Billy Graham, and He did not ask Spurgeon to be a classical pianist, or Graham to be a famous artist. He asks each of us to give back to Him the best of what He has given us. God does not ask us to be an eye when He has made us a hand, etc.

"If the foot should say, "Because I am not a hand, I am not of the body," is it therefore not of the body? And if the ear should say, "Because I am not an eye, I am not of the body," is it therefore not of the body? If the whole body were an eye, where would be the hearing? If the whole were hearing, where would be the smelling? But now God has set the members, each one of them,

in the body just as He pleased. And if they were all one member, where would the body be?" 1 Corinthians 12:15-19, see also vss 20-31.

Many in the Corinthian church were unhappy with what God had given them. They considered certain gifts more important than others. They were envious of those who possessed "greater" gifts than themselves. To continue with Paul's analogy, the finger wanted to be a hand, and the ear an eye.

God does not expect us to be a leg, when He has made us a foot. God will never call us to be something we are not. He will always equip us to function in the capacity to which He has called us.

Remember, we are one in Christ, but are accountable to Him as individuals.

Puritan Quotes:

"He who knows our heart, knows our attitude" Thomas Watson, 1620-1686.

"Envy is also frequently petulant and pouting. If it cannot have its own way it takes its marbles and goes home, and will not play with the others" John MacArthur, Jr., 1939—

THE HUMANITY OF JESUS

Reading: Leviticus 2:1-16

"When anyone offers a grain offering to the Lord" Leviticus 2:1.

The Scriptures make reference to two divisions of offering acceptable to God—sacrifices with, and sacrifices without, blood. The burnt offering in chapter one of Leviticus addresses the first class, that which required the shedding of blood. Now, chapter two speaks of the "grain-offering" (meat-offering, KJV) where no blood is required.

To us in the 21st century, there is a big difference between 'meat' and 'grain'. In 1611, when the KJV was first published, the word 'meat' meant any kind of food, including cereal crops. However, today when we speak of 'meat', we immediately think of animal flesh—this is exactly what this offering did not include.

One thing of note is that the 'burnt-offering' and the 'grain-offering' are often mentioned together (Num.15:1-16, 28:1-5; Josh. 22:23; 1 Kings 8:64; 2 Kings16:13,15).

This chapter divides into three sections and describes three kinds of grain offerings: uncooked grain (2:1-3), cooked grain (2:4-10), and the first fruits of grain (2:14-16).

It is interesting to note that each kind has "do's and don'ts" as far as the ingredients are concerned. Each kind must be made with 'fine flour' and 'oil'. Likewise, leaven and honey must not be included (2:11).

We can never forget that Jesus Christ, the Son of God, was the possessor of two distinct natures—divine and human. He was conceived by the Holy Spirit, and Mary was His mother (Matt 1:18, 20). In this Jesus is unique. As Divine, He could not sin, but in His human nature, He was tempted:

"For we do not have a High Priest who cannot sympathize with our weaknesses, but was in all points tempted as we are, yet without sin" Hebrews 4:15-16; see also Hebrews 2:18.

Just as the burnt-offering was to be of animals 'unblemished', so the 'fine flour' is indicative of Jesus' life 'without sin'. As with Christ, so with His bride:

"He did this to present her to himself as a glorious church without a spot or wrinkle or any other blemish . . . she will be holy and without fault" Ephesians 5:25-27, NLT.

Therefore, when the last citizen of His kingdom is saved, Jesus will present it to His Father (1 Corinthians.15:24), Himself included as King of kings, and Lord of lords, and it will be accepted, because both Bride and Bridegroom will be perfect, with no blemish—'holy and without fault' (Revelation 14:5).

The 'fine flour': First in the process of producing 'fine flour' was the grinding of the heads by the mill. This is significant of Isaiah 53:5, "He was crushed for our sins" (NLT). Jesus, through the 'mill' of affliction and death, saved His people from their sins and bring us to His Father.

The next step was to put sift the ground wheat until all the bran or husks were removed. Jesus was surely 'sifted' through the sieve of human experience, directly by the devil as well as by daily human temptations. As finely sieved as He was, not one husk was to be found, for He was without sin.

It was no boast when Jesus said, "I am the Bread of Life" John 6:48.

"I am the living bread which came down from heaven. If anyone eats of this bread, he will live forever" John 6:51.

If "the Man Christ Jesus" (1 Timothy 2:5) was accepted by God, and is now "seated at the right hand of God" (Ephesians 1:20), surely, there is in Him everything that should satisfy us: "The Lord will guide you continually, and satisfy your soul in drought" Isaiah 58:11.

"God never forsakes his people in the middle of the journey, but continues his kindness towards them with unwearied regularity, and for this reason promises that they shall be satisfied amidst the deepest poverty" John Calvin.

Puritan Quote:

"Let us carefully study the divine picture set before us in the life of 'the Man Christ Jesus.' How refreshing and strengthening to 'the inward man' to be occupied with Him who was perfect in all His ways, and who 'in all things must have the preeminence'" C.H. Mackintosh, 1820—1896.

THE BLOOD SACRIFICE

Reading: Leviticus 3:1-15
"the priests, shall sprinkle the blood all around on the altar" Leviticus 3:2

I would like to remain on the subject of the Peace Offering, because it presents us with a topic that is seldom heard from the pulpit. It is important to note the Peace Offering required the shedding of blood, whereas the Grain (Meat) offering did not.

Each offering was accepted by Him as a "sweet smelling odor," as was the Peace Offering. In the Burnt Offering we saw how Christ died for our sins, and His wrath was appeased toward all who "believe on the Lord Jesus Christ." The resulting affect of the shed blood of Christ not only paved the way for our sins to be forgiven (we are reconciled to God), but enabled us to be the recipients of "every blessing in Christ Jesus" Ephesians 1:3.

All mankind, believer and nonbeliever alike, are recipients of God's blessing,

"He makes His sun rise on the evil and on the good, and sends rain on the just and on the unjust" Matthew 5:45.

However, the rich blessings of God are reserved for His children, and the only way we are eligible, is because the sacrificial blood of Jesus has washed us and made us clean in His eyes. It is because of Christ's shed blood that "In Him also we have obtained an inheritance" Ephesians 1:11. Yes, not only are we reconciled to God because of His Son's shed blood, but we have been given an inheritance, and that inheritance includes all the blessings we have because we have been made one with our Savior, Jesus Christ.

Not only is our inheritance a wonderful thing, and something which we do not deserve, or have the ability to earn, but it is guaranteed:

"in whom also, having believed, you were sealed with the Holy Spirit of promise, who is the guarantee of our inheritance" **Ephesians 1:13-14.**

The Peace Offering represents our reconciliation to God and all the benefits arising from it. When God promised David He would establish a permanent house in which He would dwell, he responded with words that should be on the heart of every believer as the Holy Spirit reveals to us the magnificence of the inheritance we have in Christ:

"O Lord, for Your servant's sake, and according to Your own heart, You have done all this greatness, in making known all these great things . . . And now, Lord, You are God, and have promised this goodness to Your servant. 1 Chronicles 17:19, 26-27.

When the prodigal son returned home, before he seated him at his table and shared the bounty of his house, he clothed him in the "best robe," "put a ring on his finger" to identify him as his son, and "sandals on his feet" to separate him from the dirt of his journey, and did not hire him as a servant, but accepted and treated him as a son, then, and only then, did the father say, "Let us eat and be merry: for this my son was dead, and is alive again; he was lost, and is found" Luke 15:22-25. As it is with all true believers, their old nature is not recognized as existing before God.

The Peace Offering helps us distinguish between sin in the flesh, and sin on the conscience. The Burnt Offering addresses the sin in the flesh, our old nature, that which condemns us before God, whereas the Peace Offering speaks of the sin on our conscience. There is no peace with God until our sin has been dealt with—we cannot have fellowship with God until we are reconciled to Him.

However, God has made provision for the sins of our conscience, sins every believer commits to one degree or another, for, if we say we have no sin, we deceive ourselves, and the truth is not in us. If we confess our sins, He is faithful and just to forgive us our sins and to cleanse us from all unrighteousness" 1 John 1:8-9.

It is important that we understand the difference between how God deals with the sin of unbelievers, and the sins of believers. As an unbeliever, we must repent of our sins and seek the mercy of God for our salvation; as a believer, we must confess our sins and our heavenly Father will forgive us.

True spiritual peace comes to us when we confess our sins to God with the understanding we also receive His forgiveness. Unconfessed sin in a believers life will rob him of that peace which is his by right of his inheritance.

"**Mark the blameless man, and observe the upright; for the future of that man is peace**" **Psalm 37:37;**
"**You will keep him in perfect peace, whose mind is stayed on You, because he trusts in You**" **Isaiah 26:3.**

Puritan Quote:
"It is truly pleasant, unspeakably precious, to see God's thorough demand for spotlessness; for thus we are assured that, beyond all doubt, our reconciliation is solid. It is full reconciliation to a God who is fully satisfied" Andrew Bonar, 1810-1892.

GUILTY YET FORGIVEN

Reading: Leviticus 5:14-6:7
"If a person sins, and commits any of these things . . . though he does not know it, yet he is guilty and shall bear his iniquity" Leviticus 5:17.

The Divine Word progresses on to the Trespass Offering, which again deals with those sins of which a person is ignorant. Two distinct kinds of sin are addressed: 1) sins against God and 2) sins against man.

The holiness of God is once again brought to the forefront: "If a person commits a trespass, and sins unintentionally in regard to the holy things of the Lord . . ." The holiness of God is the standard by which all sin is judged. In Gods eyes there is no such thing as mortal sin and venial sin—any violation of God's holiness is sin, and, if not forgiven by God through the blood of Jesus Christ, will condemn a person to hell. God can forgive all manner of trespass, but He cannot pass over a single jot or tittle. He cannot sanction the slightest sin, but He can blot it out.

It is a grave error to think that, as long as a person lives up to the dictates of their conscience, they are safe from God's wrath and judgment. The glorious affect of the shed blood of Jesus, is that it makes possible our justification—to be made guiltless in the piercing judgment of God's holiness. The demands of God's holiness have been met in the person of His Son, and we who believe have been made one with Him. When God searches the heart of any redeemed person, He sees His Son in us, and adamantly declares, "NOT GUILTY."

More specifically, the Trespass Offering has to do with the personal appropriation of that which belonged to God, and that which belonged to another. Today, we often see notices posted on the boundary of someone's property that reads, "No Trespassing". In other words, by entering the property without the owner's permission, you are violating that which rightfully belongs to another. Such is the thought with the Trespass Offering: "If a soul commit a trespass, and sin through ignorance, in the holy things of the Lord . . ."

An example of trespassing was if a man kept for himself all or any part of the tithes given to God, the first-fruits, the first-born of the cattle, or the food apportioned to the officiating priest, etc. By such an act, he committed trespass by converting to his own use any thing that was dedicated to God—"the holy things of the Lord."

In the light of this, dare we examine ourselves as to that which belongs to God and that we use for our own good or advantage? What a potent question. It might be any talent God has given us, or time, or wealth, or anything that could be used in His service both in the expansion of His kingdom or the "edifying of the of the body of Christ" (Ephesians 5:12). The bottom line is, that true commitment and dedication to Jesus—not keeping anything back for ourselves—is total and complete:

"If you want to be my disciple, you must hate everyone else by comparison—your father and mother, wife and children, brothers and sisters—yes, even your own life. Otherwise, you cannot be my disciple. And if you do not carry your own cross and follow me, you cannot be my disciple" Luke 14:26-27, NLT.

The Trespass Offering brings to light that which man has defrauded of God. That which is rightfully His we are keeping and utilizing for ourselves, even if done "unintentionally" Leviticus 5:15. Again, the offering must be "without blemish."

When offered sincerely and properly, the result is "it shall be forgiven him" 5:19. How wide and deep is atonement, even stretching to include those "trespasses" of which we are ignorant.

"There is therefore now no condemnation to those who are in Christ Jesus, who do not walk according to the flesh, but according to the Spirit" Romans 8:1.

Included in the Trespass Offering are sins against a neighbor: 6:2-3. That which was borrowed and not returned, that which was given for a period of time for safe keeping; anything lent to another is included; a tool, like the prophet's borrowed axe (2 Kings 6:5), or a sum of money left in the neighbor's keeping (Exodus 22:7); in short, any stuff or articles (Exodus 22:7-14).

When asked concerning the greatest commandment, Jesus said:

"'You shall love the Lord your God with all your heart, with all your soul, and with all your mind.' This is the first and great commandment. And the second is like it: 'You shall love your neighbor as yourself.' On these two commandments hang all the Law and the Prophets" Matthew 22:37-40.

First God, then others. This is the principle taught throughout scripture—in the Trespass Offering and Jesus' teaching. How about in our life?

Puritan Quote:

"He whose sins are forgiven is willing to forgive others who have offended him. By this touchstone, we may try whether our sins are pardoned. We need not climb up to heaven to see whether our sins are forgiven, but only look into our hearts. Can we bury injuries, requite good for evil? This would be a good sign that we are forgiven of God" Thomas Watson, 1620-1686.

RECONCILIATION TO GOD AND NEIGHBOR

Reading: Leviticus 6:1-7
"If a person sins and commits a trespass against the Lord by lying to his neighbor . . ." Leviticus 6:1.

One of the important principles of Scripture is outlined in these verses: when we sin against our neighbor it is considered by God as a sin against Himself. Things considered as "small things", such as lying or twisting the truth, even when it might not adversely affect the neighbor's situation, is taken personally by God—it is "a trespass against the Lord."

"Whoever does not practice righteousness is not of God" 1 John 3:10.

This does not mean that when a believer lies to another, he loses his salvation, for the avenue of confession to God is always open (1 John 1:9), but if he continues in that sin, if it is a 'normal' part of his life and he is not convicted by the Holy Spirit of that sin, "he is not of God."

A good example of this principle, although in reverse, is found in the words of Jesus when He said:

"Assuredly, I say to you, inasmuch as you did it to one of the least of these My brethren, you did it to Me" Matthew 25:40.

Whether it be something good or something bad, whatever we do as God's child, or a citizen of His kingdom, He considers it as done unto Him—He takes it personally. The reason we are held accountable at the time of judgment, whether saved or unsaved, is because we are held accountable to God. The way we treat our neighbor is second only to the way we love God:

"You shall love the Lord your God with all your heart, with all your soul, with all your mind, and with all your strength.' This is the first commandment. And the second, like it, is this: 'You shall love your neighbor as yourself'" Mark 12:30-31.

Nothing can be more dishonoring to God than the supposition that a man may belong to God while his conduct does not reflect the law and commandments of Jesus Christ. "The Lord knows those who are His," and, "Let everyone who names the name of Christ depart from iniquity" 2 Timothy 2:19.

Sin is often taken lightly and as having no consequence, but God sees it differently (1 John 3:10). Part of "fighting the good fight" is knowing our enemy; what is expected of us, and doing it.

That which was expected of the guilty person was twofold: He was to restore whatever he had defrauded from his neighbor (plus 20%), then make his offering to God. When I was a young person (age 14), I had a serious stealing problem. When I was caught, I was made to list everything I had stolen, no matter how small, and from whom I had stolen. I was then made to go to that person, return the stolen item or the cash equivalent, and apologize. In the short-term it was a painful solution, but in the long-term it has reaped its benefits, it was a lesson well learned.

The reason for the additional 20% was to compensate the owner for the loss of use (a current insurance term) of the property during the time it was withheld. Jesus taught there is a relationship between acceptable worship and any indebtedness we have toward another person. Restoration and reconciliation comes before worship (Matthew 5:23-24). Paul warns against partaking of the Lord's Supper unworthily, and to "let a man examine himself, and so let him eat of the bread and drink of the cup" 1 Corinthians 11:28. Such is the importance of the principle taught in our reading today.

Defrauding God and a neighbor was such a serious violation that God demanded the loss of life for the offender. Bu God's grace, however, the violator could make restitution and substitute an unblemished animal to make atonement.

By God's grace, Jesus gave His life so we might receive atonement for our sins, but that does not excuse us from the importance of reconciliation and restitution to those we have wronged, however slight that may be.

"As He who called you is holy, you also be holy in all your conduct, because it is written, "Be holy, for I am holy" 1 Peter 1:15-16.

Puritan Quote:
"In bidding us to be holy like himself, the proportion is not that of equals; but we ought to advance in this direction as far as our condition will bear. And as even the most perfect are always very far from coming up to the mark, we ought daily to strive more and more" John Calvin, 1509-1564.

AS THE LORD COMMANDED

Reading: Leviticus 8:1-12
"This is what the Lord commanded to be done." Leviticus 8:5

Such was the word of the Lord honored, revered, and obeyed, that this statement is made in excess of 66 times in the Old Testament. Is it any wonder, therefore, that a person was judged by the statement that he "did what was right in the sight of the Lord." It is a thought for another time, that this is said of the kings of Judah, but not of the kings of Israel.

Anytime the word of the Lord is obeyed, that act can be said it was "right in the sight of the Lord." The poignant observation in these words is the authority of God's Word. How often we obey that which the Lord commands only when it is easy, convenient, or for our obvious well-being.

Whether it was for the dedication of the priests, or in the entire range of the sacrifices, we are brought under the authority of God's word. Phrases such as "as the Lord said," and "as the Lord told him," and "as the Lord promised," and "as the Lord directed me," are given as to the reason why Moses, Aaron, David, Jeremiah, and many others, did what they did.

These are indeed priceless words, for this is what God looks for in all His children. It does not say "This is the thing which is expedient, agreeable, or suitable; neither did he say, "This is the thing that has been arranged by the fathers or the elders. Moses recognized nothing but the authority of God.

When the word of the Lord was observed, that which every true believer happens:

"This is the thing which the Lord commanded you to do, and the glory of the Lord will appear to you" Leviticus 9:6.

God will reveal Himself to those whose life is committed in doing that which He has commanded. This is an obedience of love, not one for fear of punishment. Jesus said:

"If you love Me, keep My commandments" John 14:15.

A proof, to ourselves and to others, that we love God, is that we live a life in obedience to Him; not that we have to, but because we want to.

"For the love of Christ compels us . . . that those who live should live no longer for themselves, but for Him who died for them and rose again" 2 Corinthians 5:14-15.

This principle of obedience leaves no room for tradition, or for the arguments and dissertations of men with their various interpretations of what the word of God "surely" means. All was clear, conclusive, and authoritative. As children of God, we must always accept the word of the Lord as the final authority.

And what was the result of this strict adherence to the word of God? "The glory of the Lord will appear to you." The congregation was well rewarded for their strict adherence to the word of the Lord. They never wavered, nor deviated from what God commanded. Had they offered an animal that was blemished in any way, their sacrifice would have been rejected. However, because of their obedience to God's word,

"And Moses and Aaron went into the tabernacle of meeting, and came out and blessed the people. Then the glory of the Lord appeared to all the people, and fire came out from before the Lord and consumed the burnt offering and the fat on the altar. When all the people saw it, they shouted and fell on their faces" Leviticus 9:23-24.

The people did that which the Lord commanded, they saw the glory of the Lord, and they worshipped. This is the progression of the child of God who truly loves Him. Worship does not precede obedience, neither does God reveal Himself to those who disobey Him. Look around and see how many of us give a pretense of worship, with all its outward signs and rituals, and yet do not that which God commands. This is called "hypocrisy", and rightfully so.

Let us examine ourselves and make sure we are living in accord with the word of the Lord.

"Grace be with all those who love our Lord Jesus Christ in sincerity" Ephesians 6:24.

Puritan Quote:

"They [the people] prostrated themselves in his presence, thereby intimating the deep sense they had of HIS goodness, of their unworthiness, and of the obligation they were under to live in subjection to his authority, and obedience to his will" Adam Clarke, 1760-1832.

THE ANOINTING OF THE HIGH PRIEST

Reading: Leviticus 8:7-12
"... he poured some of the anointing oil on Aaron's
head and anointed him" Leviticus 8:12

The truth represented in the anointing of Aaron as the High Priest is extremely important and full of truth regarding Jesus Christ, our Great High Priest. Jesus was the Christ, the Greek form of the Hebrew Messiah. Both words, Christos and Messiah, mean the 'Anointed One.' The very name Jesus Christ tells us that the man Jesus was the Messiah, the 'Anointed One.' When Jesus asked Peter "Who do you say that I am?" he answered, "You are the Christ, the Son of the living God" Matthew 16:16.

The New Testament presents Jesus as the Messiah in three capacities: Prophet, Priest, and King.

When Jesus read from the book of Isaiah in the synagogue, He read: "The Spirit of the Lord is upon Me, because He has anointed Me to preach the gospel to the poor" (Luke 4: 18), He did so in the capacity of a prophet (24). The book of Hebrews announces Jesus as "a priest forever" (Hebrews 5:6; 7:24). Then, in Hebrews 1:8, we read: "Your throne, O God, is forever and ever; a scepter of righteousness is the scepter of Your kingdom. You have loved righteousness and hated lawlessness; therefore God, Your God, has anointed You with the oil of gladness more than Your companions."

These three statements are quotes from the Old Testament, reminding us that Jesus said:

"Do not think that I came to destroy the Law or the Prophets. I did not come to destroy but to fulfill" Matthew 5:17.

Jesus came as the perfect fulfillment of that which was typified in the anointing of Aaron. The one Man—Prophet, Priest, and King, anointed by God, perfect in all His ways, without sin, without blemish, the Messiah, the Christ.

Peter explained to Cornelius and his household "how God anointed Jesus of Nazareth with the Holy Spirit and with power" Acts 10:38. Just as God's children are born again by the Holy Spirit, so are we anointed:

"Now He who establishes us with you in Christ and has anointed us is God, who also has sealed us and given us the Spirit in our hearts as a guarantee" 2 Corinthians 1:21-22.

It was not only the person of Aaron that was anointed, but his garments, miter, and instruments of his office—ephod, breastplate, etc. But this is for another time.

Aaron's sons were also anointed, but not until after their father. How representative is this of Christ and His relationship to those whom God calls "sons." It is the anointing of God's sons that differentiates them from the world, the wicked, and antichrists (1 John 2: 15-27).

"But you have an anointing from the Holy One . . . But the anointing which you have received from Him abides in you" 1 John 2:20, 27).

Why were not Aaron and his sons anointed at the same time? Because the blood had not been shed. A fact perfectly in line with the anointing of Jesus and the children of God. Jesus first, then the sacrifice of Himself and the shedding of His blood, then, once our salvation was secured, we were anointed by the Holy Spirit that we might be "as He is."

"And for their sakes I sanctify Myself, that they also may be sanctified by the truth" John 17:19. Jesus first in all things, then God's children—a perfect identification with Jesus, He in us, and we in Him. This does not mean, as some wayward preachers teach today, that we have become "little Christs." There is only one Messiah, the Man Jesus. But what a privilege and joy to be made one with Him.

"You shall anoint them, as you anointed their father, that they may minister to Me as priests; for their anointing shall surely be

an everlasting priesthood throughout their generations" Exodus 40:15.

"To Him who loved us and washed us from our sins in His own blood, and has made us kings and priests to His God and Father, to Him be glory and dominion forever and ever. Amen" Revelation 1:5-6.

Puritan Quote:

"Blessed assurance! He ever liveth. He never changeth; and we are in Him, and as He is. He presents us to the Father in His own eternal perfectness, and the Father delights in us as thus presented" C.H. Mackintosh, 1820-1896.

THE SONS OF AARON

Reading: Leviticus 10:1-3
"The sons of Aaron ... offered profane fire before the Lord" Lev. 10:1

Two weeks ago, our thoughts were based on the words "they did as the Lord commanded." Unfortunately, however, this cannot be said when we look into the history of God's children. Rather than doing what the Lord commanded, man has left a trail of failure and disobedience.

Nadab and Abihu, the sons of Aaron, did that "which He (the Lord) had not commanded them" Lev. 10:1. What a contrast from chapter eight where it is stated the people "did that which the Lord commanded them."

Adam, amid all the delights of Eden, chose to listen to the devil's lie; after God's judgment on the earth, Noah, we are told, decided to get drunk; the nation of Israel, delivered from 400 years of slavery, moaned and groaned and wanted to return to Egypt; after crossing the Jordan, "they forsook the Lord God of their fathers"; these, and many other examples, lead to God's statement to Jeremiah,

"So do not pray for this people, or lift up a cry or prayer for them; for I will not hear them in the time that they cry out to Me" Jeremiah 11:14.

How merciful and how gracious is God to us today, to those of us who know Him and who have a personal relationship with Him and His Son Jesus. Since the day Jesus ascended into heaven and sat down at the right hand of His Father, He has made provision for His people when they sin. When we do not do as He has commanded, He has given us a promise:

"If we confess our sins, He is faithful and just to forgive us our sins and to cleanse us from all unrighteousness" 1 John 1:9.

The promises of God are remarkable, and, as we read His Word, we relish His promises, and claim them "by faith." Then we wonder why God does not keep His promises. 'He has failed you', Satan whispers in our ear. But, the question we need to ask, is, "Why hasn't God kept His promise?"

Whether we read God's promises in the Old or New Testament, they are always based on a condition. Do these words ring a bell? "If you will obey," "If you will confess," "If you will listen to me," "If you will hear His voice," "If you will walk in my ways, and if you will keep my commandments," etc. etc. etc. Yes, "all the promises of God in Him are Yes, and in Him Amen" 2 Corinthians 1:20, but the words "in Him" strongly imply that those who are in Christ know His Word and live accordingly, for "If you love me, you will keep my commandments" John 14:15. RSV.

The fulfillment of God's promises are based on that little word "If." God is faithful and just. He does keep His Word, both to the godly and ungodly:

"The Lord is righteous in her midst, He will do no unrighteousness. Every morning He brings His justice to light; He never fails" Zephaniah 3:5.

The basis of God's covenant with the children of Israel was, "If you will indeed obey My voice and keep My covenant, then you shall be a special treasure to Me above all people; for all the earth is Mine. And you shall be to Me a kingdom of priests and a holy nation" Exodus 19:5-6.

Puritan Quote:

"The promises [of God} are not only the food of faith, but also the very life and soul of faith; they are a mine of rich treasures, a garden full of the choicest and sweetest flowers; in them are wrapped up all celestial contentments and delights" Thomas Brooks, 1608-1680.

I AM THE LORD

Reading: Leviticus 18:1-5

"Speak to the children of Israel, and say to them: 'I am the Lord your God'"
Leviticus 18:2

Throughout Leviticus, and indeed throughout scripture, the term "I am the Lord" is prominent both as God's name for Himself and the preferred name by which His people refer to Him. Without addressing the etymology of this name, let us take a brief look at its usage in the book of Leviticus.

"I am the Lord" is used as a stamp of authority. God makes a statement, such as a command, then gives it His "stamp" of authority: "You shall observe My judgments and keep My ordinances, to walk in them: I am the Lord your God" Lev 18:4.

This phrase is used on 45 occasions in Leviticus, and 165 times in the Old Testament, which indicates the importance we should give to it. Whenever the word LORD (all capitalized), the original is Yahweh, or Jehovah, but when spelled Lord, it is "adoniai", meaning master as in a master/slave relationship.

Often, LORD is accompanied with a qualifying word such as "God." When this occurs, "God" is the Hebrew word "elohim", the plural word for God.

The prophet Ezekiel frequently uses the phrase more than any other. When God told Jeremiah not to bother praying for His people for He would not hear due to their continual disobedience and rebellion, He passed a four-fold judgment on them:

**"For they shall fall by the sword, by famine, and by pestilence ...
yet I will leave a remnant ..." Ezekiel 6:8,11.**

That remnant was taken captive by the Chaldeans for seventy years. The purpose for the judgment was "Then they shall know that I am the

Lord." Whether it was judgment against Israel or any other nation, the purpose was always that "they [you] shall know that I am the LORD" Ezekiel 6:7,10,13,14.

This is the primary purpose for God setting aside a people for Himself—that they may know Him. From the time that Adam and Eve hid themselves from the "presence of the Lord God" (Gen 3:8), God has sought a people He could call His own.

This is the reason God formed the nation of Israel:

"I will take you as My people, and I will be your God. Then you shall know that I am the Lord your God" Exodus 6:7.

Because of their rebellion and disobedience, God divorced Himself from Israel (Jeremiah 3:8). God left Himself a remnant through which Jesus would be born, through whom He would create the church with whom He has established (and is establishing) a people that know Him as their LORD God. The church, His Bride, exists for the purpose of knowing Him. God has always desired a relationship with His creation, and now He has achieved it.

To know God is to have eternal life:

"And this is eternal life, that they may know You, the only true God, and Jesus Christ whom You have sent" John 17:3.

The apostle Paul was not satisfied with just having a relationship with God, he wanted to know Him to the fullest extent possible:

"That I may know Him and the power of His resurrection, and the fellowship of His sufferings, being conformed to His death" Phil. 3:10.

There is a vast difference between "knowing God" and knowing about God. Thousands of people know a great deal about God without knowing Him. To know Him is to have a personal relationship with Him. To know Him means we are adopted into His family. To know Him gives us the privilege of calling Him Father. To know Him gives us the right to call Jesus Brother and Friend. To know Him is life eternal.

Puritan Quote:

"*God, whose name is 'the LORD' (Jehovah/Yahweh), has not only redeemed them, but has entered into a special relationship with them. What an incentive to walk in God's ways!*" Philip H. Eveson, current lecturer at London Theological Seminary.

YOU SHALL BE HOLY

Reading: Leviticus 18:1-5
"You shall be holy, for I the LORD your God am holy" Leviticus 19:2

The section of Leviticus (chap's 18-20) presents us with the personal moral status which Jehovah (the LORD) expects of those He has called to be His special people, His children. While everything mentioned may not be applicable to every individual, every individual is capable of committing these violations of His holiness.

Jehovah was their God, and He was holy, therefore they were called to be holy. God reminded them "I am the Lord" 21 times in the three chapters 18, 19, 20. God did not require of His people anything that was not true of Himself: "You shall be holy, for I the LORD your God am Holy." His people's conduct was to be founded and grounded upon what He is—Holy.

This principle of godly living is applicable to us today as it was to the Israelite nation in the days of Moses and Aaron (1 Peter 1:15-16). God does not command us then leave us to figure it out by ourselves. Yes, Paul wrote:

"Work out your own salvation with fear and trembling," but also says, **"for it is God who works in you both to will and to do for His good pleasure" Philippians 2:13.**

Any Christian who attempts to "be holy" by his own effort, will soon find he has taken on the impossible. We all need the help of the Holy Spirit. We are exhorted to "walk worthy of the Lord, fully pleasing Him, being fruitful in every good work and increasing in the knowledge of God; strengthened with all might, according to His glorious power" (Col 1:10-11), but only as we are "strengthened with all might, according to His glorious power." Paul also wrote:

"I can do all things through Christ who strengthens me" Philippians 4:13,

and Jesus said:

"With men this is impossible, but with God all things are possible" Matthew 19:26.

Once again, God reminds His people of the principle of separation:

"I am the Lord your God, who has separated you from the peoples . . . and you shall be holy to Me, for I the Lord am holy, and have separated you from the peoples, that you should be Mine. Leviticus 20:24-26.

Three times in three verses, God emphasizes "separation." God has separated His people from all other people. The primary issue is holiness—this is what separates God from sinful man, and therefore separates the true believer from the unbeliever. The true disciple of Jesus is expected to be known by his likeness to his Lord and Master. The reality of separation is true not only for this life, but is eternal. Nowhere is this separation presented more clearly than in Matthew 25:31-46:

"Come, you blessed of My Father, inherit the kingdom prepared for you from the foundation of the world" vss 25:34;
"Depart from Me, you cursed, into the everlasting fire prepared for the devil and his angels" vss 25:41.

The Promised Land was God's promise to Moses and the Children of Israel, and is described as "land flowing with milk and honey" Exod 3:8. However, should they "walk in their ordinances" (the ways of the current inhabitants), and fail to "observe My judgments and keep My ordinances," they would be "cut off" Leviticus 18:3-4. Deuteronomy 28 tells us they would be cursed.

Their enjoyment of the "milk and honey" was dependent upon their separation from the inhabitants and their ways. The parallel with the disciple of Jesus Christ and the world is evident:

> **"'Come out from among them and be separate, says the Lord. Do not touch what is unclean, and I will receive you. I will be a Father to you, and you shall be My sons and daughters, says the Lord Almighty'" 2 Corinthians 6:17-18.**

Puritan Quote:

"The fundamental issue is holiness: the set-apartness of God and also His people" Gary North, 1942—

PERFECTION REQUIRED

Reading: Leviticus 22:17-33
"It must be perfect to be accepted" Leviticus 22:21

One of the many distinctions between God and man is perfection—God is perfect (holy, righteous, faultless) in every aspect, whereas man is just the opposite. Compare the following two scriptures:

> **"No one is holy like the Lord, for there is none besides You" 1 Samuel 2:2.**
> **"The heart is deceitful above all things, and desperately wicked; who can know it?" Jeremiah 17:9.**
> **"you shall be holy; for I am holy" Leviticus 11:44; 19:2; 20:26.**

The disparity between God and man is vast and irreconcilable. It is more likely that a man can swim around the world without stopping than for God and man to be reconciled. But man, in all his supposed wisdom and creativity, continues to attempt that which he cannot possibly achieve.

Some have tried to live a godly life by shutting themselves up in a cell and meditating on God 24/7. Some commit themselves to a worthy cause hoping God will see their works and accept their effort as righteousness. These are among those who at the Day of Judgment will say to the Divine Judge:

> **"Many will say to Me in that day, 'Lord, Lord, have we not prophesied in Your name, cast out demons in Your name, and done many wonders in Your name?' And then I will declare to them, 'I never knew you; depart from Me, you who practice lawlessness!'" Matthew 7:22-23.**

Only God, man's Creator, could perform the miracle of reconciling God and man. Under the Old Covenant, when a man wanted to approach God, he was to make an offering to Him, one that was acceptable to Him. In order for God to accept his offering, several requirements had to be met:

1. "He shall offer it of his own free will" Leviticus 1:3.

It is not to be assumed that every believer enjoys the same quality of walk with God, or the same intimacy of fellowship with Him.

"Many of us have to mourn over our spiritual defects. There is lameness of walk, defective vision, stunted growth; or we allow ourselves to be defiled by contact with evil, and to be weakened and hindered by unhallowed associations" C.H. Mackintosh.

God did not force a man to make an offering to Him—he was to "offer it of his own free will." So it is with us today: "Let us therefore come boldly to the throne of grace" Hebrews 4:16.

2. He had to follow distinct procedures.

Man could choose to approach God, but he could not devise his own method of doing so. Fellow Believer, millions of professing and church-going Christians seek to enter the presence of God in ways that are not acceptable to Him. Many, Roman Catholic and Protestant alike, rely on the prayers of their priest or pastor, thinking that a cold "amen" at the conclusion of his prayer suffices the requirement of God.

It is not what is done in public, but that which is done in private, that matters (Matthew 6:5-7). The avenue that leads into God's presence, is not called priests, apostles, or idols, neither is it a godly life or good works, but is Jesus Christ, who said "I am the way, the truth, and the life. No one comes to the Father except through Me" John 14:6.

3. His offering had to be "perfect" Leviticus 22:21.

"It must be perfect to be accepted; there shall be no defect in it." That which is perfect cannot accept that which is imperfect. If God accepted the imperfect, it would make Him imperfect. This is why God provided His own Sacrifice in the Person of Jesus Christ:

"Walk in love, as Christ also has loved us and given Himself for us, an offering and a sacrifice to God for a sweet-smelling aroma" Ephesians 5:2.

Only the Perfect Sacrifice could be accepted by God, so He offered Himself in the Person of His sinless, perfect, only begotten Son (John 3:16). Jesus was the fulfillment of the unblemished sacrifice required by God in the Law of Offering and Sacrifice.

The only reason why we can approach and have audience with our Holy God, is because when we were saved by His grace, we were adorned with the robe of Christ's righteousness (perfection):

"But to him who does not work but believes on Him who justifies the ungodly, his faith is accounted for righteousness, just as David also describes the blessedness of the man to whom God imputes righteousness apart from works" Romans 4:5-6.

So now, when we approach God, we are accepted into His presence because He does not see us in our sin and imperfection, but He sees the righteousness of His Beloved Son, in whom we have been made perfect. The impossible has happened—we have been reconciled to God.

"Therefore you shall be perfect, just as your Father in heaven is perfect" Matthew 5:48.

Puritan Quote:

"There are three things that earthly riches can never do; they can never satisfy divine justice, they can never pacify divine wrath, nor can they ever quiet a guilty conscience. And till these things are done man is undone" Thomas Brooks, 1608-1680.

PERFECTION ACQUIRED

Reading: 1 Peter 1:17-21
"You were not redeemed with corruptible things . . . but with the precious blood of Christ, as of a lamb without blemish and without spot"
1 Peter 1:18-19

If there is one overriding thought in the Book of Leviticus, it is that every offering, no matter what form it takes, must be "without blemish." These words occur 18 times in Leviticus, and 52 times in the whole of scripture, therefore, this phrase must hold great significance in God's economy.

Previously, we referred to the words, "It must be perfect to be accepted; there shall be no defect in it" Leviticus 22:21, and noted how it applies to Jesus Christ who offered Himself a Sacrifice to God for our redemption (1 Peter 1:18-19). While meditating further on this wonderful reality, the words of Pilate came to mind:

"I find no fault in this Man" Luke 23:4.

Although Pilate had no divine power to scrutinize the heart of Jesus, what he said was the truth. If the Father Himself searched Jesus' heart, He also would say the same thing.

If we continue to meditate on these words, they will surely lead us to the fact that Almighty God can and does search our heart to its very core. He knows our sin—every ungodly thought and action we have ever committed. His judgment over us is eternal separation from Him, in short, hell.

However, the moment we asked God to forgive our sins, and trusted Him as our Lord and Savior, He clothed us with Jesus' righteousness:

"I will greatly rejoice in the Lord, my soul shall be joyful in my God; for He has clothed me with the garments of salvation, He has covered me with the robe of righteousness, as a bridegroom

decks himself with ornaments, and as a bride adorns herself with her jewels" Isaiah 61:9.

The Bible also tells us that we are "in Christ" (2 Corinthians 5:17), and Christ is in us (Colossians 1:27), therefore, when God looks at us now, He does not see our sin, but His Beloved Son, Jesus Christ. This is why Paul can say with such confidence, "There is therefore now no condemnation to those who are in Christ Jesus" Romans 8:1.

This glorious doctrine is called Justification. Unfortunately, so many believers think of Justification as being pardoned of our sin. Such persons are falling tragically short of the fullness of truth involved in Justification. It is much, much more than pardon. While God pardons our sins when He saves and justifies us, a wonderful happening in itself, He also does something no man has ever done or can ever do—He removes our guilt!

When a President pardons a criminal for his crime and he is set free from prison, the pardoned criminal is still a criminal—he is still guilty of his crime. When God justifies a repentant sinner, He both pardons his sins and removes all traces of guilt.

In Ezra's prayer (Ezra 9:5-15), he concluded by saying:

"O Lord God of Israel, You are righteous, for we are left as a remnant, as it is this day. Here we are before You, in our guilt, though no one can stand before You because of this!" Ezra 9:15.

Fellow believer, rejoice in the fact that we not only can stand before the Lord because every stain of sin and guilt has been removed, but we are invited to approach Him and stand before Him without fear of rejection or condemnation:

"Let us therefore come boldly to the throne of grace, that we may obtain mercy and find grace to help in time of need" Hebrews 4:16.

It is because of our relationship with Jesus Christ (He in us and we in Him) that we can approach our all-holy and righteous God:

"For through Him we both have access by one Spirit to the Father" Ephesians 2:18.

Yet how infrequently some of us take advantage of this privilege and honor that has been gained for us by the sacrifice of Jesus. Even when a Jew offered his unblemished animal as a sacrifice to God, he could not enter the presence of God in the Holy of Holies.

The path to God's throne is unobstructed for those who have been reconciled to Him by faith.

When we stand with the King of kings in glory, we shall be known as those who:

"were redeemed from among men, being firstfruits to God and to the Lamb. And in their mouth was found no deceit, for they are without fault before the throne of God" Revelation 14:4-5.

Without fault. Not guilty. Guiltless in the eyes of Almighty God. What a standing we have in the royal court of heaven. It is ours by grace, ours because Jesus offered Himself without spot to God.

"For if the blood of bulls and goats and the ashes of a heifer, sprinkling the unclean, sanctifies for the purifying of the flesh, how much more shall the blood of Christ, who through the eternal Spirit offered Himself without spot to God, cleanse your conscience from dead works to serve the living God?" Hebrews 9:13-15.

Puritan Quote:

"Christ's offering of Himself . . . was the greatest expression of the inexpressible love of Christ" John Owen, 1616-1683.

GOD'S APPOINTED TIME

Reading: 1 Peter 2:4-9
"The feasts of the Lord, which you shall proclaim to be holy convocations, these are My feasts" Leviticus 23:2

The 23rd chapter of Leviticus introduces us to the six feasts of God. God referred to them as "holy convocations" or "official days for holy assembly." Combined, the feasts foreshadow redemption to the gathering of the completed church.

Prior to the annual feasts, God reaffirms importance of the weekly Sabbath. Setting aside the seventh day was one of the Ten Commandments (Exodus.20:8). The Hebrew word Shabbat (Sabbath) comes from a word meaning to desist, cease, or rest. Shabbat does not only refer to the seventh day of the week; the first day of the seventh month (Leviticus. 23:23-25), a rest was to be given to the land every seven years (Leviticus.25:3-4), and every seven cycles of seven years was to be followed with a fiftieth year of jubilee, during which slaves were set free from their labors and the land again enjoyed rest (Leviticus.25:8-11. The practice of not cultivating a piece of land every seven years is still practiced today by some farmers as a scientifically proven benefit to future crops.

What is the spiritual application of the Sabbath? The Old Covenant shadows (Col. 2:16-17) are fulfilled (made a reality) in Jesus, therefore Jesus could say:

> "Come to Me, all you who labor and are heavy laden, and I will give you rest. Take My yoke upon you and learn from Me, for I am gentle and lowly in heart, and you will find rest for your souls. For My yoke is easy and My burden is light" Matthew 11:28-30.

The burden of carrying the law on our shoulders, the necessity of obeying all the rites, ceremonies, etc., of the Mosaic institution, made it impossible to please God in our own strength, but Jesus, who fulfilled the law in its entirety, came with a new message, "Come to Me . . . and you will find rest for your souls."

The yoke of Christ is lighter than the burden of the law. To be yoked to Christ means the believer is not alone, but is joined to Him who met the requirements of the law in its entirety. The rest God gives us in Christ is "*a rest involving removal of sin's guilt and the possession of eternal life*" Matthew Henry.

This does not give us the right to be slovenly in our daily walk with Christ, for we taught we must "fight the good fight of faith" (1 Timothy 6:12), "run with endurance the race that is set before us" (Heb. 12:1), and "work out your salvation" (Philippians 2:12). I repeat, in this venture, we are not alone, for we are yoked together with Jesus, we are one with Him:

"looking unto Jesus, the author and finisher of our faith, who for the joy that was set before Him endured the cross, despising the shame, and has sat down at the right hand of the throne of God" Hebrews 12:2.

and, as Fanny Crosby wrote in her beautiful hymn, "Blessed assurance, Jesus is mine." But,

"there remains therefore a rest for the people of God. For he who has entered His rest has himself also ceased from his works as God did from His" Heb. 4:9-10.

As with all things concerning God, our rest in Christ is eternal. Jesus has already entered His rest and is seated at the right hand of His Father, so, when we go to be with Him, we will enter the promised, perfect rest, where there will be no fight to fight, race to run, or salvation to work out.

There is a Sabbath for us to enjoy now as we walk yoked to Christ, a yoke that brings peace to our soul. The hope and expectation of all believers is eternal when we enter into that rest procured by Jesus.

"Then I heard a voice from heaven saying to me, "Write: 'Blessed are the dead who die in the Lord from now on.'"
"Yes," says the Spirit, "that they may rest from their labors, and their works follow them" Revelation 14:13.

Puritan Quote:

"In the wearisome toils of life, then, let us look forward to the 'rest' that remains in heaven, and as the laborer looks to the shades of the evening, or to the Sabbath as a period of rest, so let us look to heaven as the place of eternal repose" Albert Barnes, 1798-1870.

THE PASSOVER FEAST

Reading: Leviticus 23:4-8
"For indeed Christ, our Passover, was sacrificed for us" 1 Corinthians 5:7.

Of all the feasts of Israel, none foreshadows our redemption in Jesus Christ in such beautiful detail as the festival of Passover. The Feast of Passover is immediately followed by the Feast of Unleavened Bread. The Passover was celebrated on the 14th day of Nissan (March/April), and the Feast of Unleavened Bread from the 15th to the 21st.

This Feast remembers the day when Israel was finally released from 400 years of captivity to the Egyptian nation (Exodus 12:1-12). This release from their Egyptian captors did not come easily. Pharaoh's heart was hardened, although the Lord had demonstrated His power over the gods of Egypt through nine plagues. The final plague, the destruction of the firstborn throughout the land, broke through the stubbornness of the Pharaoh, and he released them,

The identifying mark for the Israelite household was the blood of the sacrifice applied to the doorposts of their house:

"For the Lord will pass through to strike the Egyptians; and when He sees the blood on the lintel and on the two doorposts, the Lord will pass over the door and not allow the destroyer to come into your houses to strike you" Exodus 12:23.

How beautifully this application of the lamb's blood speaks to the blood of our Sacrifice redeeming God's people, and "not allow[ing] the destroyer to come into your house to strike you."

"Oh, give thanks to the Lord, for He is good! For His mercy endures forever. Let the redeemed of the Lord say so, whom He has redeemed from the hand of the enemy" Psalm 107:1-2.

While the entire lamb was sacrificed, it was the blood the Lord saw to identify His people. The word the Lord used was "the blood shall be a <u>sign</u> for you." Exodus 12:13.

Throughout scripture, God has used signs (tokens) to identify people. The first use of the word is found in Genesis 4:15 when God placed a mark on Cain to protect him: "And the Lord set a mark [NASB, "sign"] on Cain, lest anyone finding him should kill him." Circumcision was the 'mark' by which the Israelites were identified, if they were not, even a stranger could not take part in the celebration of the Passover unless he had been circumcised (Exodus 12:48).

Born again believers are identified by God, not by circumcision, but by the blood of our Sacrifice, Jesus Christ:

"Therefore, brethren, having boldness to enter the Holiest by the blood of Jesus, by a new and living way which He consecrated for us, through the veil, that is, His flesh, and having a High Priest over the house of God, let us draw near with a true heart in full assurance of faith, having our hearts sprinkled from an evil conscience . . ." Hebrews 10:19-22.

During the seven days of the Feast of Unleavened Bread, no leaven of any kind was to be consumed. Leaven represents "malice" (the evil habit) and "wickedness" (evil coming out in word and deed) as opposed to "sincerity" and "truth" (1 Corinthians 5:7).

The Jews searched with extreme care their houses, to purge out every particle of leaven. So Christians ought to search their hearts and purge out every corruption (Psalm 139:23-24). It also symbolizes corrupt doctrine and practices. Jesus told His disciples "Take heed and beware of the leaven of the Pharisees and the Sadducees" Matthew 16:6.

The life and behavior of any believer must reflect the sacrifice by which he has been redeemed—without blemish and unleavened.

"But if we walk in the light as He is in the light, we have fellowship with one another, and the blood of Jesus Christ His Son cleanses us from all sin" 1 John 1:7.

". . . knowing that you were not redeemed with corruptible things, like silver or gold, from your aimless conduct received by tradition from your fathers, but with the precious blood of Christ, as of a lamb without blemish and without spot" 1 Peter 1:18-19.

Puritan Quote:
"Redeemed, how I love to proclaim it!
Redeemed by the blood of the Lamb;
Redeemed through His infinite mercy,
His child and forever I am"
Fanny Crosby—1820-1915.

THE FEAST OF TABERNACLES

Reading: Leviticus 23:38-44
"You shall rejoice before the Lord your God . . .
your generations may know" Leviticus 23:40, 43.

The Feast of Tabernacles (or booths) is considered the greatest of all the feasts, and is sometimes referred to as "The Holiday." It was a time of rejoicing and a time of remembering.

For this occasion, booths were to be made, and each family was to live in them for the eight days of the festival. There are many and diverse interpretations of this feast, including that of the restitution of the Jewish nation at the return of their Messiah in the last days. However, this seems to be inconsistent with the other Feasts which find their fulfillment in Jesus Christ, and are shadows of His work and ministry during the church or gospel age.

These celebratory Feasts are no longer to be a part of the life of God's people, for they have been fulfilled in the Person of Jesus Christ (Matt 5:17). However, the design and purpose of the Feasts remains.

The only feast God has initiated for His people to celebrate is the Lord's Supper. It too is to be a time of remembering and rejoicing. Rather than remembering how God provided for His people during forty years of Wilderness wandering, we are to remember how God has provided for our salvation in the sacrifice of Jesus—the offering of His body and blood:

"When He had given thanks, He broke it and said, 'Take, eat; this is My body which is broken for you; do this in remembrance of Me.' In the same manner He also took the cup after supper, saying, 'This cup is the new covenant in My blood. This do, as often as you drink it, in remembrance of Me'" 1 Corinthians 11:23-25; Matthew 26:26-29.

The New Covenant's Feast, established by none other than Jesus Himself, is to be one of thanks and remembrance, not one of sorrow and the beating of one's breast. Many animals were to be sacrificed during the weeklong Feast, but the body and blood of one Man is sufficient to fulfill the reality of which they spoke.

When we remember the Lord's death, we are to give thanks. That which God has provided for His people is cause for rejoicing: "rejoice in God through our Lord Jesus Christ, through whom we have now received the reconciliation" Romans 5:11.

It is also worth noting that the Feast of Tabernacles is referred to repeatedly in the New Testament as proof of the Messianic credentials of Jesus Christ:

"And the Word became flesh and dwelt among us, and we beheld His glory, the glory as of the only begotten of the Father, full of grace and truth" John 1:14.

The Greek word for "dwelt" used here means to dwell as in a tabernacle or tent, to abide in a temporary shelter. In his writings, Paul makes it clear that as born again children of God, we are "in Him" and He is in us. Our dwelling place is in Jesus Christ. Jesus not only tabernacles with us, but we tabernacle in Him—He is our booth, our tabernacle in who we abide.

At the time of Jesus, the drawing of water had been added to the celebration. Thousands of people were in Jerusalem to celebrate the Feast of Tabernacles, including Jesus and His disciples. Finally, on the last day of the feast, Jesus made His great proclamation:

"On the last day, that great day of the feast, Jesus stood and cried out, saying, 'If anyone thirsts, let him come to Me and drink. He who believes in Me, as the Scripture has said, out of his heart will flow rivers of living water'" John 7:37-38.

Jesus did not whisper these words to His disciples, but He 'stood' and 'cried out' so all could hear. The stunned crowd hears, and everyone understood what He meant. To the first-century Jewish mind, pouring water on the altar at the Feast of Tabernacles symbolized the pouring out of the Holy Spirit in the days of the Messiah. Jesus was therefore declaring that He was the Messiah, and everyone that believed in Him would receive the gift of the Holy Spirit, the Living Water.

The Feast of Tabernacles does not speak of an event yet to come, but of that which Jesus fulfilled and in which we are to both remember and rejoice.

Puritan Quote:

"They (the Jews) rested in the type and shadow, and sought their full joy from the mere feast and its gladsome ceremonies, instead of looking through these rights to the future" Andrew Bonar, 1810-1892.

THE BREAD OF THE TABERNACLE

Reading: Leviticus 24:5-9
"take fine flour and bake twelve cakes with it" Leviticus 24:5

The common name for these loaves is Shewbread, and, like everything else offered to the Lord, it must be made of that which is pure and uncompromised—"take fine flour." All impurities have been removed; just as the sacrificial animals must be "without blemish." As we have previously noted in this series, anything that has any element of imperfection cannot be received by God, let alone be reconciled to Him and have communion with Him.

How wonderful then is our justification, for by it we are pardoned of every sin, to the extent that even our guilt has been removed, and we are declared pure and without blemish in the eyes of Him who knows all, sees all, even to the intent of our heart. When our heavenly Father sees us with His all-penetrating vision, He does not see our imperfections, but clothed in the perfect righteousness of Jesus Christ.

The number twelve in the Old Testament speaks of the twelve tribes of Israel, and just as the twelve names were written on the High Priest's breastplate, so each tribe was represented by the twelve loaves. All of God's people were represented.

This number is important to those who believe the physical Israel of God has a place in the economy of God. It is also important to those of us who believe that God has divorced His earthly people (Israel) (see Jeremiah 3:8), and is now building His church that includes both Jew and Gentile, the new "hope of Israel" Acts 28:20.

"For He Himself is our peace, who has made both one, and has broken down the middle wall of separation, having abolished in His flesh the enmity, that is, the law of commandments contained in ordinances, so as to create in Himself one new man from the two, thus making peace, and that He might reconcile them both

to God in one body through the cross, thereby putting to death the enmity. And He came and preached peace to you who were afar off and to those who were near. For through Him we both have access by one Spirit to the Father" Ephesians 2:14-18.

The New Covenant is often seen as built on the twelve apostles, whereas the Old Covenant was restricted to the twelve tribes. The gospel message is to Jew and Gentile:

"He came to His own, and His own did not receive Him. But as many as received Him, to them He gave the right to become children of God, to those who believe in His name: who were born, not of blood, nor of the will of the flesh, nor of the will of man, but of God" John 1:11-13.

The table upon which the twelve loaves were placed, was made of gold, and gold speaks of divinity. The tribes did not stand alone; their laws, moral, spiritual, and economic, were based on their relationship to God: "I will be their God" was God's promise to the tribes, however, that promise was based on the condition that they "shall keep My covenant, you and your descendants after you throughout their generations" Genesis 17:8-9.

The showbread also speaks of Him who came to fulfill the law and the prophets, Jesus Christ, the Architect and Builder of the church. Did He not say of Himself,

"I am the bread of life. He who comes to Me shall never hunger, and he who believes in Me shall never thirst" John 6:35.

Jesus is foreshadowed in the loaves that "Every Sabbath he shall set it in order before the Lord continually" Leviticus 24:8. It was renewed weekly, every Sabbath, therefore it never molded, and was always fresh. So is Jesus to every child of God who continually feeds on Him who is the Bread of Life. No matter how long we live, or how frequently we go to Him for spiritual sustenance, He will refresh our soul.

It is interesting to note the bread was to be eaten by the priests, not burnt like the animal sacrifices. The Hebrew word for "bread" means "the bread of the presence." How significant that we, as priests in His kingdom, are invited into and blessed by God's presence.

What a beautiful meaning this brings to us when we participate in the Lord's Supper—we eat the bread of His presence. Every time we read His Word, let us realize, as priests to our God, the Holy Spirit can use this activity to draw us close to Him, and refresh our soul.

"I will bring a morsel of bread, that you may refresh your hearts"
Genesis 18:5.
"Among the smooth stones of the stream is your portion" Isaiah
57:6.

Puritan Quote:

"Jesus is the representative of His people before the Lord and, as we humble ourselves and receive Him as our representative and substitute offering, God remembers His covenant and we are accepted" Philip H. Eveson, Principal of London Theological Seminary.

INTRODUCTION

Reading: Proverbs 30:1-9

"What is His name, and what is His Son's name . . . ?" Proverbs 30:4

"Who has ascended into heaven, or descended? Who has gathered the wind in His fists? Who has bound the waters in a garment? Who has established all the ends of the earth? What is His name, and what is His Son's name . . . ?" Proverbs 30:4

"My people shall know My name . . ." Isaiah 52:6

The primary way God has revealed Himself to us is by the use of His name, what it means, and the context in which it is used. The name of God reveals His character.

Before we begin to delve into this marvelous aspect of God, we need to understand the difference between a name and a title. Is there a difference between 'Name' and 'Title'?

Yes. For instance: Queen Elizabeth: Queen is her title, Elizabeth her name; President Obama; Judge Janine; Pastor Scott, etc. God is not God's name. The God of the universe has a name, but 'God' isn't it. "God" is what God is. "Human being" is not your name, "Human being" is what you are. You also have a name. Whether it is Barbara or Tom, you have your own personal name. So does God.

In today's economy, there are numerous reasons for naming our children the way we do: after another person—one we admire, a relative, etc., we like the name, or because we hope our child will grow into a person the name characterizes.

I would suggest there are three reasons for studying the name of God:

1) God has commanded us to honor His name—"You shall not take the name of the Lord your God in vain, for the Lord will not hold him guiltless who takes His name in vain" Exodus 20:7. This means more than using God's name in a slang or profane way, but

those who are in a personal relationship with Him are to honor His name in their lives. We become accountable for reflecting His character.

2) Because of the inherent greatness of His name—"O Lord, our Lord, how excellent is Your name in all the earth, Who have set Your glory above the heavens!" Psalm 8:1; also 48:10; 75:1; 76:1. Meditation on the name of God will encourage us to praise and worship Him.

3) Our protection is in His name—"The name of the Lord is a strong tower; the righteous run to it and are safe" Proverbs.18:10. God's name is like a fortress that provides protection for the believer.

The primary <u>title</u> of God is Elohim. Elohim describes what He is, not who He is. Elohim was a common word used to describe any group of gods or leaders—see Genesis1:26; 3:22; 11:7.

Elohim is the first title of the Supreme Being in the Bible: "In the beginning Elohim created the heavens and the earth" Genesis 1:1. The word Elohim is used 39 times in Genesis and 2,346 times in the O.T. when referring to the Hebrew God. Other uses include judge; goddess; and angels.

The meaning of Elohim is might, strength, almighty, powers: "In the beginning the Mighty One (or Powers) created the heavens." This title shows God to be the Mighty One, the First Great Cause of all.

It is interesting to note how many names of the prophets include 'el, (elohim is the plural form of el, and occurs about 250 times; the title indicates strong and first, and shows God to be the Mighty One, the First Great Cause of all. There are six names that contain 'el': Samuel—asked of God; Elijah—whose God is Jehovah; Elisha—God his salvation; Ezekiel—God strengthens; Daniel—God has judged; Joel—Yahweh is God.

The title 'el is often combined with one or more of the divine attributes: el shaddai which means **Almighty God**—Genesis.17:1; el Olam—**Everlasting God**—Genesis.21:33; qanaa' el—**Jealous God**—Exodus 20:5; chay el—**Living God**—Joshua.3:10—; rachuwm el—**Merciful God**—Deuteronomy 4:31; emaan el—**Faithful God**—Deuteronomy7:9: el elyon—**Most High God**—Genesis14:19.

Each attribute of God (el) is infinite—one infinite eternal love, one infinite almighty power, and so on; therefore the attributes are connected generally with the title el in the singular, and not the plural elohim.

Other forms of 'el include Eloah, from Ahlah, and means to worship, adore, and presents God as the One supreme object of worship, the Adorable One. i.e. Deuteronomy 32:15,17, and is frequently used in Job.

The questions are often asked: "To whom should I pray—the Father, Jesus, or the Holy Spirit? Can I pray to each person of the Trinity individually?"

When we pray to God, we are addressing Elohim, the "us" in the Godhead.

Elohim has also revealed themselves to us in their individual Persons. Father, Son, and Holy Spirit are one in essence, one in attributes, one in love, etc. As far as I can understand, the Bible teaches us to pray to our heavenly Father: "In this manner, therefore, pray: Our Father in heaven, Hallowed be Your name" Matthew 6:9.

We are taught to pray in the name of Jesus: "And whatever you ask in My name, that I will do, that the Father may be glorified in the Son. If you ask anything in My name, I will do it" John 14:13-14.

"And when He (the Holy Spirit) has come, He will convict the world of sin, and of righteousness, and of judgment: of sin . . . He will guide you into all truth; for He will not speak on His own authority, but whatever He hears He will speak; and He will tell you things to come. He will glorify Me, for He will take of what is Mine and declare it to you" . . . John 16:8, 13-14.

I hope these few thoughts give a foundation for our future contemplations on the name of God. Names applied to God are few, but titles are many.

I AM
Yahvah (Yawheh, Jehovah)

Reading: Exodus 3:13-15

"And God said to Moses, 'I AM WHO I AM.'" Exodus 3:14

Throughout scripture, God reveals Himself based on the various needs of His people. When Abraham faced the extreme test of his faith, the sacrifice of his son Isaac, God revealed Himself as "Jehovah-jireh"—"the Lord will provide," Genesis 22:14. When Gideon was at war with the Midianites, God revealed Himself as "Jehovah-shalom"—"the Lord is peace," Judges 6:24.

When God sent Moses with a message to His people, Moses asked, "when they say to me, 'What is His name?' what shall I say to them?" Elohim's answer was "'I AM WHO I AM.' And He said, 'Thus you shall say to the children of Israel, 'I AM has sent me to you'"

So, what has God's answer have to do with Israel's situation? Remember, Israel had been in captivity to Egypt for 400 years. They ate what Pharaoh provided, they worked the jobs Pharaoh gave them, they were ruled and governed by Pharaoh—the people knew nothing else. The word translated "I am that I am" EHYEH SHER EHYEH means "the self-existent one"—hence "Alpha and Omega, Beginning and the End, First and the last" Revelation 1:8,11. The word comes from the Hebrew verb "to be." It speaks of the unchangeableness of His character, it transcends time, past, present, and future.

Whatever His people's needs, and whenever they need Him, He will meet their need, for He the I AM. By revealing Himself as I AM, God basically gave His people a blank check. Whatever our need, we make the check out for that need. Therefore, if we want life, Christ says "I am the life;" if we want righteousness, He is "The Lord our Righteousness;" if we want peace, "He is our Peace." The only limitation is that we ask according to His will, and in His name:

**"If you ask anything in My name, I will do it" John 14:14.
"Now this is the confidence that we have in Him, that if we ask
anything according to His will, He hears us. And if we know
that He hears us, whatever we ask, we know that we have the
petitions that we have asked of Him" 1 John 5:14-15.**

YAHWEH's name, the "I AM", reveals the fullness of His being. All
of His nature and attributes are embodied in His name. In other words,
rather than a cryptic mystery, "I AM" tells us everything that can be known
about YAHWEH. The name Yahweh occurs more than 6,800 times in the
O.T., and is found in every book other than Esther, Ecclesiastes, and Song
of Solomon.

I would suggest Yahweh (Jehovah) is the only name for God (Elohim),
given by Himself for Himself. So precious was this name to the people,
that it was only spoken by priests worshipping in the temple. After the
destruction of the temple in AD 70, the name was not spoken at all, adonai
was substituted. That is why the Bible translators use "Lord" for Adonai,
and "LORD" for Yahweh. We can tell which word is used in the original
Hebrew because Yahweh (Jehovah) is capitalized (LORD), and Adonai is
not (Lord).

"I am who I am . . . this is My name forever." Read Exodus.3:14-18—
"the LORD God"—Yahweh (I am that I am) elohim (God)—"Yahweh, the
elohim of your fathers, the elohim of Abraham," etc.

Jesus claimed to be the "I am." Note the reaction of the Jews to Jesus'
statement: John 8:24, 54-59.

Note how John capitalizes on this name: "I am the Bread of Life" 6:48;
"I am the Light of the World" 8:12; 9:5; "I am the door of the sheep" 10:7-
9; "I am the good shepherd" 10:11,14; "I am the resurrection and the life"
11:25; "I am the way, the truth, and the life" 14:6; "I am the true vine" 15:1,
5; "I am the Alpha and the Omega, the Beginning and the End" Revelation
1:8; "I am the first and the last" Revelation 1:11; 22:13; "I am the Root and
the Offspring of David, the Bright and Morning Star" Revelation 22:16.

In other words, we can place any of God's attributes after "I am"—"I
am your strength, comfort, intercessor, provider, shield, fortress, etc. see
Psalm 18:2.

Note how angry the Jews became when Jesus proclaimed Himself to be "I AM" John 8:52-59. He was charged with blasphemy. Not only did Jesus speak the word, but He claimed to be "I AM", and they tried to stone Him, the punishment for blasphemy (Leviticus 24:13).

Note also the power in the name "I AM". When the soldiers came to arrest Jesus. and asked Him to identify Himself, He said "I am, and they drew back and fell to the ground" John 18:6. The word "He" is in italics, indicating it is not in the original.

"I will sing unto Yahweh, For He is exalted, The horse and his rider hath He cast into the sea! My might and melody is Yah, and He became mine by salvation. This is my El and I will glorify Him, the Elohim of my father, and I will set Him on high. Yahweh is a warlike one, Yahweh is His name" Exodus 15:1-3, Sacred Name Bible.

"Now I know that the Lord (Yahweh) is greater than all the gods (elohims); for in the very thing in which they behaved proudly, He was above them" Exodus 18:11.

Recommended book: Restoration of Original Sacred Name Bible; published by: Missionary Dispensary Bible Research. Copyright 1976. This book uses the original names of God throughout, and has a very good section explaining the names of God. Available through Amazon used books.

Puritan Quote:

"Nothing can be more interesting or practically important in its way than to follow out those great dispensational titles of God. These titles are always used in strict moral consistency with the circumstances under which they are disclosed; but there is, in the name "I AM," a height, a depth, a length, a breadth, which truly pass beyond the utmost stretch of human conception" C.H. Mackintosh, 1820-1896.

GOD ALMIGHTY
El Shaddai

Reading: Genesis 17:1-8

"I am Almighty God; walk before Me and be blameless" Genesis 17:1

God was about to tell Abram something that to the human mind was incomprehensible: "I will multiply you exceedingly." The ninety-nine year old Abram was married to a ninety-year-old woman, and he reacted the same way most of us would, "he fell on his face and laughed." Let us not be too hard on Abram—he heard the promise of God, thought it was impossible, and laughed. We might not fall on our face and laugh, but how often do we read a promise of God and dismiss it as being impossible?

God's response was to reveal Himself to Abram as El Shaddai: "I am Almighty God." There is no conclusive meaning of the word 'Shaddai', but the word 'Almighty' expresses it quite well. It speaks of power, and the ability to accomplish whatever 'El wants. This name of God is used 48 times in the Old Testament, but generously in the Book of Job—31 times. One needs only to examine the life of Job to understand why 'El Shaddai is the name of choice.

'El Shaddai' reminds us that God is all-powerful, and that nothing is impossible with Him. When Jesus told His disciples "How hard it is for those who have riches to enter the kingdom of God," they were 'greatly astonished' and asked, 'who then can be saved?' Jesus answered by using the meaning of 'El Shaddai by saying:

"With men it is impossible, but not with God; for with God all things are possible" Mark 10:27.

This is a fundamental truth for us all to grasp and believe. No matter the circumstance we are in, or the challenge that faces us, our God is 'El Shaddai. When Job was wallowing in his misery (and who can blame him?), he asked God questions like, "Why have You brought me out of the womb?"

(Job 10:18), and pleaded "Cease! Leave me alone, that I may take a little comfort" (Job 10:20). Zophar, one of his friends pointed him in the right direction:

> **"Can you search out the deep things of God? Can you find out the limits of the Almighty (Shaddai)? They are higher than heaven—what can you do? Deeper than Sheol—what can you know? Their measure is longer than the earth and broader than the sea" Job 11:7-9.**

In response, Job finally agrees, "But I would speak to the Almighty, and I desire to reason with God" Job 13:3. One of the benefits of understanding the names and titles of God, is that we can address Him in the capacity of our need. If we need guidance, we can speak to Him as our Shepherd who goes before His sheep and leads us along the right path, or if we embattled in spiritual warfare, we can call on Him who is our Peace.

Job had questioned the manner in which 'El Shaddai was treating him, so he wanted to address Him as "the Almighty." While it is true God will hear our prayer no matter in which name we address Him, how much more will it enhance our soul when we are conscious of the specific capacity in which we commune with Him.

The Greek word translated as 'Almighty' is used nine times in the New Testament, eight of which are found in Revelation. One example is:

> **"The four living creatures, each having six wings, were full of eyes around and within. And they do not rest day or night, saying: 'Holy, holy, holy, Lord God Almighty, Who was and is and is to come!" Rev 4:8.**

The first three references address the eternal aspect of God: "Who was and is and is to come" (1:8; 4:8; 11:17); the next two address the righteousness of God's works (15:3; 16:7), the next two of the wrath and judgment of God (16:14; 19:15), and concludes with the reference to the "Lord God Almighty" in conjunction with "the Lamb" (21:22).

It is in this name and in all it stands for, that Jesus will rule and govern His eternal kingdom.

"He who dwells in the secret place of the Most High shall abide under the shadow of the Almighty. I will say of the Lord, 'He is my refuge and my fortress; My God, in Him I will trust'" Psalm 91:1-2

Puritan Quote:

"*The God with whom we have to do is a God that is enough. [1.] He is enough in himself; he is self-sufficient; he has everything, and he needs not anything. [2.] He is enough to us, if we be in covenant with him: we have all in him, and we have enough in him, enough to satisfy our most enlarged desires, enough to supply the defect of everything else, and to secure to us a happiness for our immortal souls" Matthew Henry, 1662-1714.*

LORD OF HOSTS
Yahvah Tsebaoth

Reading: 1 Samuel 17:37-51
"I come to you in the name of the Lord of Hosts" 1 Samuel 17:45

This is one of the most well-known stories in the Bible, one of the first we learn as a child in Sunday School. Whenever the underdog has an unexpected result, it is spoken of as a "David and Goliath" event. The title "LORD of Hosts" brings to mind a general, astride his white horse, with masses of troops waiting to be led into battle. When David looked out from Saul's tent and saw the Philistine giant audaciously challenging God's people, he did not see himself going out as a single person to fight, but as a representative of his all-powerful God with masses of troops in support.

With 245 references in the Old Testament, the "LORD of Hosts" is used most often in the context of war or opposition. Fifty-four of these references are found in the Prophecy of Isaiah. When the prophet saw the Lord, the Cherubim surrounding Him were singing, "Holy, holy, holy is the Lord of hosts; the whole earth is full of His glory!" Isaiah 6:3. The Commander was surrounded by the hosts of heaven singing His praises, acknowledging His holiness.

In four chapters, Malachi uses this titles 24 times. It is a very important concept of God in the Old Testament, and speaks continually of His authority and power. When He accused His people of sacrificing blemished animals, He said,

"'But cursed be the deceiver who has in his flock a male, and takes a vow, but sacrifices to the Lord what is blemished—For I am a great King,' says the Lord of hosts, 'And My name is to be feared among the nations'" Malachi 1:14.

When Elisha's servant saw the "great army" that surrounded the city of Dothan, he was afraid, and said, "Alas, my master! What shall we do?" Elisha answered:

"'Do not fear, for those who are with us are more than those who are with them.' And Elisha prayed, and said, 'Lord, I pray, open his eyes that he may see.' Then the Lord opened the eyes of the young man, and he saw. And behold, the mountain was full of horses and chariots of fire all around Elisha" 2 Kings 6:16-17.

Elisha knew his God was The LORD of Hosts, that he was not alone. Elisha was one of those prophets

"who through faith subdued kingdoms, worked righteousness, obtained promises, stopped the mouths of lions, quenched the violence of fire, escaped the edge of the sword, out of weakness were made strong, became valiant in battle, turned to flight the armies of the aliens" Hebrews 11:33-35.

He could see with the eye of faith beyond that which the human eye could see. How often are we limited to what we see around us—unsolvable problems, walls that cannot be breached, etc. Our eye of faith, that which sees the invisible, is blinded.

The Lord asked the same question of Jeremiah, Amos, and Zechariah, "What do you see? Jeremiah 1:11,13; 24:3; Amos 7:8; 8:2; Zechariah 4:2; 5:2. In each case, God had a meaning behind what the human eye could see. This is a very important principle in our spiritual life.

It is only by the eye of faith we can see the plan and purpose of God in situations and circumstances that come our way. It may not be until the problem has passed that we see what God had in mind. If it is not clear at the time, then that is when we exercise our faith that He is in control and knows what He is doing. As difficult as it may be, we need to pray with all sincerity and faith, "Thy will be done."

The eye of faith sees the reality of the divine presence and protection where all is empty or darkness to the natural eye.

"The angel of the Lord encamps all around those who fear Him, and delivers them" Psalm 34:7.

Whether or not this statement speaks of the "angel of the Lord," the Lord Jesus Christ fulfilling His promise, "I will never leave you or forsake you," or as the Captain of our Salvation leading the hosts of heaven, matters not.

The Angel, the Lord, at the head of all the hosts of heaven, surrounds with his army, the circumstances of His people. Like hosts waiting in the trenches, so are the ministering spirits encamped around the Lord's chosen, to serve and comfort, to defend and protect them.

Those very same hosts that were ready to come to our Savior's assistance (Matthew 23:56) are ready and waiting to come to the assistance of God's people.

On every side the watch is kept by warriors who do not sleep, and the LORD of Hosts is one whose ability none can resist. We do not know how many coincidental events we owe to those unseen hands that are charged to bear us up lest we dash our foot against a stone:

"For He shall give His angels charge over you, to keep you in all your ways. In their hands they shall bear you up, lest you dash your foot against a stone" Psalm 91:11-12.

Puritan Quote:
"O my blessed Jesus, increase this faith. Lead me from faith to faith, that, while I am travelling heaven-wards, mine eye and my heart may be sore simply fixed upon Thee" William Romaine, 1714-1795.

THE LORD MY BANNER
Yaḥvaḥ Nissi

Reading: Exodus 17:8-16
"Moses built an altar and called its name, The-Lord-Is-My-Banner"
Exodus 17:15

When the Israelites faced the Amalekites in battle, Moses took his rod to the top of the mountain, the tool with which he used to part the Red Sea, and held it over the battlefield. So, it is recorded, "When Moses held up his hand, that Israel prevailed; and when he let down his hand, Amalek prevailed." When the Amalekites were defeated, "Moses built an altar and called its name, 'The-Lord-Is-My-Banner.'"

Unlike fabric flags, ancient banners were usually made out of wood or metal, and shaped into various figures or emblems that could be seen from a long distance. The banner was always visible, and soldiers in the midst of a battle, could look at the banner and be encouraged. They were reminded as to why they were fighting and for whom.

In this case, they were fighting the first battle after their deliverance from 400 years of captivity in Egypt. When they looked on the banner, they were reminded of the power and ability of God in their deliverance—the same God, the same power, the same ability.

To the Christian, our banner is the cross of Jesus Christ. When we look at the cross we are reminded of Jesus who was sacrificed on it. The empty cross reminds us it could not hold our Savior, but that He rose again, and is living at the right hand of His Father.

The cross is the rallying point for believers as they are engaged in fighting the good fight of faith (1 Tim 6:12). The cross is where we renew our strength as we run the race set before us. The cross is where Satan was defeated and our victory was secured. The cross is more than a piece of jewelry to be hung around the neck:

"let us run with endurance the race that is set before us, looking unto Jesus, the author and finisher of our faith, who for the joy that was set before Him endured the cross, despising the shame, and has sat down at the right hand of the throne of God" Hebrews 12:1-2.

Another banner for the believer is the empty tomb. It is where Jesus was. It is reminds us death could not hold Him. It reminds us that "Death is swallowed up in victory."

"'Death, where is your sting? O Hades, where is your victory?' The sting of death is sin, and the strength of sin is the law. But thanks be to God, who gives us the victory through our Lord Jesus Christ" 1 Cor 15:55-57.

As great as these banners are, they fall short of the banner built and named by Moses: "The LORD is My Banner." Tragically, the cross and empty tomb speak only of the One who occupied them. "The LORD is My Banner" Moses cried. Jehovah, the great "I AM," it is from Him we should gain our strength: "Finally, my brethren, be strong in the Lord and in the power of His might" Eph 6:10; "looking unto Jesus" the writer to the Hebrews wrote. Not to bullocks, sheep, or goats, but to Him of whom they spoke.

The cross and empty tomb cannot replace the One who occupied them. "I am the Way, the Truth, and the Life," Jesus said, not the cross or tomb. We have the joy and privilege of a personal relationship with this Man named Yahvahshua, Jesus, the Son of God. How many millions bow before the cross, and flock to Jerusalem to see the place where Jesus died? He is not there. He lives in the hearts of those who believe in Him. He is our Banner—nothing else.

If the cross reminds us of Him who died on it, and the tomb of Him who walked away from it, then they are a memorial only. Both are empty. You will find the Christ only by repenting of your sin, and believing in Him as your Savior. Then, and only then, can you look on Him as your Banner.

Unlike the altar Moses built, our Banner is of a different material:

"He brought me to the banqueting house, and his banner over me was love" Song of Songs 2:4.

David said it well: "You have given a banner to those who fear You, that it may be displayed because of the truth" Psalm 60:4.

Puritan Quote:

"So long as soldiers see their banner uplifted, they flock round it with confidence. But when it is prostrate their spirits and hopes fall. The banner is a pledge of safety, and a rallying point to those who fight under it. A. R. Faussett, 1821-1910.

THE LORD IS PEACE
Yahvah Shalom

Reading: Judges 6:1-24

"So Gideon built an altar there to the Lord, and called it
The-Lord-Is-Peace" Judges 6:24.

Shalom is a common term for greeting or farewell in modern Israel, and Yahvah Shalom is more a title than a name. We have previously established the name of Elohim as "I AM" (Yahvah, Yahweh, Jehovah), and various titles were applied to Jehovah based on His accomplishments on behalf of His people. A common practice was to erect a memorial in memory of that event, and to give it a name.

The first thing to note in this passage is that "the children of Israel did evil in the sight of the Lord." This was nothing new, and was to repeated time and time again throughout their history. In this case, God "delivered them into the hand of Midian for seven years." Whatever the Israelites did, God destroyed it via the might of the Midianites.

Without repeating the entire story, for it is in the scripture reading above, let it suffice to say Gideon was the chosen man of God through whom He would deliver His people. Gideon's heart was in turmoil; he had questions; the entire circumstance did not make sense to him:

"If the Lord is with us, why then has all this happened to us? And where are all His miracles which our fathers told us about, saying, 'Did not the Lord bring us up from Egypt?' But now the Lord has forsaken us and delivered us into the hands of the Midianites" Judges 6:13.

The messenger of Jehovah met with Gideon and assured Him of victory over the Midianites, and so it came to pass.

There is much in this story that aligns with the spiritual life of every believer. But let's stick to the main principle—peace. There are many facets that go into spiritual peace. How many believers experience turmoil in their hearts. They want to believe the Word of God and God's promises, but encounter nothing but unrest when "God does not keep His promises."

The problem is not with God, but with us. "The promises of God in Him are Yes, and in Him Amen, to the glory of God through us" 2 Corinthians 1:20. One thing we can count on is "He who promised is faithful" Hebrews 10:23. Just because we do not see an immediate answer to our prayer, does not mean God is saying "No."

One thing that hinders answered prayer is our sin, our uncleanness before God. The first step in answered prayer is having nothing standing in its way. One aspect of God's faithfulness is His forgiveness:

"If we confess our sins, He is faithful and just to forgive us our sins and to cleanse us from all unrighteousness" 1 John 1:9.

One of the charges against the prophets and priests in the Old Testament was their message proclaiming a false peace:

"And from the prophet even to the priest, everyone deals falsely. They have also healed the hurt of My people slightly, saying, 'Peace, peace!' when there is no peace" Jeremiah 6:14; 8:11; Ezra 13:10

So today, and throughout all time, there have been false prophets, preaching one thing when God has not instructed them to do so. The true gospel is one of peace (Romans 10:15), yet all around us in our churches and individual relationships, we see friction, unrest, accusations, divisions, and even violence. Is this the fruit of those who preach the gospel of peace, and whose God is the God of Peace?

Isaiah, in his wonderful prophesy of Jesus Christ, speaks of Him as the "Prince of Peace" (Isaiah 9:6). Paul frequently refers to God as the "God of peace" (Romans 15:33). The third expression listed in the fruit of the Spirit is 'peace' (Galatians 5:22). It makes sense that one who is walking in the Spirit and whose God is the God of peace, should experience peace in his soul as well as with other believers with whom he has fellowship.

One thing we know: "'There is no peace,' says my God, 'for the wicked'" Isaiah 57:21. Apart from Christ there is no peace.

Peace is not a quality of life that is automatically endowed on one who says he is a Christian. As with all things there is a qualifier:

"You will keep him in perfect peace, whose mind is stayed on You, because he trusts in You. Trust in the Lord forever, for in Yah, the Lord, is everlasting strength" Isaiah 26:3-4.

"The work of righteousness will be peace, and the effect of righteousness, quietness and assurance forever" Isaiah 32:17.

"Be anxious for nothing, but in everything by prayer and supplication, with thanksgiving, let your requests be made known to God; and the peace of God, which surpasses all understanding, will guard your hearts and minds through Christ Jesus" Philippians 4:6-7.

Puritan Quote

"Get near to God, believer, and you will be calm. Commune with heaven and be at rest. The peace of God passeth all understanding, and it is this which Jesus waits to give you. There is no reason why you should be heavily burdened; return unto your rest, for the Lord hath dealt bountifully with you" C.H. Spurgeon, 1834-1892.

THE ETERNAL GOD
El Olam

Reading: Genesis 21:22-33
"There he called upon the name of the LORD, the Eternal God"
Genesis 21:33

Whenever scripture speaks of one calling on the "name of the LORD", it must be understood that they are invoking the name "Yahweh, Jehovah, see series #2). Here, the name of God is not El Olam (Eternal God), but as revealed in Exodus 3:14. The eternal aspect of God is not a name, but an attribute of "I AM."

The human mind is incapable of comprehending eternity. We are a product of time, and everything with which we have to do is governed by time, and time has a beginning and an end. There is no "forever" in time. We are born and we die. We have never experienced eternity. Eternity is not our experience, but our "hope." Mankind was created in time, and will come to an end in time.

However, the God whom we love and trust is eternal. God's existence, His plans and purposes, are eternal.

"Before the mountains were brought forth, or ever You had formed the earth and the world, even from everlasting to everlasting, You are God" Psalm 90:2.

God was when nothing else was.

"The everlastingness of which Moses speaks is to be referred not only to the essence of God, but also to his providence, by which he governs the world. He intends not merely that he is, but that he is God" John Calvin.

In this Psalm (90), before Moses speaks of the brevity and depravity of mankind, he reminds them of the eternal God with whom they (as a nation) had a refuge. Man is transient, but Jehovah is eternal, "He is from everlasting to everlasting." He does not open the gates to His refuge for a specific time each day, for He is eternal.

Therefore, when Jesus, who is eternal, came into the world as a man (governed by time), he brought Him an unimaginable message:

"For God so loved the world that He gave His only begotten Son, that whoever believes in Him should not perish but have everlasting life" John 3:16.

That which belonged to God, that which God is, that where God dwells, man can now be a participant of—everlasting life. Jesus spent the next three years preaching this message. As a man He died, as a man possessing everlasting life, He rose from the dead, and forty days later, ascended into heaven, the realm of eternity. There He was given an "everlasting dominion, which shall not pass away . . . and His kingdom the one which shall not be destroyed" Daniel 7:13-14.

The message of the gospel is the fulfillment of the following prophecy: "the saints of the Most High shall receive the kingdom, and possess the kingdom forever, even forever and ever" Daniel 7:18.

The One whom we love and worship is the King of His kingdom, He is "King of Kings and Lord of Lords" Revelation 19:16. There is no weakness in Him that He should ever fail us: "For though He was crucified in weakness, yet He lives by the power of God. For we also are weak in Him, but we shall live with Him by the power of God toward you" 2 Corinthians 13:4.

"These will make war with the Lamb, and the Lamb will overcome them, for He is Lord of lords and King of kings; and those who are with Him are called, chosen, and faithful" Revelation 17:14.

There is a definite relationship between the eternal King and the citizens of His everlasting kingdom. Never let us glide over the qualifications of those who have been brought into the everlastingness of Jehovah's kingdom: they are "called, chosen, and faithful."

"Then the King will say to those on His right hand, 'Come, you blessed of My Father, inherit the kingdom prepared for you from the foundation of the world'" Matthew 25:34.

"These will make war with the Lamb, and the Lamb will overcome them, for He is Lord of lords and King of kings; and those who are with Him are called, chosen, and faithful" Revelation 17:14.
"Then the King will say to those on His right hand, 'Come, you blessed of My Father, inherit
"'I am the Alpha and the Omega, the Beginning and the End,' says the Lord, 'who is and who was and who is to come, the Almighty.'" Revelation 1:8.

Puritan Quote:

"His duration is as endless as His essence is boundless: He always was and always will be, and will no more have an end than He had a beginning; and this is an excellency belonging to the Supreme Being" Stephen Charnock. 1629-1680.

GOD THE JUDGE
El Yahweh Shophet

Reading: Psalm 94:1-23
"Rise up, O Judge of the earth; Render punishment to the proud"
Psalm 94:2.

Spiritually, mankind is divided into two groups: 1) Those who do not know God, and who are designated in God's Word as lost, sinners, wicked, and unrighteous, and apart from Christ; 2) Those who know God, and who God's Word refers to as saved; born again, righteous, and God's children, and in Christ.

The Bible states clearly, and with no room for debate, "all the world may become guilty before God" Romans 3:19; "All have sinned and fall short of the glory of God" Romans 3:23; "For the wages of sin is death" Romans 6:23. "the Scripture has confined all under sin" Galatians 3:22. The Psalmist wrote, "Behold, I was brought forth in iniquity, and in sin my mother conceived me" Psalm 51:5.

Sin is a violation of God's holiness, and He will not sit idly by and let it take its course. God does not judge sin, but the sinner. How can we trust God to make the correct judgment? We must remember that God's justice is ultimately rooted not in a collection of rules or laws, but in the character and nature of God—in His holiness.

The Psalmist declares, "God is the Judge: He puts down one, and exalts another" Psalm 75:7, and again, "Arise, O God, judge the earth; for You shall inherit all nations" Psalm 82:8. The writer to the Hebrews speaks of "God the Judge of all" Hebrews 12:23.

God does not sit on the fence and wait to see what man decides to do with Him. When He sees iniquity, He Judges it.

The Old Testament is filled with examples of God's judgments. The prophets spend more time preaching judgment than anything else, including the promises connected to the coming Messiah. Among the notable of God's judgments were when He almost destroyed His creation with a flood (Genesis 7:23-24), and when He fulfilled His word against His own people, Israel. After numerous warnings from the prophets, God brought His judgment against the Northern kingdom (Israel) who fell victim to the Assyrians, and Judah to the Babylonians (2 Kings 17; 22:15-17; 23:26-27).

When it came time to administer judgment against Judah, God told the prophet

"Do not pray for this people, for their good. When they fast, I will not hear their cry; and when they offer burnt offering and grain offering, I will not accept them. But I will consume them by the sword, by the famine, and by the pestilence" Jeremiah 14:11-12.

This was the fulfillment of Deuteronomy 28:15-68. The first 14 verses of this chapter show the blessings God will bestow on His people if they "diligently obey the voice of the Lord your God, to observe carefully all His commandments which I command you today" (vs 1).

Even after witnessing God's judgment on the ten northern tribes (Israel), Judah "did not fear, but also went and played the harlot" Jeremiah 3:8. They did not learn, and continued to live with the thought that will never happen to me. So, the promised judgment fell on Judah.

The greatest of all judgments was when Jesus bore God's judgment for our sins, "Christ died for our sins" 1 Corinthians 15:3; Jesus "committed Himself to Him who judges righteously; who Himself bore our sins in His own body on the tree" 1 Peter 2:23-24.

Do not think God stepped down as Judge, and all sins and wickedness were washed away by love. God was, is, and always will be the Judge of all the earth.

The New Testament also has many references to God's judgment: Judgment falls on the Jews because they rejected the Messiah (Matt 21:43-44; 1 Thess 2:14-16), on Ananaias and Sapphira for lying to God (Acts 5:1-10), on Herod for his pride (Acts 12:21-23), on Elymas, because he opposed the gospel message (Acts 13:8-11), When Jesus ascended into heaven, all judgment was given to Him, "For the Father judges no one, but has committed all judgment to the Son" John 5:22. Jesus Christ, who is the world's Savior, is also its Judge.

A major theme running throughout the New Testament is that of a coming judgment. Not only does God administer judgment during our lifetime, but will make a final judgment known as the Great White Throne judgment" Revelation 20:11-15. God's people, however, will not participate. They have their own meeting with Christ when they will be judged for rewards, based on their works (1 Corinthians 3:5-15).

At the Great White Throne judgment, there will be no plea bargaining, no lawyers arguing different positions, and the only witness will be God. There will be no wondering what the judgment will be, and no question as to whether or not the judgment is just.

Paul reminds us that we must appear before Christ's judgment seat as "the terror of the Lord" 2 Corinthians 5:11. The same things apply to this judgment, other than we will not know until the moment whether God will judge our works as "gold, silver, precious stones, wood, hay, [or] straw" 1 Corinthians 3:12.

The Judge is "faithful and True." "These things says the Amen, the Faithful and True Witness, the Beginning of the creation of God: "I know your works" Revelation 3:14-15. He is "the righteous Judge" 2 Timothy 4:8. The Judge is Jesus Christ "who is ready to judge the living and the dead" 1 Peter 4:5; Acts 10:42. "God will judge the secrets of men by Jesus Christ" Romans 2:16.

Jesus said, "the Father judges no one, but has committed all judgment to the Son . . . and has given Him authority to execute judgment also, because He is the Son of Man. Do not marvel at this; for the hour is coming in which all who are in the graves will hear His voice and come forth—those who have done good, to the resurrection of life, and those who have done evil, to the resurrection of condemnation" or, as the New Living Translation says, "and those who have continued in evil will rise to experience judgment." John 5:22, 27-29.

Every act, thought, and intent is known to Him who knows us better than we know ourselves. The wicked priests in Ezekiel's day thought they could hide from the all-seeing eye of God, but they were wrong:

"Then He said to me, 'Son of man, have you seen what the elders of the house of Israel do in the dark, every man in the room of his idols? For they say, 'The Lord does not see us'" Ezekiel 8:12. "'My eye will not spare, nor will I have pity; I will repay you according to your ways, and your abominations will be in your midst. Then you shall know that I am the Lord who strikes" Ezekiel 7:9.

The character of God is the guarantee that everyone will be judged in righteousness. There will be no errors in judgment, and no miscarriages of Justice.

Puritan Quote:

"Ascend thy judgment seat and be acknowledged as the ruler of men: and, moreover, raise thyself as men do who are about to strike with all their might; for the abounding sin of mankind requires a heavy blow from thy hand" C.H. Spurgeon, 1834-1892.

GOD THE JUDGE — CONT'D
El Yahweh Shophet

Reading: Psalm 94:1-23
"Because they have rejected the law of the Lord of hosts . . .
the anger of the Lord is aroused" Isaiah 5:24-25

As a continuation of the previous thought of God, the righteous Judge, let us consider the wrath of God. The wrath of God cannot be understood as a divine reaction to an unexpected circumstance, but rather a divine action taken against that which violates who God is—holy, righteous, perfect, and without sin.

The Bible does not say God gets upset or is disappointed when you rebel against Him and disobey His commandments. God's wrath is always regarded in the Bible as just, righteous, and as an expression of His holiness, therefore, as long as there is sin in this world, the wrath of God will exist.

"Because they have rejected the law of the Lord of hosts, and despised the word of the Holy One of Israel. Therefore the anger of the Lord is aroused against His people; He has stretched out His hand against them and stricken them, and the hills trembled. Their carcasses were as refuse in the midst of the streets" Isaiah 5:24-25, see also 42:24-25; Jeremiah 44:6.

God's wrath is as much an attribute as His love, mercy and grace, and, because love is a more pleasant and desired attribute found in humankind, we project it more in God because we enjoy it more.

"A study in the concordance will show that there are more references in Scripture to the anger, fury, and wrath of God, than there are to His love and tenderness" A.W. Pink, *The Attributes of God.*

The Bible clearly teaches that God is good to those who trust him, as much as He is terrible to those who do not. The following passage, written by the prophet Nahum, expresses this thought in his prophecy of the coming judgment on Nineveh:

> "The Lord is a jealous God, filled with vengeance and wrath. He takes revenge on all who oppose him and continues to rage against his enemies! The Lord is slow to get angry, but his power is great, and he never lets the guilty go unpunished . . . Who can stand before his fierce anger? Who can survive his burning fury? His rage blazes forth like fire, and the mountains crumble to dust in his presence. The Lord is good, a strong refuge when trouble comes. He is close to those who trust in him. But he will sweep away his enemies . . . He will pursue his foes into the darkness of night" Nahum 1:2-8. NLT.

The New Testament continues the theme of God's wrath against those (nations and individuals) who defy Him: Luke 21:22-24; Romans 1:18; 2:5-6; 5:9, Revelation 6:12-17; 16:19, and so forth.

We often ascribe attitude to God, but God does not have attitude. The dictionary defines attitude as "a feeling or emotion toward a fact or state." While in a broad sense this can be applied to God, God is not governed or controlled by feelings or emotions. Rather, God acts based on His Sovereignty and Holiness. God does not feel angry at sin or the sinner, He is angry because He is Holy.

> "You are of purer eyes than to behold evil, and cannot look on wickedness" Habakkuk 1:13.

Holiness and sin cannot exist together. They are diametrically opposed.

The judgment that God serves on wicked and unrepentant mankind is not universal in its severity—"I will repay them according to their deeds and according to the works of their own hands" Jeremiah 25:14. This is a principle of God's justice—severity of punishment is equal to the severity of the crime, and only God knows the degree of both for it is based solely on His holiness. One thing of which we can be sure, His judgment will be just, for He is "the righteous Judge" 2 Timothy 4:8.

Against what or whom is God angry? Does God hate the sin but love the sinner? What does God hate?

"God is angry with the wicked every day!" Psalm 7:11. God is not angry merely against the sin apart from the sinner, but against the sinner himself! Some people have labored hard to make it appear that God is angry at sin, yet not at the sinner; that He hates the theft, but loves the thief; that He abhors adultery, but is pleased with the adulterer.

The sin cannot be separated from the sinner. The act of sin is nothing, apart from the sinful actor. What God hates and disapproves of is not the act committed, as distinct from the actor, but He hates the actor himself!

The following scriptures may give us pause:

"Jacob I have loved; But Esau I have hated" Malachi 1:2-3; Romans 9:13.
"The boastful shall not stand in Your sight; You hate all workers of iniquity" Psalm 5:5
"The wicked and the one who loves violence, His soul hates!" Psalm 11:5.
"The LORD detests all the proud of heart. Be sure of this: They will not go unpunished!" Proverbs 16:5.
"The LORD is a jealous and avenging God; the LORD takes vengeance and is filled with wrath. The LORD takes vengeance on His foes and maintains His wrath against His enemies!" Nahum 1:2.
"Whoever rejects the Son will not see life, for God's wrath remains on him" John 3:36.
"But for those who are self-seeking and who reject the truth and follow evil—there will be wrath and anger!" Romans 2:8.

In the light of these scriptures, we must remember that God is the righteous Judge, and every judgment He makes will be just. There will be no mistrial in the courthouse of God. He is the only witness, and He is "faithful and true."

Puritan Quote:

"The root cause of our unhappiness seems to be a disquieting suspicion that ideas of wrath are in some way unworthy of God" J.I. Packer, Knowing God.

THE LORD OUR RIGHTEOUSNESS
Yahweh Tsidqenu

Reading: Jeremiah 23:5-6; 33:15-16
"This is His name by which He will be called:
THE LORD OUR RIGHTEOUSNESS" Jeremiah 23:6

Personally, the righteousness that is God, is one of, if not the, most glorious truths expounded in Scripture. The knowledge that 1) God is Righteous, and 2) He is OUR Righteousness, exports me into a realm only God's wisdom and power can conceive and achieve.

The two references above are the only times Yahweh Tsidqenu are used in the Old Testament, yet they prophesy of such an enormous and important event in God establishing a personal relationship between Himself and His people:

"But now the righteousness of God apart from the law is revealed, being witnessed by the Law and the Prophets, even the righteousness of God, through faith in Jesus Christ, to all and on all who believe. For there is no difference; for all have sinned and fall short of the glory of God, being justified freely by His grace through the redemption that is in Christ Jesus, whom God set forth as a propitiation by His blood, through faith, to demonstrate His righteousness" Romans 3:21-25.

There is only one way whereby sinful man can be seen by the All-Holy God as righteous, and that is if we are as righteous as He is. Impossible, you say? Yes, impossible except the God of the impossible achieves it on our behalf, "through faith in Jesus Christ, to all and on all who believe . . . by His grace through the redemption that is in Christ Jesus."

"By making satisfaction to the justice of God for the sin of man, he has brought in an everlasting righteousness, and so made it over to us in the covenant of grace that, upon our believing consent to that covenant, it becomes ours. His being Jehovah our righteousness implies that he is so our righteousness as no creature could be. He is a sovereign, all-sufficient, eternal righteousness. All our righteousness has its being from him, and by him it subsists, and we are made the righteousness of God in him." Matthew Henry.

The word 'tsedeq' is usually translated as 'righteousness', but can also be translated as 'honest', 'right', 'accurate', 'justice', 'truth', or 'integrity'. In the Old Testament, people were often said to 'be righteous' if they observed the law, but Jesus and the apostles stress that righteousness is not merely an outward behavior, but one of the heart—of thoughts, motives, and desires.

The goal of every genuine Believer is not merely to do what God says, but to become like Him. This does not mean, as some preachers claim today, that we actually become "little gods", but that when God looks at us as born again Believers, He sees Himself, He sees us as new creatures, as holy beings, as righteous—He sees the righteousness of His only begotten Son, for it is that which has been imputed into us.

We have been made one with Christ—He is in us, and we in Him. This is a personal relationship, one that satisfies the justice of God on our behalf. This is what caused Paul to say:

"There is therefore now no condemnation to those who are in Christ Jesus, who do not walk according to the flesh, but according to the Spirit" Romans 8:1.

This relationship is not only a personal one but an unbreakable one. In the same chapter, Paul writes:

"For I am persuaded that neither death nor life, nor angels nor principalities nor powers, nor things present nor things to come, nor height nor depth, nor any other created thing, shall be able

to separate us from the love of God which is in Christ Jesus our Lord" Romans 8:38-39.

The key to righteous living is found in the words of Jesus: "My judgment is righteous, because I do not seek My own will but the will of the Father who sent Me" John 5:30. One who is a new creature in Christ will seek to do the will of God. "If you love me, you will keep my commandments" John 14:15, RSV. This is not a command as in the KJV, but a statement of fact. The proof that Jesus Christ is indeed "The LORD OUR RIGHTEOUSNESS" is that we keep His commandments, that we live in accordance with His will.

Not only does our heavenly Father see the righteousness of His Son in us, but so should everyone else: "Let your light so shine before men, that they may see your good works and glorify your Father in heaven" Matthew 5:16.

Puritan Quote:

"If, then, we desire to have God as our righteousness, we must seek Christ; for this cannot be found except in him. The righteousness of God has been set forth to us in Christ; and all who turn away from him, though they may take many circuitous courses, can yet never find the righteousness of God. Hence Paul says that he has been given or made to us righteousness,—for what end? that we might be made the righteousness of God in him" John Calvin, 1509-1564.

GOD MOST HIGH
El Elyon

Reading: 2 Samuel 22:2-16
"The Most High uttered His voice" 2 Samuel 22:14

When studying the numerous times God is spoken of as "The Most High," its association with His voice is both appropriate and effective. The word 'Elyon' means "to go up," and is used of persons or things to indicate their elevation or exaltation. When applied to God, it speaks of Him being the "Exalted One," as being lifted far above all gods and men. The name emphasizes the might and power of God.

> **"The Lord thundered from heaven, and the Most High uttered His voice. He sent out arrows and scattered them; lightning bolts, and He vanquished them. Then the channels of the sea were seen, the foundations of the world were uncovered, at the rebuke of the Lord, at the blast of the breath of His nostrils" 2 Samuel 22:14-16.**

Is there any wonder that the commandments were accompanied by thunder and lightning? (Exodus 20:18-19). Are we surprised that at the death of Jesus there were earthquakes and the rocks were split? (Matthew 27:51-54). These things, among others, are an expression of the limitless authority and power of the God Most High.

In the Old Testament Yahweh is known as the Most High: "And will sing praise to the name of the Lord Most High" Psalm 7:17. In the New Testament Jesus is known as the Son of the Most High: "Jesus, Son of the Most High God," while the Holy Spirit is the power of the Most High. All who belong to Christ are called "the servants of the Most High God, who proclaim to us the way of salvation" Acts 16:17.

The fourth chapter of Daniel is a wonderful study of God the Most High—as is the entire book of Daniel. Thirteen times the term Most High is used in the first seven chapters. It is an acknowledgment of the greatness of God and His everlasting kingdom and dominion. As God, the Most High, is exalted, so Nebuchadnezzar, the king whose word was never to be disobeyed, is diminished.

The great kings of the earth offer no comparison to the God Most High. There kingdoms will come and go, "But the saints of the Most High shall receive the kingdom, and possess the kingdom forever, even forever and ever" Daniel 7:17-18.

Paul grasps the magnitude of this truth when he writes about Jesus, and

"the riches of the glory of His inheritance in the saints, and what is the exceeding greatness of His power toward us who believe, according to the working of His mighty power which He worked in Christ when He raised Him from the dead and seated Him at His right hand in the heavenly places, far above all principality and power and might and dominion, and every name that is named, not only in this age but also in that which is to come. And He put all things under His feet, and gave Him to be head over all things to the church, which is His body, the fullness of Him who fills all in all" Ephesians 1:18-23.

Jesus is the "Son of the Most High God," and as Man, He has been elevated to a position higher than any other. All authority has been given to Him (Matthew 28:18), and we have been made one with Him. What an exalted position we have been given in Christ—a position above that of the devil himself.

Because all dominion has been given to Jesus, so Paul can write, "sin shall not have dominion over you" Romans 6:14. There is, however, order in the kingdom of heaven, an order that is too often ignored. We cannot simply snap our fingers and the devil will cower under our authority and position in Christ. James writes:

"Therefore submit to God. Resist the devil and he will flee from you. Draw near to God and He will draw near to you" James 4:7-8.

Note the order: "Submit to God," "Rebuke the devil," "Draw near to God." The devil will "flee from you" only as we live our life in submission to God. We have no authority or power when we live according to the flesh. It is only as we live in submission to God that our fight against the devil and our prayer life is effective.

It is one thing to stand on the sideline and cheer the exalted position of God Most High, but another to participate with Jesus in His authority and power.

"Oh, clap your hands, all you peoples! Shout to God with the voice of triumph! For the Lord Most High is awesome; He is a great King over all the earth" Psalm 47:1-2.

I remember standing in front of Buckingham Palace waving and cheering as Queen Elizabeth and her family stood on the balcony accepting the admiration of her subjects, but there was an iron fence, guards, and a parade ground that separated us. How indicative of many Christians who stand cheering God on the sidelines when He has invited us to stand with Him on the balcony. We recognize His power and authority, but do not and cannot participate with Him.

> **"Hear attentively the thunder of His voice, and the rumbling that comes from His mouth. He sends it forth under the whole heaven, His lightning to the ends of the earth. After it a voice roars; He thunders with His majestic voice, and He does not restrain them when His voice is heard. God thunders marvelously with His voice; He does great things which we cannot comprehend" Job 37:2-5.**

Puritan Quote:

"O Fountain of all good: Nothing exceeds Thy power, Nothing is too great for Thee to do, Nothing too good for Thee to give. Infinite is Thy might, boundless Thy love, Limitless Thy grace, glorious Thy saving name" Puritan Prayer. The Valley of Vision.

THE SAVIOR
Yahvahshua

Reading: Matthew 1:18-23

"Thou shalt call His name YAHVAHSHUA—for He will save His people from their sins" Matthew 1:21 (Sacred Name Bible).

It is well established that the name of God (Elohim) is Yahvah (Yahweh, Jehovah) Exodus 3:14. The Son of Yahvah said, "I have come in My Father's name" John 5:43. His Father's name is Yahvah, therefore Yahvah's Son is called Yahvahshua. The title SHUA means Savior, therefore Yahvah Savior or Jehovah Savior. The meaning of the name is given in the following words, "He shall save His people from their sins." His name is not Jesus, but Yahvahshua.

Whether your translation uses the name Jesus or Yahvahshua is a matter of semantics. The important thing to consider is the meaning of the name—"He shall save His people from their sins." But, who are "His people?" Does this wonderful promise include you and me, or just the Children of Israel who are classified as such? "I will walk among you and be your God, and you shall be My people" Leviticus 26:12.

The answer is "yes." Since through His Son, Yahvahshua, Yahvah "has broken down the middle wall of separation," between Jew and Gentile, He has created "in Himself one new man from the two, thus making peace, that He might reconcile them both to God in one body through the cross" Ephesians 2:15-16. This is what is meant by "God so loved the world," not every individual, but both Jew and Gentile.

Now we know "who" His people are, what does it mean to be saved from our sins? It does not mean Yahvahshua saves His people from sinning or even from the temptation to sin. Yahvahshua has freed us from the ramification of sin—God's wrath and judgment.

God is still angry with those who remain outside of His family, His kingdom. But for those who have been made one with His Son, and for those who have been washed clean by Yahvahshua's blood, He is no longer angry. Do we still sin? Yes, However, for those of us who are His people, He has provided relief:

"If we say that we have no sin, we deceive ourselves, and the truth is not in us. If we confess our sins, He is faithful and just to forgive us our sins and to cleanse us from all unrighteousness" 1 John 1:8-9.

This is made possible because Yahvahshua died for His people. This is a glorious element of our salvation—we have a faithful and just Father. If we confess our sins to Him, He has promised to forgive us. He does not require we do penance, whether it be something physical, or the repetition of the Lord's Prayer, or a certain number of "Hail Mary's". What He does require is that we confess our sin. When one who is walking with the Lord sins, the Holy Spirit will convict him, and he will confess. The Holy Spirit is faithful to convict us, and the Father is faithful to forgive us. This is a personal matter between the Believer and his heavenly Father without the assistance of pastor or priest. As children of the Living God, we have direct access to Him.

Unlike the Old Covenant, when only the High Priest was permitted into the Holy of Holies, and that but once a year, we, because of the work of Yahvahshua on the cross, have immediate and direct access into the Father's presence.

"Tell Aaron your brother not to come at just any time into the Holy Place inside the veil, before the mercy seat which is on the ark, lest he die" Leviticus 16:2.
"Let us therefore come boldly to the throne of grace, that we may obtain mercy and find grace to help in time of need" Hebrews 4:16.
"For through Him we both have access by one Spirit to the Father" Ephesians 2:18.

The reason this remarkable privilege is possible, is because Yahvahshua, our Great High Priest, ascended into the very presence of His Father, and remains at His right hand interceding on our behalf. When He died bearing our sins and all of the guilt attached to them, the veil that separated the Holy of Holies from the rest of the tabernacle, was torn from top to bottom (Matthew 27:51).

The obstacle, keeping God's people from His immediate presence, was removed. It was torn from "top to bottom" indicating it was an act of God. Because of Yahvahshua, there is nothing to keep God's people from His presence. The Cherubim that kept Adam and Eve from returning to the Garden of Eden, lay aside their swords when they see one of God's people approaching, dressed in the robe of righteousness, with which we have been adorned.

"I will greatly rejoice in the Lord, my soul shall be joyful in my God; for He has clothed me with the garments of salvation, He has covered me with the robe of righteousness, as a bridegroom decks himself with ornaments, and as a bride adorns herself with her jewels" Isaiah 61:10.

Why are so many of us reluctant to pray? I think one of the reasons is because we do not feel worthy to be in God's presence. We are ashamed to continually acknowledge our failures. It is not that we actively avoid prayer, but the devil, knowing how we feel, plays on those feelings, and is quick to cause interruptions—phone calls, television, visiting friends, etc. I think we all experience these things.

Remember the name of our Savior—Yahvahshua. He shall save His people from their sins; from every ramification of their sins. By so doing, we are invited to come BOLDLY to the Throne of Grace. Reluctance, timidity, ashamedness, fear, none of these things should keep us from approaching Him—they certainly do not keep Him from granting us an audience.

The moment we say, "Abba, Father," we have His ear, and He introduces us the court of Heaven as "This my son."

Puritan Quote:

"The starting point, then, is confession of sin and repentance towards God. Yet, amazingly, we are bidden to seek this mercy 'boldly'—not hesitantly of fearfully, but eagerly and with full assurance" Edgar Andrews, 1932—.

EMMANUEL
Emmanoueel

Reading: Matthew 1:18-23
"Behold, the virgin shall be with child, and bear a Son, and
they shall call His name Immanuel" Matthew 1:23

It is remarkable that in the one declaration of the angel to Joseph, the
Messiah is given two names. He is first given the name Yahvahshua (He
shall save His people from their sins) v 21, and then Emmanuel (God with
us) v 23.

The work of Yahvahshua could not be accomplished by any man, but
by divine intervention, therefore it is written "that which is conceived in her
is of the Holy Spirit" v 20.

These words of the angel are a direct quote from Isaiah 7:14. At the
time God gave these words to Isaiah, Judah had been decimated by Pekah,
king of Israel. 120,000 persons had been killed in one day, and 200,000
taken away into captivity. It is no wonder that Ahaz was afraid his enemies
would prevail and destroy Jerusalem and the kingdom of Judah. This would
also mean the line of David would be annihilated, the line promised by
God to endure forever.

To assure Ahaz his fears were groundless, God sends Isaiah to him
with the promise:

**"Therefore the Lord Himself will give you a sign: Behold, the
virgin shall conceive and bear a Son, and shall call His name
Immanuel" Isaiah 7:14.**

The angel tells Joseph the promise to Ahaz is to be fulfilled in the
person of his son, Yahvahshua. The line of David is to be continued
through Him, and the only way this is possible is by God becoming man,
Emmanuel, "God with us." The Divine and human natures combined in one

man—a miracle accomplished by divine power, an event never seen before and never to be seen again.

The word translated Emmanuel actually means "Mighty One with us." He who is spoken of in the Old Testament as the all-powerful, most high, almighty God, is to be the "Savior."

God is to be with us in a way never before known. God's people were not only to be influenced by God, or seen in dreams and visions, or in promises and prophecies, by Yahvah, Jehovah, living among them as a man. Only as such will He be able to save them from their sins. He will live among them, face their temptations, battle the devil, and yet be victorious.

"By the light of nature, we see God as a God above us; by the light of the law, we see him as a God against us; but by the light of the gospel, we see him as Immanuel, God with us, in our own nature, and (which is more) in our interest. Herein the Redeemer commended his love. With Christ's name, Immanuel, we may compare the name given to the gospel church (Ezek 48:35). Jehovah Shammah—The Lord is there; the Lord of hosts is with us" Matthew Henry.

The wonderful and most comforting knowledge of all is that Yahvahshua is still Emmanuel. The Bible never tells us the Christian life is easy. It is not. It tells us we are in a fight against an enemy who is very powerful, cunning, and dedicated to see we fail. We are in a race in which we will become tired. We can win the battles and win the race by remembering that our Savior is Emmanuel—the Mighty One with us.

Circumstances may dictate otherwise, nevertheless the God of Abraham, Moses, David and the prophets, remains with us in a way the patriarchs of old never knew.

"And without controversy great is the mystery of godliness: God was manifested in the flesh" 1 Timothy 3:16.

"And the Word became flesh and dwelt among us, and we beheld His glory, the glory as of the only begotten of the Father, full of grace and truth" John 1:14.

The word translated Emmanuel literally means "the strong one with us." No matter the opposition, God, the Most Highly Exalted, Almighty One, is with His people. We need not face our enemy alone, for God is with us in the person of Yahvahshua, our Savior and Redeemer.

Puritan Quote:

"*God with us, by the influences of his Holy Spirit-in the holy sacrament-in the preaching of his word-in private prayer. And God with us, through every action of our life; that we begin, continue, and end in his name. He is God with us, to comfort, enlighten, protect, and defend us in every time of temptation and trial, in the hour of death, in the day of judgment; and God with us, and in us, and we with and in him, to all eternity*" Adam Clark, 1760-1832.

MESSIAH/CHRIST
Mashach / Christos

Reading: John 1:1-3, 10-14
"God has made this Jesus, whom you crucified, both Lord and Christ"
Acts 2:36

Most of us are as familiar with the title "Christ" as we are with "Jesus" because they are often used together. "Christ" is the Greek form of the Hebrew "Messiah," and both mean "anointed one." The phrase "anointed one" refers to someone who has been set apart for a special purpose.

The Jews were looking for the promised Messiah, but they were expecting Him to be the king who would deliver them from their enemies, especially the Roman authorities. They certainly didn't expect their Messiah to be born in a stable housing farm animals.

It wasn't until Jesus began His ministry that He was called "Messiah." Andrew, Peter's brother, introduced Jesus to him, "He first found his own brother Simon, and said to him, "We have found the Messiah" (which is translated, the Christ). And he brought him to Jesus" John 1:41-42.

Andrew and Simon (Peter) learned from John the Baptist that the Lamb of God that takes away the sins of the world was indeed the Messiah (John 1:29,36,40). This is why Andrew was so excited when he told his brother, "We have found the Messiah."

Jesus was indeed a king, but not one who would lead His troops into battle riding a white horse—this will come later (Rev. 19:11-16).

In order to avoid the false concept the Jews had for their expected Messiah, Jesus avoided this title throughout most of His life. The only other reference to Jesus as the Messiah was when He revealed Himself as such to a foreigner, a Samaritan woman:

"The woman said to Him, "I know that Messiah is coming" (who is called Christ). "When He comes, He will tell us all things." Jesus said to her, "I who speak to you am He" John 4:25-26.

Finally, shortly before His death, Jesus answered the high priest's question, "Are You the Christ, the Son of the Blessed?" Jesus said, "I am." Mark 14:61-62.

Throughout the Old Testament, priests and kings, among others, were anointed with oil, but the Messiah was anointed with the Holy Spirit: "God anointed Jesus of Nazareth with the Holy Spirit and with power" Acts 10:38. Oil is the symbol of the Holy Spirit, therefore, when we are born again, it is with the power of the Holy Spirit.

As God's people. We are His anointed ones:

"Now He who establishes us with you in Christ and has anointed us is God, who also has sealed us and given us the Spirit in our hearts as a guarantee" 2 Corinthians 1:21-22.

The anointing represents being set apart to a specific service, hence the prophet, priest, and king. Jesus was anointed with the Holy Spirit, being set apart to the highest office ever held in the world as Prophet, Priest, and King.

As believers, we are set apart by the Holy Spirit to serve God in whatever capacity He calls us. We may be called to serve in the church as elders or deacons, teachers or evangelists, or in our everyday lives by comforting the sick and lonely. Do you have the gift of saying an encouraging word to the depressed and disappointed?

It is our responsibility to discover the gift(s) God has given us, and to apply ourselves to it.

"You are the light of the world. A city that is set on a hill cannot be hidden. Nor do they light a lamp and put it under a basket, but on a lampstand, and it gives light to all who are in the house. Let your light so shine before men, that they may see your good works and glorify your Father in heaven" Matthew 5:14-16.

This same Spirit, this same anointing, is given us as a seal and guarantee of our salvation. "But you have an anointing from the Holy One, and you know all things" 1 John 2:20. It is only by such that we "become a sweet savour of Christ" for we are anointed with the same Oil (Holy Spirit) as Jesus Christ.

In response to Jesus' question "Who do you say that I am?" Simon Peter answered "You are the Christ (Messiah—Anointed One), the Son of the living God." What a vital and important response this was, for Jesus went on the say, "on this rock (statement) I will build my church." Everything in God's purpose for sending His Son into the world depends on the Messiahship of Jesus. He was anointed by God to bring the gospel to mankind, and we are anointed to continue His work as He builds His Church.

Puritan Quote:

"They are confirmed by the Holy Spirit. He does establish Christians in the faith of the gospel; he has anointed them with his sanctifying grace, which in scripture is often compared to oil; he has sealed them, for their security and confirmation; and he is given as an earnest in their hearts" Matthew Henry, 1662-1714.

HALLOWED BE YOUR NAME

Reading: Matthew 6:8-13
"Our Father in heaven, Hallowed be Your name" Matthew 6:9

Recently, we have considered some of the names and titles given by and applied to God. Jesus, in these words, I believe is referring not to the specific name that God revealed to Moses, but to who He is in every aspect of His name and titles. The following thoughts are taken from our series on the Lord's Prayer of September 21ˢᵗ, 2011 (Meditations on the Lord's Prayer #3).

In these days when the name of God is blasphemed without thought or concern, these words of Jesus at the beginning of His prayer carry great import.

The first of seven petitions in this prayer is for God's name to be hallowed. The word 'hagiazo' occurs 29 times in the New Testament, and all but twice is translated "sanctify(ied)." "Our Father who is in heaven, let Your name be venerated" Wuest's Expanded Translation. The NLT translates it as, "May your name be honored." The Septuagint says, "Sanctified be thy name."

The placement of this petition shows us that the honoring of God's name must come before all other things. We pray for our daily necessities to be provided—"Give us this day our daily bread"—but not before we honor the name of the Provider. How readily we neglect God's holy name, and begin our prayers with "Give us."

The hallowing of God's name was not a new concept to the disciples. Jesus reminded them of God's words to Moses:

"You shall not profane My holy name, but I will be hallowed among the children of Israel" Leviticus 22:32.

"As the vessels of the sanctuary were said to be hallowed, so, to hallow God's name, is to set it apart from all abuses, and to use it holily and reverently. In

particular, hallowing God's name is to give Him honor and veneration, and render His name sacred" Thomas Watson.

To honor the name of God means to give to the Lord the glory due to His name. When David brought the Ark of the Covenant to Jerusalem, he unabashedly sang and danced before God and the people: "Give to the LORD the glory due His name," he sang. In his heart and by his actions, he was honoring the name of God.

How do we hallow God's name? David continues in his song to show us:

"Bring an offering, and come before Him. Oh, worship the LORD in the beauty of holiness! Tremble before Him, all the earth" 1 Chronicles 16:29-30.

Here are four ways of honoring the name of God: 1) Bring an offering, 2) Come before Him, 3) Worship the Lord, 4) Tremble before Him.

God no longer requires the offerings of bulls and sheep, but rather that of ourselves.

"I beseech you therefore, brethren, by the mercies of God, that you present your bodies a living sacrifice, holy, acceptable to God, which is your reasonable service. And do not be conformed to this world, but be transformed by the renewing of your mind, that you may prove what is that good and acceptable and perfect will of God" Romans 12:1-2.

We hallow God's name when we separate ourselves from the world both physically and mentally. Where do our desires lay? Whenever we choose God over the world, we honor His name. Every act of obedience to God's commandments hallows His name. Honor, respect, reverence, venerate, are all words to describe the hallowing of God's name.

When Ezekiel and John fell on their faces in awe and worship, they honored the name of God (Ezekiel 1:28; Revelation 1:17).

Again, David said, "For our heart shall rejoice in Him, because we have trusted in His holy name" Psalm 33:21. Every time we trust God, we honor

His name. When God told Abraham he and Sarah would have a son in their old age,

"He did not waver at the promise of God through unbelief, but was strengthened in faith, giving glory to God, and being fully convinced that what He had promised He was also able to perform" Romans 4:20-21.

Abraham trusted God, and in so doing gave "glory to God." Unbelief leads to disobedience, and disobedience is an affront to God. Trust in God and His Word brings glory to His name. "He who does not believe God has made Him a liar" (1 John 5:10)—strong words, indeed.

At Christ's birth, the angels sang: "Glory to God in the highest" (Luke 2:14)—may this be the desire and intent in each of our lives, for then we shall hallow God's glorious name.

Puritan Quote:

"We hallow and sanctify God's name when we never make mention of it but with the highest reverence. His name is sacred, and it must not be spoken of but with veneration. To speak vainly or slightly of God is profaning His name, and is taking His name in vain" Thomas Watson, 1620-1686.

THE LAMB OF GOD

Reading: Genesis 22:2-14
"Behold! The Lamb of God who takes away the sin of the world!"
John 1:29

What a glorious and consuming study is the name by which Jesus Christ is referred—"The Lamb of God." From the well known account of Abraham and Isaac in Genesis 22:2-14, to the profound position and activity of the Lamb in Revelation, Yahvahshua, the Messiah, is portrayed as a Sacrifice to a Victor occupying the Throne of God. One is tempted to lay aside every other project and put pen to paper (as we used to say before the era of computers), and commence the writing of a book on the subject, but we are restricted in this venue to a few brief thoughts.

The "Lamb" is mentioned 70 times in the Old Testament—52 times in Exodus, Leviticus, and Numbers, where the foundation of Redemption was laid. In the New Testament the word is used 32 times with 26 times in Revelation. In the Old Testament the Lamb speaks of Sacrifice and the Messiah, whereas in the New Testament it primarily address the Sovereignty of the Messiah, the Son of God.

Sacrifice: Although never stated conclusively, many believe the coverings with which God supplied Adam and Eve were made of lamb skins (Genesis 3:21). This makes perfect sense as it sets the precedence of a sacrifice being made in the redemption of God's people.

The account of Abraham and Isaac, where Abraham made the well-known prophecy, "God will provide for Himself the lamb for a burnt offering" (Genesis 22:8) continues the theme. The blood smeared of the homes of God's people at the first Passover, was the blood of lambs (Exodus 12:1-5).

Son (Messiah): The use of lambs in the laws of sacrifice (Leviticus 3:6), and the tribal leaders offering at the dedication of the altar (Numbers 7:15), all point forward to the time when John the Baptist introduced Jesus as "The Lamb of God who takes away the sin of the world!" John 1:29.

The Ethiopian was reading from Isaiah (Acts 8:32-33):

"He was led as a lamb to the slaughter, and as a sheep before its shearers is silent, so He opened not His mouth" Isaiah 53:7.

The one theme running through the sacrifice of a lamb (as well as other animals) is that it must be without blemish and with spot, and which was fulfilled when the Son of God offered Himself for the redemption of God's people:

"You were not redeemed with corruptible things, like silver or gold . . . but with the precious blood of Christ, as of a lamb without blemish and without spot" 1 Peter 1:18-19.

Sovereign: Beginning with chapter five, eleven of the next seventeen chapters of Revelation speaks of the "Lamb." The fifth chapter of Revelation is the transition between Sacrifice and Sovereignty.

When no one could be found worthy, the Lamb was "worthy to open the scroll and the seals, because "You were slain, and have redeemed us to God by Your blood" (5:9).

In Chapter six, the Sovereign Lamb opens the seven seals. Seal 5 is the cry of those martyred for Christ—to the 'Sovereign Lord' (Lord (despotes) means absolute ruler, not 'kurios' as in Lord Jesus Christ). Seal six speaks of the "wrath of the Lamb" (16), a scenario not usually associated with a furry, gentle lamb skipping playfully on the green grass of meadows, etc.

The Lamb is equal with His Father, and is worthy to be praised (7:10-12), and His role is reversed when the Lamb becomes the Shepherd:

"for the Lamb who is in the midst of the throne will shepherd them and lead them to living fountains of waters" 7:17.

The following is a brief synopsis of the Lamb as the Sovereign Lord:
Chapter 12: The blood of the Lamb is the source of victory (11)
Chapter 13: The Lamb owns the Book of Life (8)

I hope these few thoughts will encourage you to study this wonderful theme that is knit like a red cord throughout the Word of God. The Lion of the Tribe of Judah is the Redeemer of God's people, portrayed as "the Lamb of God that takes away the sins of the world."

Puritan Quote:

"*Let us hence learn what benefit the reading of the Law brings us in this respect; for, though the rite of sacrificing is abolished, yet it assists our faith not a little, to compare the reality with the type, so that we may seek in the former what the latter contains.*

"*Peter, by applying this to Christ, teaches us that he was a suitable victim, and approved by God, for he was perfect, without any blemish; had he had any defect in him, he could not have been rightly offered to God, nor could he pacify his wrath*" John Calvin, 1509-1564.

WE WILL REMEMBER THE NAME

Reading: Psalm 20:1-9

"Some trust in chariots, and some in horses; but we will remember the name of the Lord our God" Psalm 20:7

In this powerful and comforting Psalm of David, the King of Israel mentions the name of God three times, on each occasion bringing forth different aspects of the believer's relationship with his Lord and Master.

Protection: "May the name of the God of Jacob defend you" vs1. Jesus never promised a life free of trouble to His followers, rather the opposite:

> **"Then Jesus said to His disciples, "If anyone desires to come after Me, let him deny himself, and take up his cross, and follow Me. For whoever desires to save his life will lose it, but whoever loses his life for My sake will find it" Matthew 16:24-26.**

How easy it is in our "day of trouble," whatever that may be, to seek solace in all but the "name of God." David refers to "the God of Jacob," for he remembers when Jacob fled from his brother Esau, at Bethel, and Jacob said to his household, 'Let us arise, and go up to Bethel; and I will make there an altar unto God, who answered me in the day of my distress, and was with me in the way which I went.' Genesis 35:3.

Over the past few weeks, we have considered some of the names and titles given to God. I would suggest there are some names that mean more to us personally than others. Every name and title of God are there for us to draw on. In the time when we need guidance and protection, perhaps the words of Jesus when He said, "I am the good shepherd; and I know My sheep, and am known by My own" are our meditation, and are the means of comfort and strength.

No matter our trouble or need, Jehovah, the great "I AM," the God of Jacob, the God of His people, is always there "that we may obtain mercy and find grace to help in time of need" Hebrews 4:16.

Participation: "And in the name of our God we will set up our banners!" vs5. Is there a greater name under whose banner we can fight our enemy? We are not asked to fight the devil in our own strength. The "Captain of our salvation" is Jesus Christ, and it is His name that is on our banners. It is He who leads His army to victory. It is the "Lion of the Tribe of Judah" with whom we, as children of God, participate in our spiritual warfare.

If we face the enemy with our name on the banner, we are doomed to defeat. Tragically, so many of us yield to temptations because we raise our own standard. Prayer, and an understanding of God's Word, are the greatest banners we can raise in this world of trouble. Is there any better way to grow in our knowledge of God than by prayer? Is it any wonder that the apostle wrote "pray without ceasing" 1 Thessalonians 5:17.

Power: "Some trust in chariots, and some in horses; but we will remember the name of the Lord our God" Psalm 20:7.

It is not just a remembering, but calling upon the name of the "Lord our God." We have no power against the troubles that we face other than the power and strength of God:

"Be strong in the Lord and in the power of His might" Ephesians 6:10.

The Hebrew words "LORD our God," are "Yahweh Elohim." As we have previously noted (# 2 of this series), Yahweh, Jehovah, is the name by which God revealed Himself to Moses, and Elohim is the plural name of our God. We should take great encouragement in that our God (Elohim) is three in one and one in three:

"For there are three that bear witness in heaven: the Father, the Word, and the Holy Spirit; and these three are one" 1 John 5:7.

Not one, but the power and work of the three persons of our Godhead, together in unison are with us and for us. Because of this, the Psalmist could write:

"They have bowed down and fallen; But we have risen and stand upright" Psalm 20:8.

This is the position of those whose trust is in the LORD our God. Unlike those who trust in "horses and chariots," or anything else that takes the place of God in their lives, we have been raised with Christ, and "stand upright" before our heavenly Father, free of guilt and condemnation, for the righteousness of Christ is imputed to those whose trust is in the Lord.

"There is therefore now no condemnation to those who are in Christ Jesus, who do not walk according to the flesh, but according to the Spirit" Romans 8:1.

Puritan Quote:

"And I resolved to try what "the name of the God of Jacob" would do, having the Father's fixed decrees, the Son's unalterable responsibility, and the Spirit's invincible grace and operation around me" Joseph Irons, 1785-1852.

THE LION OF JUDAH

Reading: Revelation 5:1-5

"Behold, the Lion of the tribe of Judah, . . . has prevailed" Revelation 5:5

The apostle John, privileged to witness the happenings of Jesus Christ following His resurrection and ascension into heaven, broke down in tears because "no man was found worthy to open and read the book" (5:4). Not one of the prophets, priests, or kings that had played such a great part in the plan of God, was, in all their greatness and devotion to God, found worthy.

The weeping apostle heard the words, "Weep not." Are we not used to hearing these words from the lips of our Master Himself? When the ruler was told of the death of his daughter, Jesus told him, "Do not weep" Luke 8:52. Only Jesus could say this with authority because He has the power over death.

When Mary went to the tomb and found it empty, she wept, until "she turned around and saw Jesus" John 20:14. She did not recognize Him until He spoke her name, and she immediately responded, "Master."

John's tears were now stopped when his vision was turned to Jesus, "Behold, the Lion of the tribe of Judah." He was the one that was found worthy. He alone had the authority and the power to do that which no other man could do. He alone conquered death and gained the victory over the devil.

"His designation as the Lion of the Tribe of Judah denotes His oneness with our human nature by virtue of the incarnation. The tribe of Judah was the tribe of David from whom the kingly line proceeded and to whom the promise was given of a son, the throne of whose kingdom would last forever (2 Samuel 7:13, 16)" Philip Edgcumbe Hughes, 1915-1990.

The scripture that immediately comes to mind is found in Hebrews 12:2:

"looking unto Jesus, the author and finisher of our faith, who for the joy that was set before Him endured the cross, despising the shame, and has sat down at the right hand of the throne of God."

No matter the cause of our weeping, we are invited to "Behold, the Lion of the tribe of Judah." When we see Him as such, we see Him as the conqueror, the all-powerful one. The lion is the most courageous and majestic beast, the king of the forest, an emblem of strength and valor.

"All weeping ceases when we look away from our defeated and unworthy selves, and put our trust in him, through whom all tears are wiped away" Phillip E. Hughes.

Again, John is invited to "Come and see." It was not enough to read about it, or hear about it, but to see for yourself: "And I looked, and behold, a white horse. He who sat on it had a bow; and a crown was given to him, and he went out conquering and to conquer" Revelation 6:1-2.

It is true we cannot see Him visibly, but God's children have been given the eye of faith, who like Moses:

"By faith he forsook Egypt, not fearing the wrath of the king; for he endured as seeing Him who is invisible" Hebrews 11:27-28.

Do we not need to place our faith and trust in Him who the conqueror over "all principality and power and might and dominion, and every name that is named, not only in this age but also in that which is to come"?

Jesus, the "Lion of the tribe of Judah" is the fulfillment of Genesis 49:9: "Judah is a lion's whelp." The tribe of Judah, the tribe of David, the tribe of Joseph, and the tribe of Yahvahshua (Matthew 1:16). Jesus, the "root of David," with whom, and in whom, we are made one.

"Though now you do not see Him, yet believing, you rejoice with joy inexpressible and full of glory, receiving the end of your faith—the salvation of your souls" 1 Peter 1:8-9.

Puritan Quote:

"Christ is the great Conqueror. The victory has been achieved, it remains only to celebrate the triumph. That is what opening the book, i.e. revealing and bringing to pass all the mighty prophecies in it concerning the triumphant course and the glorious consummation of the kingdom, signifies" R.C.H Lenski, 1864-1936.

"I AM"

Reading: John 18:1-11

"When He said to them, "I am He," they drew back and fell to the ground"
John 18:5

For more than one reason, this account of Jesus in the Garden of Gethsemane is a passage to which I often return. But what has it got to do with the names or titles of God? In translating from the original language, it is difficult, if not impossible, to be accurate or precise. Sometimes, in order to make sense to the English reader, a word has to be added—when this is done, the word[s] is printed in italics. Such is the case in the words of Jesus when He said "I AM *He.*"

Jesus did not say "I AM He," but simply "I AM" ("*Ego eimi*"). It is very important to understand this because of the effect it had on the "detachment of troops, and officers from the chief priests and Pharisees" that came to arrest Him.

When asked for Jesus of Nazareth to identify Himself, Jesus spoke His name (Exodus 3:14). How significant this is for Jesus to claim the self-proclaimed name of God. I cannot imagine Jesus hanging His head and nervously saying "I AM He," for "He went forward [stepped toward them], and said with divine authority "I AM."

The power and authority in the name of God is clearly associated here. It is the same power as when Jesus stilled the waves of the sea (Mark 4:39), and cast out demons (Luke 9:42), and healed and raised Lazarus from the dead (John 11:43). What judgment will those face who so flippantly use the name of God. How carelessly some of us who love God tack His name on to the end of our prayers as a matter of ritual, not remembering why we do so (John 14:13).

As we read in the gospels, in particular the apostle John, Jesus often declares Himself as that which we need:

"I am the bread of life" John 6:35;

"I am the light of the world" John 8:12;

"I am the door" John 10:9;

"I am the Good Shepherd" John 11,14;

"I am the resurrection and the life" John 11:25;

"I am the way, the truth, and the life" John 14:6;

"I am the true vine" John 15:1;

"I am the Alpha and the Omega, the Beginning and the End" Rev 1:11;

"I am the First and the Last" Revelation 1:11;

"I am the Root and the Offspring of David, the Bright and Morning Star" Revelation 22:16.

To these, and many more, we can claim Jesus as being whoever and whatever we need. "I am—and fill in the blank. I do not mean to be irreverent, but practical. "Lord, whatever is my need, I can find satisfaction and fulfillment in You."

As we grow older, our needs change, and we find we need Jesus in different ways. Perhaps we look to Him as our Comforter more than we used to. If so, then I am encouraged and strengthened by His words, "I, even I, am He who comforts you" Isaiah 51:12.

Perhaps we can no longer be as active in our ministry, and the devil tells us we are no longer of any use to God. How wonderful then are His words:

"You are My servant, I have chosen you and have not cast you away: Fear not, for I am with you; be not dismayed, for I am your God. I will strengthen you, Yes, I will help you, I will uphold you with My righteous right hand" Isaiah 41:4.

It is as if Jesus is telling us, "No matter what you need, I AM." The words of God to Paul also apply to us, "My grace is sufficient for you, for My strength is made perfect in weakness" 2 Corinthians 12:9.

The voice of God to some is as a "still small voice" (1 Kings 19:12), comforting and strengthening, but to others it is damning and destroying, "He will strike the earth with the rod of his mouth, and will slay the wicked by the breath of his lips" Isaiah 11:4.

Some will hear:

"Depart from Me, you cursed, into the everlasting fire prepared for the devil and his angels," and some **"Come, you blessed of**

My Father, inherit the kingdom prepared for you from the foundation of the world" Matthew 25:41,34.

The same voice—different people. To some comfort, strength and assurance, to others condemnation. Let those who love and serve Him know Him as the Great "I AM," but to those who ignore and reject Him, take heed, for "I, the Lord, am the first; and with the last I am He."

Puritan Quote:

"There is, in the name "I AM," a height, a depth, a length, a breadth, which truly pass beyond the utmost stretch of the human conception. When God would teach mankind His name, He calls Himself the great "I AM," and leaves a blank—believers may supply those things for which we pray. C.H. Mackintosh, 1820-1896.

THE HONOR OF YOUR NAME

Reading: Psalm 138:1-8

"You have magnified Your word above all Your name" Psalm 138:2

Upon the first reading of these words in the KJV and other modern translations, these words appear confusing and complicated. For the past nineteen weeks, we have considered the names and titles of our God, our Elohim, and have been impressed with the glory, honor and majesty they contain. Now, to read there is something greater than His name, seems contradictory to the balance of scripture.

Once more, as always, the words must be considered within their context. The most important aspect of God is that He has revealed to us is His Name. It tells us who He is, and everything He stands for. "Your name" means more than just "God" or "LORD", it means everything that God is.

David begins this song with his full commitment to Jehovah—"with my whole heart," specifically because of His "lovingkindness and truth." God's name means nothing to us unless it is revealed by His acts toward us. Nature alone is not sufficient to convince us of our sin, and of God's love in sending His Son to die for us.

In the Bible we read of God's promises to His people, and most importantly how He has kept those promises. Promises made does not mean promises kept—unless God made those promises. The New Living Translation and The Living Bible both translate the Hebrew as "Your promises are backed by all the honor of your name."

There is nothing more honorable or trustworthy in heaven or earth than God's name.

"I am satisfied David means to declare that God's name is exalted above all things, specifying the particular manner in which he has exalted his name, by faithfully performing his free promises" John Calvin.

Unlike promises made by any man or woman, God's promises are not empty words—they can be trusted and relied upon. There is always a chance that human promises will not be kept, for they are made by one whose character is flawed by sin, however righteous he may appear. But, when God speaks, we must listen and believe, because He is holy, and "it is impossible for God to lie" Hebrews 6:18.

"The Word is the glass in which we see God, and seeing him are changed into his likeness by his Spirit. If this glass be cracked, then the conceptions we have of God will misrepresent him unto us; whereas the Word, in its native clearness, sets him out in all his glory unto our eye" William Gurnall, 1617-1679.

Calling on his past experience, David immediately gives an example of His Lord's faithfulness:

"In the day when I cried out, You answered me, and made me bold with strength in my soul" Psalm 138:3.

Then, not satisfied with past blessings from the Lord, he tells us of his current trust in God's promises:

"Though I walk in the midst of trouble, You will revive me; You will stretch out Your hand against the wrath of my enemies, and Your right hand will save me" Psalm 138:7.

How easy it is to remind ourselves of past blessings, yet fall short when we are faced with today's trials and temptations. Do not misunderstand me, for we can be encouraged and strengthened by remembering God's faithfulness to us in days gone by. Yesterday's victories will not win today's battles.

Our faith and walk with God must be a daily, present, experience. We can be strengthened by God's faithfulness in the past, and also by reading of His promises in His Word. We cannot, however, live in the past.

Call to mind the glory, honor, and majesty of God's name, and the divine authority that is contained in His promises.

Note the order of time when Jesus said, "'I am the Alpha and the Omega, the Beginning and the End,' says the Lord, '**who is** and **who was** and **who is to come**, the Almighty'" Revelation 1:8

Remember the "I AM"s of Jesus, not "I WAS" or "I WILL BE."

Yesterday's bread will not satisfy today's hunger, but knowing and feasting on the Bread of Life, will.

Puritan Quote:

"Thy word", or, "Thy promise." So great are God's promises, and so faithful and complete is his performance of them, as even to surpass the expectations which the greatness of his name has excited.—Annotated Paragraph Bible—1856.

LET HIM KISS ME

Reading: Song of Songs 1:1-4

"Let him kiss me with the kisses of his mouth" Song of Songs 1:2

As we noted previously (God's Name series #21), this song was the most excellent of all the "one thousand and five" that he penned (1 Kings 4:32). I believe also it is the most excellent of all songs period, including that of Moses (Exod 15

The author of this Song of Songs is also the author of Ecclesiastes, where he refers to the "vanity of vanities" Eccl. 1:2. Solomon spends the entire book specifying what these vanities are—33 times he uses this phrase. But, now his thoughts are on a different subject—the love story between the Bridegroom and His Bride. This is the romance of the King of kings, and the Lord of lords.

Solomon was a very prolific writer: "He spoke three thousand proverbs, and his songs were one thousand and five" 1 Kings 4:32, and we have the joy and privilege of knowing the "Song of Songs," the most excellent of them all.

In the days when this song was written, especially among royalty and those of a high society standing, it was the custom to marry a person, not for love, but that which would enhance the political standing of the groom, or the joining together of nations. But, this is not the case of the Groom and Bride in the Song of Songs.

It is generally accepted that the Bridegroom is the Messiah, Yahvahshua, Jesus, He that would save His people from their sins. The Bride speaks of you and me as individuals in the church, in the body of Christ. The Daughters of Jerusalem represents the church as a body, as in "I will build my church" Matthew 16:18.

At the very beginning of this Song of Songs, the name of its main character is referred to. The bride has asked to be kissed, and immediately she was blessed with revelation concerning her Bridegroom's name. She wasn't going to be satisfied with a "peck on the cheek," she wanted an intimate relationship with her betrothed.

"Your name is ointment poured forth." What is His name? God told Moses, "I AM WHO I AM," (Exodus 3:14), or "The Self-existent One." (see #2 in God's Name series.) This Hebrew word "Yahvah," is also given to Jesus as "Yahvahshua" Matthew 1:21. And, as we saw recently from John's Gospel, Jesus referred to Himself as "I AM" eight times, such as "I Am the Good Shepherd", etc.

This most wonderful name is to the Bride "as ointment (perfume) poured forth." The perfume speaks of the internal thoughts and emotions of Jesus. We so often dwell on what He did, but His works are the expression of His thoughts.

"Let this mind be in you which was also in Christ Jesus" Philippians 2:5.

His innermost being, when revealed to His own, is like "perfume poured forth." The more we learn of Him, the more we love Him. "The kisses of His mouth" is an expression of His intimate love for us.

Through us, God pours forth His fragrance:

"Now thanks be to God who always leads us in triumph in Christ, and through us diffuses the fragrance of His knowledge in every place. For we are to God the fragrance of Christ among those who are being saved and among those who are perishing. To the one we are the aroma of death leading to death, and to the other the aroma of life leading to life. And who is sufficient for these things? For we are not, as so many, peddling the word of God; but as of sincerity, but as from God, we speak in the sight of God in Christ" 2 Corinthians 2:14-17.

We should each one examine our heart and ask "What does the name of Jesus mean to me?" Is His name just another name? Or is it "as perfume poured forth"?

His name is not just any name, just as His perfume is not just any perfume:

"Because of the fragrance of your <u>good</u> ointments" S of S 1:3.

It was Mary, the sister of Lazarus, who anointed the feet of Jesus with "fragrant oil" Luke 7:38. This was not inexpensive oil, it was "fragrant" oil—that which had a special aroma, and which pleased the Lord. As Jesus blesses us with His "good ointments," so we in turn, by the pouring forth of His name, bring a special aroma to His nostrils.

"Therefore be imitators of God as dear children. And walk in love, as Christ also has loved us and given Himself for us, an offering and a sacrifice to God for a sweet-smelling aroma" Ephesians 5:1-2.

Puritan Quote:
"By kisses, we suppose to be intended those varied manifestations of affection by which the believer is made to enjoy the love of Jesus."

"O Lover of our souls, be not strange to kiss us; let the lips of Thy blessing meet the lips of our asking; let the lips of Thy fullness touch the lips of our need, and straightway the kiss will be affected" C.H. Spurgeon, 1834-1892.

LET HIM KISS ME

Reading: Song of Songs 1:1-4

"Let him kiss me with the kisses of his mouth" Song of Songs 1:2

Previously (God's Name series #21), this song was the most excellent of all the "one thousand and five" that Solomon penned (1 Kings 4:32). I believe also it is the most excellent of all songs period, including that of Moses (Exod 15) and Deborah and Barak (Judges 5).

In this beautiful love story, it is generally accepted that the Bridegroom is the Messiah, Yahvahshua, Jesus. The Bride speaks of you and me as individuals in the church, in the body of Christ. The Daughters of Jerusalem represent the church as a body, as in "I will build my church" Matthew 16:18.

The great wish of the Bride is, "Let him kiss me with the kisses of his mouth." She has no doubt of His love for her, but that is not enough, she seeks after the manifold expressions of that love.

Here lies a challenge for us—are we satisfied with just the knowledge that Jesus loves us, or do we desire to experience the expressions of that love? A verse that often amazes me is Ephesians 1:3:

"Blessed be the God and Father of our Lord Jesus Christ, who has blessed us with every spiritual blessing in the heavenly places in Christ."

This scripture tells us we have been blessed with <u>every</u> spiritual blessing in Christ Jesus—not with spiritual blessings, which would be wonderful, but with everyone. God has no more blessings He can give us. "The kisses of His mouth" is an expression of His intimate love for us.

I am often reminded of the story of the Prodigal Son when his father "fell on his neck and kissed him" (Luke 15:20). All the time his son was in "far country," his father loved him, but it was not until he returned that he experienced the expressions of that love.

The Bride cannot enjoy the "kisses of His mouth" unless she brings herself to the position where she can be kissed. Mary "sat at Jesus' feet and heard his word" (Luke 10:39), and John, who was known as the disciple who "leaned on His [Jesus'] breast" (John 21:20). It is incumbent upon every believer to "Draw near to God," then He will "draw near to you" (James 4:8).

The person who is to kiss, is "'him,'" the Bridegroom; He who is the most excellent person in the world, He is the "altogether lovely one" (5:16). The person whom he is to kiss, is "me," a contemptible despicable creature; for so the Bride was in herself (vss 5-6).

What a transformation! The one who was dead in trespasses and sins now has a personal relationship with him who is "altogether lovely."

Throughout this Song, it is made clear that Christ has a way of communicating His love to believers, and not to those who do not belong to Him"

"For the message of the cross is foolishness to those who are perishing, but to us who are being saved it is the power of God" 1 Corinthians 1:18.

God will not ignore the heart's desire of those who seek Him. It is the promise of the Bridegroom, and He if faithful and true to His word.

"He who has My commandments and keeps them, it is he who loves Me. And he who loves Me will be loved by My Father, and I will love him and manifest Myself to him . . . If anyone loves Me, he will keep My word; and My Father will love him, and We will come to him and make Our home with him" John 14:21,23.

One who desires an intimate relationship with Jesus Christ will be blessed by Him, for such a person will spend time in meditation and prayer. This is placing yourself in the position where we can receive the expressions of His love.

Puritan Quote:

"An high esteem of Christ, is no ill argument in pressing for, and pursuing after his presence; for to those that thus love and esteem him, he will manifest himself" James Durham, 1622-1658.

THE KING'S CHAMBERS

Reading: Song of Solomon 1:1-4
"The king has brought me into his chambers" Song of Solomon 1:4

The thought this week was originally shared on October 8th, 2008, and, after rereading it, I felt it again says exactly that which I would like to share in this series.

The more the Holy Spirit works in my heart the more convinced I become that our text is not merely rhetoric or a part of a love story. There is a place of quiet rest where those who can call God "Abba, Father" are invited to visit. It is the place where Jesus meets with those whom He has redeemed. It is the place where chaos is replaced with calm; doubt with assurance; sorrow with joy; turmoil with peace; weakness with strength; burdens with sustenance; tears with smiles; darkness with light; ad infinitum. The chamber of Jesus is the Holy of Holies to the believer, the place where God dwells. The difference between the Holy of Holies and the inner chamber is that the entire number of redeemed are invited to spend time there. It is a special place of which, unfortunately, many are unaware of its existence.

The inner chamber is where you and Jesus spend time alone. It is where true love is exchanged. One beautiful example provided by the scriptures is of the mother bird with her chicks:

"He shall cover you with His feathers, and under His wings you shall take refuge" Psalm 91:4.

"Keep me as the apple of Your eye; Hide me under the shadow of Your wings" Psalm 17:8,

"Like an apple tree among the trees of the woods, so is my beloved among the sons. I sat down in his shade with great delight, and his fruit was sweet to my taste" Song of Solomon 2:3

"As rivers of water in a dry place, as the shadow of a great rock in a weary land. The eyes of those who see will not be dim, and the ears of those who hear will listen" Isaiah 32:2-3.

These are but a few of the descriptions of Christ's inner chamber. How long I walked as a child of God without understanding of what these words were speaking. Time spent daily with Jesus in His inner chamber will change your life. The light of Christ will shine in your face and His peace will reign in your heart. Your attitude will be a reflection of His righteousness and your prayers will echo His gentleness. This is reality, not just head knowledge.

"I had never heard anyone pray like that. There was a simplicity, a tenderness, a boldness, a power that hushed and subdued me, and made it clear that God had admitted him to the inner circle of His friendship. Such praying was evidently the outcome of long tarrying in the secret place, and was as dew from the Lord" From Hudson Taylor's Spiritual Secret, Chapter sixteen—Overflow.

The inner chamber is not reserved for special Christians. The only qualification for entrance is that you are born again and that you are a new creature in Jesus Christ. If He is your Savior and Redeemer then His invitation is for you. Do not languish in that state of uncertainty and non-communion with your Lord. Do not be a Christian whose thirst is never quenched. Do not be hard of hearing when the Spirit of God speaks.

"Take time. Give God time to reveal Himself to you. Give yourself time to be silent and quiet before Him, waiting to receive, through the Spirit, the assurance of His presence with you, His power working In you. Take time to read His Word as in His presence, that from it you may know what He asks of you and what He promises you. Let the Word create around you, create within you a holy atmosphere, a holy heavenly light, in which your soul will be refreshed and strengthened for the work of daily life. From The Secret of Adoration by Andrew Murray—Introduction.

I have a friend in the Faroe Islands who, when he prays, is obviously in the King's chamber and he takes me inside with him. You know what I mean—most of us have experienced this when another prays. He addresses our Heavenly Father with his language's word for 'Daddy', and I am very aware it is natural with him and not an attempt to impress. Such sincerity and simplicity is part of our communion with God, and is available for all who are sons of God and joint heirs with Jesus.

May the Holy Spirit guide us into this chamber where we may bask in the glorious presence of Him who loves us and gave Himself for us.

Puritan Quote:

"The King has brought me into his chambers; and now I see how truly royal he is. The King has done it. The King, not a king; but that King who is King of all kings, the most royal of all monarchs, 'the Prince of the kings of the earth,' even my Lord Jesus, hath brought me into his chambers" C.H. Spurgeon—1834-1892.

"Being brought into the chamber, We have what we would have. Our desires are crowned with unspeakable delights; all our griefs vanish, and we will be glad and rejoice" Matthew Henry—1662-1714.

WE WILL REJOICE IN YOU

Reading: Song of Solomon 1:1-4
"We will be glad and rejoice in you" Song of Songs 1:4

In this fourth verse of chapter one, the sense changes from the Bride as an individual "me" into the corporate "we." I am, of course, included in the "we" because I am a member of the church Jesus is building.

Three responses to Christ's love are given in this verse:

"We will run after you,"
"We will be glad and rejoice in you,"
"We will remember your love."

As I look at the "we", the church, the body of Christ, is this what I see among its members? Apart from a few individuals, the answer is an emphatic "no." Instead, I see arguing, conflict, and division. All of the outward practices are there, such as hymn and chorus singing, the Lord's Supper and Baptism, elders and deacons, tithing, and the plethora of council meetings, but little else. Of course, there are exceptions, but they are few.

As I make these observations, I must ask myself where I fit into this scenario? If I am honest, I must admit I am not a part of the exception, but of the norm. Do the words of verse four apply to me? Do I run after Christ? Do I rejoice in Him? Do I remember His love? Questions we must all ask ourselves.

Most believers have periods when they can say "yes", that explains my walk with the Lord, but those times are not consistent. They do not describe my perpetual walk with my Savior.

My personal condition cannot be blamed on Christ, for He does indeed "Draw me away." He can be found knocking at the door of my heart, seeking entrance to my inner life (Revelation 3:21). He is not begging for me to "let Him in" so He can save me, for I am already His bride.

Can my pursuit of Him be described as running after Him? Is there determination in my step? Do I remain on the ground when I trip over the obstacles in my way, or do I jump up and continue my pursuit?

Then there is the matter of rejoicing. There are many Christians who exhibit an outward form of rejoicing, but is it an outward expression of an inward condition? It should be. If our heart does not rejoice when we are alone in the presence of our Bridegroom, we cannot claim to truly be glad. This should be the permanent state of our soul, one of gladness and rejoicing.

"Though now you do not see Him, yet believing, you rejoice with joy inexpressible and full of glory, receiving the end of your faith—the salvation of your souls" 1 Peter 1:8-9.

The only real joy and gladness is "in" Him. All true spiritual blessings are found "in Him." Be blessed as you meditate on these scriptures: Eph.1:4,10,11,13; 2:18; 3:6; Col 1:19; 2:6; 2:7; 2:9-11; 1 John 2:5.

David expressed it so well:

"I have set the Lord always before me; because He is at my right hand I shall not be moved. Therefore my heart is glad, and my glory rejoices; my flesh also will rest in hope" Psalm 16:8-9.

In setting the Lord before us always in all we think and do, making Him the sole purpose for living, then our heart will be made glad and rejoice.

Is there any better medicine than to "remember your [His] love"? This is the remedy the Physician of our souls prescribes for our depression and disappointment we face. We are often told "you cannot live in the past", but there is nothing wrong in remembering the times God has blessed us, either from His Word or from the miracles He has performed in our life. Remember His love when He gave His life for your salvation. Remember His love when, as a prodigal son, He welcomed you home with hugs and kisses from your backsliding days. Remember His love when He performed those small everyday miracles we so often take for granted.

"Let the hearts of those rejoice who seek the Lord! Seek the Lord and His strength; Seek His face evermore! Remember His marvelous works which He has done, His wonders, and the judgments of His mouth" 1 Chronicles 16:10-12.

Puritan Quote:

"All our joy shall centre in God: We will rejoice, not in the ointments, or the chambers, but in thee. It is God only that is our exceeding joy, Psalm 43:4. We have no joy but in Christ, and which we are indebted to him for" Matthew Henry, 1662-1714.

THE GENTILE BRIDE

Reading: Song of Solomon 1:5-6
"I am dark, but lovely" Song of Songs 1:5

There are several interpretations of these words, but, to me, the woman standing before the daughters of Jerusalem made them indignant. She was not an Israelite, but a treaty wife of the king. She is black, or dark-skinned: a Gentile without the rights of an Israelite woman. She was a foreigner, yet the king had chosen her, and given her his heart.

She mentions the "tents of Kedar," which were made from the hair of goats. The word Kedar means dark, and such were the tents of the second son of Ishmael (Genesis 25:13), tents which the Jews avoided (Psalm 120:5). This was the same attitude the Jews displayed in Jesus' day concerning foreigners—He told His own people that salvation was not only for them, but for Gentiles also—the world:

"He was in the world . . . and the world did not know Him. He came to His own, and His own did not receive Him. But as many as received Him, to them He gave the right to become children of God, to those who believe in His name: who were born, not of blood, nor of the will of the flesh, nor of the will of man, but of God" John 1:10-13.

The hated Samaritans, who were half Jew and half Gentile, understood this—John 4:9, 39-42. What an accurate picture this is of us. The gospel made available to Gentiles to become His Bride, for in Him, there is no difference between Jew and Gentile: "But now in Christ Jesus you who once were far off (Gentiles) have been brought near by the blood of Christ" Ephesians 2:13.

The Bride continues: "I am . . . like the curtains of Solomon." The curtains represent the veil in Solomon's Temple that divided the holy place from the holy of holies, a place where no one but the High Priest could enter but once a year.

The veil represented Christ's flesh:

"Therefore, brethren, having boldness to enter the Holiest by the blood of Jesus, by a new and living way which He consecrated for us, through the veil, that is, His flesh" Hebrews 10:19-20.

Jesus took all of our sins and bore them in His own body on the cross making us clean in God's eyes—1 Peter 2:24. Because of the work of Jesus Christ, the Father looks at our spirit, and sees us as clean and righteous as His Son.

This is a fact we, His Bride, must accept by faith. When we look at ourselves, we know we are given to sin, and sin separates us from God. We are therefore unworthy to be called His sons—Luke 15:18-19. Praise God, we are as righteous as Jesus Christ in His eyes; we have been made worthy because He has clothed us with His robe of righteousness—Romans 4:11.

It is a favorite ploy of Satan to tell us we are still sinners and unacceptable to God. He takes it even further by accusing God's children constantly before God. But God knows His children, and that "nothing shall be able to separate us from the love of God which is in Christ Jesus our Lord" Romans 8:39.

Puritan Quote:

"Believers, their observing of their sinfulness, should not make them deny their grace; and their observing their grace, should not make them forget their sinfulness" James Durham, 1622-1658.

"As Isaiah makes clear, 'all our righteousnesses are as filthy rags' (Isaiah 64.6). Similarly in Ephesians 5.26 Christ promises that He will keep and nourish His church, as a man does a maiden, and will present her to Himself a glorious church, holy and without blemish, but it is made clear that this results from the fact that He has first cleansed her and clothed her in the splendor of His righteousness (compare 1 Corinthians 1.30; 2 Corinthians 5.21). Having been made clean, His people are to be beautiful in Him with the beauty of holiness (Psalm 96.9)"—Dr. Peter Pett, BA; BD; (Hons-London) DD, is a retired Baptist minister and college lecturer.

CHRIST'S POINT OF VIEW

Reading: Song of Solomon 1:7-10
"I have compared you, my love, to my filly among Pharaoh's chariots"
Song of Songs 1:9

It is interesting to know how Jesus compares His Bride as He sits at the right hand of His Father. Here, in this first chapter of Solomon's song, He compares us to "My filly among Pharaoh's chariots," or "you remind me of my favorite mare in the chariot spans of Pharaoh" Amplified.

Egypt was famous for the high quality of its horses, and Solomon obtained the very best for himself (2 Chron.1:17; Isa.31:1). The horse is often spoken of when referring to strength and endurance:

"Have you given the horse strength? Have you clothed his neck with thunder? Can you frighten him like a locust? His majestic snorting strikes terror. He paws in the valley, and rejoices in his strength; He gallops into the clash of arms. He mocks at fear, and is not frightened; nor does he turn back from the sword. The quiver rattles against him, the glittering spear and javelin. He devours the distance with fierceness and rage; nor does he come to a halt because the trumpet has sounded. At the blast of the trumpet he says, 'Aha!' He smells the battle from afar, the thunder of captains and shouting" Job 39:19-25.

So the Bridegroom sees his Bride: strong, fearless, bold, and victorious. "And will make them as His royal horse in the battle" Zechariah 10:3. Now, says the Bridegroom, if these be lovely, strong and stately, then so are you, for, 'I have compared you' to such.

From this comparison we can take much encouragement: First, there is an excellent courage and boldness, wherewith the believer is furnished beyond others—"the righteous are bold as a lion" Proverbs 28:1.

"Yet in all these things we are more than conquerors through Him who loved us. For I am persuaded that neither death nor life, nor angels nor principalities nor powers, nor things present nor things to come, nor height nor depth, nor any other created thing, shall be able to separate us from the love of God which is in Christ Jesus our Lord" Romans 8:37-39.

Second, there is a cause for our strength and boldness. The Groom claims the responsibility. A closer translation of the words "I have compared you" is "I have made you comparable," or "made you to be like them." Believers, in ourselves, belong to Christ, so whatever spiritual strength and courage we have, it is His, and from Him.

The next thing Jesus sees in believers, is "Your cheeks are lovely with ornaments" vs 10. Scripture tells us that our righteousness is like "filthy rags" Isaiah 64:6, and this is how God sees us apart from Christ. But now, because He has made us His Bride, He sees as beautifully adorned:

"I clothed you in embroidered cloth and gave you sandals of badger skin; I clothed you with fine linen and covered you with silk. I adorned you with ornaments, put bracelets on your wrists, and a chain on your neck. And I put a jewel in your nose, earrings in your ears, and a beautiful crown on your head" Ezekiel 16:10-13.

This entire passage is not about how we view ourselves, for we know we so often yield to the things of the flesh, we know we sin, and we hate ourselves for it. But, that is not important, although it keeps us humble and dependant on God. The important question is, "How does God see us?"

He sees us as justified, clothed in the righteousness of Jesus Christ. He sees us as perfect in His Son, one with Him, and beyond the vile accusations of Satan. Instead of filthy rags, He sees His children adorned with "lovely ornaments and chains of gold" vs 10.

It is all of Him, His mercy, love, and grace.

David Peckham

Puritan Quote:

"We are weak in ourselves, but if Christ make us as horses, strong and bold, we need not fear what all the powers of darkness can do against us" Matthew Henry, 1662-1714.

THE ROSE OF SHARON

Reading: Song of Solomon 2:1-3
"I am the Rose of Sharon" Song of Songs 2:1

The chapter division is unfortunate, and should have occurred in chapter one, verse 15. Because of this break, many Christians consider the words of our text as belonging to the Bridegroom, but Hebrew commentators apply them to the Bride, which makes more sense.

These descriptions are a continuation of the unworthiness of the Bride. What the Bride is saying, is *"I am like an ordinary, plain flower, how is it You love me as You do? I am common. There is nothing special about me. I am a foreigner unworthy of of any consideration from You, my king."*

The "rose" is the white narcissus, the same as referred to in Isaiah 35:1, a common plant, one among thousands in the Valley of Sharon. This is the Bride who speaks of herself as lowly, though lovely, in contrast with the lordly "apple" or citron tree (the Bridegroom) of 2:3; the "lily" is also applied to her (2:2).

The more a believer learns about how unworthy he is, the greater the love and grace of his Savior is to him. How many times do we ask Him, "Why do You love me as You do?" You are not alone in these feelings. Paul had the same questions:

"For I am the least of the apostles, who am not worthy to be called an apostle, because I persecuted the church of God. 10 But by the grace of God I am what I am" 1 Corinthians 15:9-10

The devil likes to focus us onto ourselves and miss the infinitely, costly value living in us, for it is not I, but Christ who lives in us—Galatians 2:20.

"As the lily among thorns,"—this is the state of every believer. Lest we become proud, we must remember this is how Christ sees us. He knows we are surrounded by "thorns" every day. The "thorn" represents the curse brought on Adam and Eve through sin (Genesis 3:17-18; Matthew 13:7; Hebrews 6:8).

There is little that is beautiful to the Lord. Sin has marred even creation itself. Jesus bore the curse by wearing a crown of thorns. The only thing beautiful in His eyes is His Bride.

The Groom disagrees with her assessment of herself. In the warmth of his affection, he insists she as much surpasses all other maidens as the flower of the lily does the bramble.

Who are we? We are an heir of God and joint heirs with Jesus (Romans 8:17). We are the Bride of Christ (Revelation 19:7-9; 21:9). We are a holy, royal priest (1 Peter 2:5,9). We have been given authority to rule (Ephesians 2:6; Revelation 5:10. Rejoice, we are something special in His eyes.

While this is very true, we must be careful not to think of ourselves more than we should:

"Because of the privilege and authority God has given me, I give each of you this warning: Don't think you are better than you really are. Be honest in your evaluation of yourselves, measuring yourselves by the faith God has given us" Romans 12:3.

Rejoice in that Christ has made you a "new creation"; be thankful old things have passed away, and all things have become new, but be sure to give all the credit to Him who made it all possible. The "better than thou" attitude with which some Christians present to the world, is degrading to the gospel, and offensive to God.

Puritan Quote:

"It is rather the bride who thus speaks of herself, as lowly, though lovely, in contrast with the lordly "apple" or citron tree, the Bridegroom (Song 2:3)" Jamieson, Fausset, and Brown Commentary.

"Amazing love! How can it be that Thou, my God, shouldst die for me? 'Tis mystery all! The Immortal dies! Who can explore His strange design? In vain the firstborn seraph tries to sound the depths of love Divine" Charles Wesley, 1707-1788.

MY TASTE

Reading: Song of Solomon 2:1-3
"And his fruit was sweet to my taste" Song of Songs 2:3

Every person who knows Jesus Christ as their Savior feeds on Him as their Provider. Jesus said, "I am the Bread of life," and "whoever drinks of the water that I shall give him will never thirst" John 4:14.

"I am the bread of life. He who comes to Me shall never hunger, and he who believes in Me shall never thirst" John 6:35.

Sadly, there are many Christians who do not partake of this plenteous fruit, but He does provide it in abundance to those who abide under his shadow. Those who choose to wander around the orchard with their eyes cast down, looking for fruit that has fallen from the tree, will never know the true sweetness of the fruit Christ gives by His Spirit; fruit freshly picked by the Master and given only to those who rest in the shadow of His branches.

Well I remember as a child the tomatoes my father grew in his greenhouse. There was nothing so sweet to my taste as a tomato picked straight from the vine. It was warm and had a taste that was unique, a taste that it possessed only when eaten as it was harvested. That same tomato served with a meal later in the day had already lost some of that peculiar, fresh picked taste. The fruit of the Spirit comes to us freshly picked, direct from the hand of the Master Gardener.

When Israel crossed the Jordan River and entered into the Promised Land, it is recorded that "they ate of the fruit of the land of Canaan" Joshua 5:12. Sermons are preached and songs sung that tell us crossing the River Jordan is a picture of the believer dying and going to heaven. It is not. It is a picture of the believer leaving behind the struggles of a worldly existence and entering into the abundance of life in Christ; for it is there the fruit of the Spirit grows. How many Christians still wander in the desert feeding on bread and water when they can cross the Jordan and feast on the fruit of God?

"My fruit is better than gold, yes, than fine gold" Proverbs 8:19. Don't look down for fruit that has fallen from the branches, but rather reach up and accept the fruit that Jesus offers whenever you want it. There is an abundant supply, and no matter how much you eat of it, like the widow's oil, there will always be more.

David wrote: "Oh, taste and see that the Lord is good" Psalm 34:8, and "How sweet are Your words to my taste, sweeter than honey to my mouth!" Psalm 119:103.

Faith is spoken of as many senses of the spiritual life: It is *hearing*— "Hear, and your soul shall live" Isaiah 55:3; It is *sight*—"Look to Me, and be saved" Isaiah 45:22; It is *smelling*—"All Your garments are scented with myrrh" Psalm 45:8, and "Your name is ointment poured forth—" Song of Songs 1:3; It is *touch*—"a woman who had a flow of blood for twelve years came from behind and touched the hem of His garment . . . Be of good cheer, daughter; your faith has made you well" Matt 9:20-22. Faith is equally the spirit's *taste*.

One way the Holy Spirit feeds us the fruit of the Bridegroom is from the Word of God. It is God's food for our soul. How often, when our soul is depressed or disappointed, does the Word of God encourage us?

When God told Ezekiel to eat the scroll, an unpleasant prospect, he found it to be other than he thought:

"And He said to me, 'Son of man, feed your belly, and fill your stomach with this scroll that I give you.' So I ate, and it was in my mouth like honey in sweetness." Ezekiel 3:3.

The word translated "feed" actually means "digest." We must learn how to digest God's Word; it is not enough to simply read it, we must take it to heart, only then will it be "like honey in sweetness." This thought is captured in our verse: "I sat down in his shade with great delight, and his fruit was sweet to my taste." She did not run or even walk through the orchard, but sat down and rested. There is a great difference between reading through the Bible in one year, and meditating in it, absorbing it, and digesting it. It is not a challenge that must be met, but a feast of God's blessings and love. In today's turmoil, we must learn to rest in the Lord, and enjoy Him.

That which is "sweet to my taste" is seen in the "fruit of the Spirit"—"the fruit of the Spirit is love, joy, peace, longsuffering, kindness, goodness, faithfulness, gentleness, self-control. Against such there is no law. And those who are Christ's have crucified the flesh with its passions and desires. If we live in the Spirit, let us also walk in the Spirit. Let us not become conceited, provoking one another, envying one another" Galatians 5:22-26.

This is the Tree of Life, for there is life in none other than Jesus Christ. To rest in its shadow guarantees rest, peace, strength, encouragement, and victory.

"He who dwells in the secret place of the Most High shall abide under the shadow of the Almighty" Psalm 91:1.

This is not an easy thing, for the enemy of our soul will keep us busy, occupying our day with anything that will keep us from being quiet with Christ. When, at the close of the day, we realize have been too busy to "sit down under his shadow," we have a sense of loss.

"Rest in the Lord, and wait patiently for Him; do not fret because of him who prospers in his way" Psalm 37:7.

"Come to Me, all you who labor and are heavy laden, and I will give you rest. Take My yoke upon you and learn from Me, for I am gentle and lowly in heart, and you will find rest for your souls. For My yoke is easy and My burden is light" Matthew 11:28-30.

Puritan Quote:
"Like some rich, luxuriant, and generous tree, which not only shelters the traveler from the scorching heat, but holds forth on its branches delicious fruit to regale and satisfy for food; so Jesus, by his person, work, and righteousness,

protects his people from all evil; and by the fruits of his blood and redemption, supplies them all with good" Robert Hawker, 1753-1827.

"There is always something over, when we, from the Father's hand,
Take our portion with thanksgiving, praising for the things He's planned.
Satisfaction, full and deepening, all our need He doth supply,
When the heart has tasted Jesus Its desires to satisfy" Johann C. Lavater, 1741-1801.

HIS BANNER

Reading: Song of Solomon 2:4-7
"He brought me to the banqueting house, and his
banner over me was love" Song of Songs 2:4.

Once again, there are various interpretations as to what this "banqueting house" is? Some believe it is the covenant of redemption, while others think it is the church. However, I, along with many others, consider it another aspect of the believer's relationship with their Savior.

In a previous meditation (ch:2:4), we considered the "fruit" provided by the Groom to His Bride, but here He has prepared a "banqueting House" for her pleasure. This is the place where He communes with her, where the two can enjoy a banquet together. The food is prepared by Him, food that is necessary and nutritious for her well-being. He would not tempt her to eat anything that is detrimental to her; after all, "His banner over her was love."

This food can be found in the Word of God, for, as the prophet said:

"Your words were found, and I ate them, and Your word was to me the joy and rejoicing of my heart; for I am called by Your name, O Lord God of hosts" Jeremiah 15:16.

And David, the King:

"Oh, how I love Your law! It is my meditation all the day" Psalm 119:97.

In the Word of God, spiritual milk may be found for "babes" in Christ, for those that are newly born again, and require nutrition for the development of their young bones, and meat for us to grow into the mature man of God, one who exhibits the fruit of the Spirit in his daily walk with God.

Notice, also, it was He who brought you into the banqueting house. You had nothing to with it. You did not gate-crash the party, or talk your way into it. We may attend church, read the Bible, and follow ordinances, even participate in the Lord's Supper, but unless Jesus, by His Holy Spirit, leads us, we are never going to experience the delicacies of His banquet table. You are there by invitation. You are there because He wanted you to be there. He wants the company of His Bride—you are pleasing to Him. It was his love that brought her there.

In Hebrew, the "banqueting house" is literally the "house of wine."

"The ancients preserved their wine, not in barrels or dark cellars underground, as we do, but in large pitchers, ranged against the wall in some upper apartment in the house, the place where they kept their most precious effects" Adam Clark's Commentary.

Wine is a predominate element in the Song of Songs (1:2,4; 4:10; 5:1; 7:9; 8:2.), and the Groom's love is likened to it. As Mary, the mother of Jesus said, "He has filled the hungry with good things" Luke 1:53.

In this song of songs, there are four references to a "vineyard", and vine[s] six times. Wine, which makes glad "the heavy heart" (Psalm 104:15) of one ready to perish, so that he "remembers his misery no more." So, in a "greater" sense, Christ's love (Habakkuk 3:17-18). Jesus' first miracle turned water into wine, and was the promise given of His love at the last supper.

Earth's wine could not compare with Her Beloved's love; it was all encompassing, and filled her heart. From what she was, to what she has become, so excites His heart, that he takes her by the hand, and escorts her into his house of wine. Allow a little imagination—once she is seated at the table, he unfurls a banner, holding it over her for all to see. It says, "This is my love! This is my chosen one. She may be a gentile, but that does not matter; she is mine, and I love her."

"Those who have gathered it (new wine) shall eat it, and praise the Lord; those who have brought it together shall drink it in My holy courts" Isaiah 62:9.

Puritan Quote:

"... He, who of his own grace placed us there, must shew it us: nor can we of ourselves know the depths and mysteries of the sacred writings; they open the book and our understandings to look into it; nor will his church, with all the ordinances of it, be a banqueting house unto us, unless he himself be present with us" John Gill, 1697-1771.

HIS HANDS

Reading: Song of Solomon 2:4-7
"His left hand is under my head, and his right hand embraces me"
Song of Solomon 2:6

What believer does not need the reassurance of the comfort and encouragement of their Redeemer? We may know it in theory, but do we feel it? True Christianity is not a matter of beautifully sculptured idols, stained-glass windows, multi-colored paintings, or even crosses and crucifixes. It is also not a matter of emotions only, for thousands of people are "converted" by their momentary emotions. A spurious conversion does not register with God. True conversion is accomplished by the Holy Spirit.

When that occurs, our spirit is joined together by the Spirit of God into an inseparable union with Jesus Christ. True conversion is a personal relationship with the King of kings, and Lord of lords—our Bridegroom.

In our text, the Bride is in need of comfort and strength, and she knows it is her Beloved alone who can give it to her. She was an outcast, a Gentile, hated by most Jews, for they were the chosen of God—but then, so was she.

It was not enough that her Beloved had brought her into the "house of wine," and she could eat of the fine foods and drink spread before her—she needed more. She needed his personal touch. The wonderful thing is that he understood that need and embraced her. The warmth of his body was just the tonic she needed. He sustains her in his arms.

"The eternal God is your refuge, and underneath are the everlasting arms" Deuteronomy 33:27.

With his arms around her, she was safe, knowing that his right hand was strong enough to protect and strengthen her, and his left hand under her head, gave her peace and assurance of his love. Christ's love is a real thing, and is able to support the heart under its greatest weakness and need.

Christ is tender to all his people, and at all times, especially when they feel depressed, doubtful, and disappointed.

His left hand controls a believer's thoughts, and will instill to their heart wisdom, knowledge, and understanding:

"But of him are ye in Christ Jesus, who of God is made unto us wisdom, and righteousness, and sanctification, and redemption"
1 Corinthians 1:30, KJV.
"attaining to all riches of the full assurance of understanding, to the knowledge of the mystery of God, both of the Father and of Christ, in whom are hidden all the treasures of wisdom and knowledge" Colossians 2:2-3.

There is an important thought in this statement of the Bride—"until He pleases" (2:8). There are times when believers are guilty of marring Christ's fellowship with them, and they might enjoy Christ's company much longer if their sins did not interfere, and make his presence seem far way.

I remember, many years ago, when I was in missionary training, the feeling that God had deserted me. I wrote:

O God, I seek to know the reason why
The heavens seem as brass.
My soul seems barren, empty, dry.
I'm withering like the grass.

It seems as if You've closed your ears,
That You've withdrawn your hand.
That now I face the coming years
To live in barren land.

The touch of Your love which once I knew
Seems weak, pathetic, lean.
Your love was as the morning dew,
Which once my soul had seen.

Why are my prayers unheard, O Lord?
Why do I cry in vain?
My heart is cold, as hard as board,
My heart cries out in pain.

I cry along with Job of old,
"O that I had been taken
From the womb to the grave so cold,"
Where my faith had not been shaken.

I know that there within Your word
It tells me my position:
Made one with Christ, by God adored,
O glorious condition.

It tells me that You cannot lie,
That all Your words are sure,
That Yourself, O Lord, you can't deny,
That You're honest, true, and pure.

Fulfill Your promises unto me,
That through the weeks have meant
A source of strength, of hope, of glee,
On which my soul has leant.

Teach me not to question why,
Nor to doubt Your word.
Teach me to rest and not to cry,
To trust my precious Lord.

Refresh my soul, thou Living Water,
Feed my heart, thou Living Bread.
I kneel right now before Your alter
And feast upon Your spread.

My soul refreshed, my heart is fed,
I'm satisfied within.
No longer dry; alive, not dead;
Forgiven of all my sin.

Rejoice my soul, He's faithful still,
My Savior changes never.
His promises He will fulfill,
His love he ne'er will sever.

Satan's attacks have not diminished—it continues to be one of his greatest and effective weapons. He constantly accuses us before God that we have sinned—and he is correct. However, God does not condemn us, for "if we confess our sin, He is faithful and just to forgive our sins, and to cleanse us from all unrighteousness" 1 John 1:9. God looks for and welcomes our confession, for when we confess, our fellowship with Jesus Christ is restored.

"You have also given me the shield of Your salvation; Your right hand has held me up, Your gentleness has made me great. You enlarged my path under me, so my feet did not slip" Psalm 18:35-36.

The restoration of fellowship with our Beloved is "as he pleases," but thankfully, it is based on His faithfulness.

Puritan Quote:

"It is, therefore, by the benefit of prayer that we reach those riches which are laid up for us with the Heavenly Father. For there is a communion of men with God" John Calvin, 1509-1564.

LET ME SEE YOU

Reading: Song of Solomon 2:10-14

"Let me see your face, let me hear your voice" Song of Songs 2:14

How well we understand what the Bride is experiencing. I am sure there are times when our heart longs to be in communion with Christ, but we feel so unworthy to be in His presence. We know there is sin in our life, and although we have confessed it time after time, we feel like a hypocrite asking Him to hear and listen to us.

Remember the prodigal son of Luke 15—he wanted to go home, but because of his waywardness, he did not think his father would accept him as his son:

"Father, I have sinned against heaven and before you, and I am no longer worthy to be called your son. Make me like one of your hired servants" Luke 15:18-19.

But he was wrong. He underestimated the love his father had for him. When his father saw him in the distance, he ran to meet him, threw his arms around him and kissed him, so much so that the son could not complete his prepared speech. He felt unworthy, but even when he left home, and wasted every part of his inheritance, he never stopped being his father's son. His feelings were overpowered by his father's love.

Believe me when I say, "I have been there." The feeling of unworthiness is immense, but the love of our heavenly Father is greater. Words cannot describe the feeling when He wraps His arms around you and kisses you. The love of God is beyond measure. How happy was the Shepherd when He found his lost lamb, and carried him on his shoulders back to the fold? Luke 15:6. How pleased was the widow when she found the lost coin? Luke 15:9.

Rather than hiding from our Savior and Friend, listen to His voice:

"O my dove, let me see your face, let me hear your voice; for your voice is sweet, and your face is lovely" 2:14.

These are not the words of the Shulamite, but of the Bridegroom. A similar picture is drawn in Revelation 3:20: "Behold, I stand at the door and knock. If anyone hears My voice and opens the door, I will come in to him and dine with him, and he with Me." The scriptures are full of invitations from God to His people. He wants to "dine" with us. He wants to "see our face, and hear our voice."

The Groom calls her by a new name, "my dove." He had called her his "love," and his "fair one," but not his "dove" until now, although he had compared her eyes to dove's eyes (1:15).

The dove is very beautiful, so are his elect: they are washed in Christ's blood, justified by his righteousness, and sanctified by his grace, pure and spotless, beautiful in his eyes. The bride of Christ is "like the wings of a dove covered with silver, and her feathers with yellow gold" Psalm 68:13.

The dove is also an innocent and harmless creature, therefore Jesus said to His disciples, "Be wise as serpents and harmless as doves" Matthew 10:16.

Stop hiding from God; He knows where we are, He knows what we have done, and He says, "Oh, my dove, come out from where you are hiding; I want you to know my love."

God does not force us into communion with Him. "Let me see—let me hear" is His invitation:

"Come to Me, all you who labor and are heavy laden, and I will give you rest. Take My yoke upon you and learn from Me, for I am gentle and lowly in heart, and you will find rest for your souls. For My yoke is easy and My burden is light" Matthew 11:28-30.

"Let us come before His presence with thanksgiving" Psalm 95:2

Listen to the tone of his voice. He doesn't brow beat her. He presents Himself who is hurt because she is hiding from him, and yearns for her fellowship. "My beloved spoke, and said to me: "Rise up, my love, my fair one, and come away" 2: 10. Seven times in these eight chapters, the Groom asks her to "Rise up" from where she is hiding, or "come" and join him.

"For your voice is sweet, and your face is lovely" 2:14. These are precious words from the lips of the Bridegroom, for it shows us how He who sits on at the right hand of His Father sees His Bride. He does not see us as unclean or "filthy rags," but clean, washed in His blood, and lovely, clothed in His righteousness. When we commune with Him in prayer, our voice is sweet to His ears. It is these things He misses when we are hiding in the clefts of our emotions, and feelings of unworthiness. If only we could see ourselves as He sees us—worthy of His love, clothed in the garments of His righteousness, and welcome into His presence.

"I will greatly rejoice in the Lord, my soul shall be joyful in my God; for He has clothed me with the garments of salvation, He has covered me with the robe of righteousness, as a bridegroom decks himself with ornaments, and as a bride adorns herself with her jewels" Isaiah 61:10; see also Zechariah 9:16, Malachi 3:17.

Puritan Quote:

"One of the immediate results of that cordial reconciliation which is now established between the most high God and yourself, through your grateful acceptance of the propitiatory sacrifice of the Redeemer, is your filial return to your Father's house, where you enjoy free and open access, at all times, to His enduring presence" John Bradford, 1510-1555.

I WILL RISE

Reading: Song of Solomon 3:1-5
"I will rise now," I said, "and go about the city" Song of Songs 3:2

We must never forget, while reading this wonderful song, that it portrays the relationship between the bride and her Beloved. A personal relationship had already been established, therefore speaking of a born again person and Jesus Christ—not that of an unsaved person still in their sins and at enmity with God.

How frequently the Bridegroom called for His Bride to "Rise up" and "come away," but she continued to hide because she felt unworthy of him. Now, however, she decides to seek him, but in her current condition, she failed—he could not be found. How significant that it was nighttime, and she lay on her bed, alone.

Was she expecting her beloved to suddenly appear and make everything right? It was night, indicating she was in a condition of darkness. A consciousness of darkness overcomes the believer when, because of his sin, Christ seems absent. He is not absent, but she is not aware of His presence.

She was on her bed, not his bed or "our bed" (1:16). The old adage: "You've made your bed, now you must lie in it" is also true of the believer. Christ will never join us when we are on the bed of our choosing. It was we who sinned, not Him.

Realizing she was not going to find him in her current condition, she decided to do something about it: "I will rise now, and go about the city."

There are three steps shown here: To rise, to go, to seek. How often does the Holy Spirit convict our heart, and in response we "rise," fully intending to correct our situation, but before we know it we find ourselves back on our bed reclining in our self pity. The bride rose from her apathy, and went to the city. She followed the stirring of the Spirit with action, she pursued her Beloved. When he was not immediately found, she continued to seek after him. She did not give up—she pursued him.

It was obvious she had heard the voice of her beloved, but it was only now that she listened and obeyed. There is a big difference between hearing and listening. We may hear the voice of the Holy Spirit, but not listen. To listen means to think on it followed by action.

She searched the "streets and squares," but he was not to be found. She then asked a watchman of the city if he knew where she could find him, and he pointed her in the right direction. God has appointed His "watchmen" whose ministry is to direct the wanderer to Jesus Christ. Tragically, there are many self-appointed "watchmen" whose directions cannot be trusted. But this "watchman" was faithful to his calling, and pointed her in the proper direction.

It was but a short distance to where she found her beloved. Oh, what joy returned to her heart. She "held him, and would not let him go." She clung to him, as Ruth clung to Naomi, her mother-in-law (Ruth 1:14). Ruth made the decision:

"Entreat me not to leave you, or to turn back from following after you; for wherever you go, I will go; and wherever you lodge, I will lodge" Ruth 1:16.

Oh, what a decision; one that every true believer will make during their Christian life.

"On that hill named Calvary Jesus took His stand,
While the depths of hell vented all of its fury.
But it's His shout of vict'ry that rings in my ears,
And from this day on it's a different story.

I, too, have decided to stand on that hill,
By the side of my Savior; to make a new start.
I'll stand tall and firm, no longer ashamed,
For that look in His eyes has conquered my heart."

We must commend the Bride for her persistence. She searched the "streets and squares," but could not find her beloved, but she did not give up.

"But from there you will seek the Lord your God, and you will find Him if you seek Him with all your heart and with all your soul. When you are in distress, and all these things come upon you in the latter days, when you turn to the Lord your God and obey His voice (for the Lord your God is a merciful God), He will not forsake you" Deuteronomy 4:29-31.

The promises of God are real and genuine, for He who makes them is faithful and true. "He is a rewarder of those who diligently seek Him" Hebrews 11:6. The rewards for those who fellowship with their Savior are great, for we have been blessed with every spiritual blessing in Him. Not only do we enjoy His presence, but all the benefits (rewards) He provides.

Puritan Quote:

"O you who love Christ, go beyond the means of grace! Go beyond ordinances, go beyond preachers, go beyond even the Bible itself, into an actual possession of the living Christ; labor after a conscious enjoyment of Jesus himself, till you can say with the spouse, 'I found him whom my soul loveth'" Charles H. Spurgeon, 1834-1892.

YOU ARE FAIR

Reading: Song of Solomon 4:1—15
"Behold, you are fair, my love!" Song of Songs 4:1

The more I concentrate on this beautiful song, the more I am impressed with the words and sentiment of the Bridegroom to his beloved. Throughout my life, I have heard preachers take one or two verses and automatically apply the words to Jesus. That which is blessing my heart are the words that actually apply to the Beloved, Jesus Christ.

What we have here is an amazing revelation of what our Savior sees in us. Do these words speak of how my Savior sees me? Am I beautiful (fair) to Him? Am I really precious in His sight?

"For you are a holy people to the Lord your God; the Lord your God has chosen you to be a people for Himself, a special treasure above all the peoples on the face of the earth" Deuteronomy 7:6; 14:2; 26:18; Malachi 3:17
"Since you were precious in My sight, you have been honored, and I have loved you" Isaiah 43:4.

Is it any wonder that Christ sees us as beautiful? It is, after all, His own beauty and perfection He sees. "There is no spot in you," He says, a necessary requirement in those He calls His own. This was the requirement of the animals sacrificed as symbols of Himself, and that which He accomplished for His church:

"... that He might present her to Himself a glorious church, not having spot or wrinkle or any such thing, but that she should be holy and without blemish" Ephesians 5:27-28.

When you saw your bride walking down the aisle, she was the most beautiful woman alive, dressed in her wedding dress. She smiled as she looked forward to a lifetime with you. How could we be in His presence if He could see our faults and weaknesses?

Although we often wander from Him, and grieve His Holy Spirit, He does not allow them to affect His love for us. He will chastise us, but never stops loving us.

One of the many allegories found in this chapter, is a flock of sheep, "Which have come up from the washing" 4:2. How do believers, like sheep, come up from the washing, but by the washing of regeneration: "To Him who loved us and washed us from our sins in His own blood" Revelation 1:5.

"But you were washed, but you were sanctified, but you were justified in the name of the Lord Jesus and by the Spirit of our God" 1 Corinthians 6:11.

This is how Jesus sees His Bride, the image of Himself. Hard to believe? Yes, it is one of those unfathomable miracles of regeneration.

Jesus is not unaware of the struggles we have in this world, and in His compassion tells His Bride: "Until the day breaks, and the shadows flee away, I will go my way to the mountain of myrrh, and to the hill of frankincense" 4:6.

What day is this? It is the day "when He comes, in that Day, to be glorified in His saints and to be admired among all those who believe" 2 Thessalonians 1:10. Tried and tested believer, look toward that great day when your Redeemer's coming will light up the sky with His glory, and take you to that place where there will be no more pain, temptation, or valley.

"He does not cherish ill thoughts of us, but He pardons and loves as well after the offense as before it. It is well it is so, for if Jesus were as mindful of injuries as we are, how could He commune with us?" C.H. Spurgeon.

Where will we resort until then? "I will go my way to the mountain of myrrh, and to the hill of frankincense." This does not imply he will separate himself from us, but that he will take us with him to this "mountain of myrrh," and "hill of frankincense." Are we not a part of Him? Are we not one with Him, in Him, and the object of His love?

As part of our reading, we must contemplate the security his bride enjoys with her Beloved: "A garden enclosed is my sister, my spouse, a spring shut up, a fountain sealed" 4:12. The wild animals are kept at bay and can wreak no harm within this "enclosed garden." What a wonderful analogy of God's people who are "safe in the arms of Jesus."

"You have hedged me behind and before, and laid Your hand upon me. Such knowledge is too wonderful for me; it is high, I cannot attain it" Psalm 139:5-6.

Puritan Quote:

"The Lord has fragrant places of safety and repose for His people until He comes to fetch them to glory. Until we see Him face to face, let us cling closer and closer to Christ, whose name is "as ointment poured forth" to the Lord's faint and weary ones." Octavius Winslow, 1808-1878.

CHRIST'S PERFECTION

Reading: Song of Solomon 5:1—16
"What is your beloved more than another beloved?"
Song of Solomon 5:12

The first aspect of this question that comes to mind is, is this person of whom you are being questioned known as "your Beloved?" Does your life so radiate Jesus that others would refer to Him as this such? I can readily understand the question "What is your God more than another god?" Jesus was the Beloved of His Father, as He told us on two occasions. But what is He to you?

The balance of this chapter contains the response of the Shulamite woman, and is far too descriptive for us to go into at this time. However, the conclusive and definitive answer is found in verse 16:

"Yes, he is altogether lovely. This is my beloved, and this is my friend" Song of Songs 5:16.

After describing His skin, head, hair, eyes, cheeks, lips, hands, body, legs, countenance, and mouth, the conclusion is "He is altogether lovely." There is nothing about Him of which I can be critical. He is faultless. He is beautiful. After sharing her feelings when she could not find her Beloved, the women of Jerusalem asked, "so, what makes him so special that we should take time to find him for you?" She responded, "Because He is absolute perfection, and He is my friend." What a beautiful and wonderful relationship.

Every person who considers themselves a member of the Body of Christ should ask themselves this question. What is Jesus to you? Describe Him. Tell me what He is like. How well do you know Him? One who is truly committed to Jesus knows the answer. He does not have to search for words.

"With him, Christ is first, Christ is last, Christ is midst, Christ is all in all; and when he speaks about anything connected with Christ, his words come with such a solemn earnestness that men are impressed with what he says, and they turn round to him, and ask, as the daughters of Jerusalem enquired of the spouse, "What is thy Beloved more than another beloved, that thou dost so charge us?" C.H. Spurgeon.

When asked this very pertinent question, the woman did not say, "Wait a moment, I must read up on the subject and become better acquainted with the Him. She answered from her heart. She was a part of Him and knew Him well. Her answer was given from personal experience. "Is my Beloved better than any other beloved? Certainly he is, and here are the reasons." Upon hearing the question, she immediately responded, and gave an entire list of reasons. She puts them together, one after the other, without pausing. Her one concise answer was "He is altogether lovely."

Dear reader, answer the question right now to yourself. If it helps, write your answer down on a piece of paper. Bernard of Clairvaux (1090-1153) expressed it well:

Jesus, the very thought of Thee
With sweetness fills my breast;
But sweeter far Thy face to see,
And in Thy presence rest.

Nor voice can sing, nor heart can frame,
Nor can the mem'ry find
A sweeter sound than Thy blest name,
O Savior of mankind.

O hope of every contrite heart,
O joy of all the meek,
To those who fall, how kind Thou art,
How good to those who seek.

But what to those who find? Ah this
Nor tongue nor pen can show
The love of Jesus, what it is,
None but His loved ones know.

More than her opinion of her Beloved, "Yes, he is altogether lovely," is that "He is my Beloved," and even more so, "He is my friend" 5:16. She tells the women, "I have a personal relationship with him. I can turn to him and share my innermost thoughts. He listens to my problems and concerns—he is my friend. This one in whom there is no fault or defect, is *my* friend. I can trust him. I love him.

Puritan Quote:
"*Nor earth, nor seas, nor sun, nor stars,*
Nor heaven, his full resemblance bears;
His beauties we can never trace,
Till we behold him face to face."
                            Author unknown.

CREATOR/FRIEND

Reading: Song of Solomon 5:1—16
"This is my beloved, and this is my friend" Song of Songs 5:16

To be a friend of God, the Creator of all things, is one of those spiritual realities beyond my comprehension. If Jesus Himself had not designated me as such, I would fear I was regarding my relationship with Him frivolously. To have a personal relationship with the Almighty, Omniscient, Creator, before whom the hosts of heaven bow in continuous worship, is in itself gloriously remarkable, but to know He considers me a friend is . . . beyond words.

From the very beginning, God and Adam were friends—they enjoyed each other's company as they walked together in the coolness of the evening—the words imply this was a regular feature of their day. Sin ruined this very special friendship, and God drove Adam and Eve from the garden, and blocked their return by appointing sword-carrying angels at the garden's gate.

Only two men, Abraham and Moses, are spoken of as being a friend of God throughout the Old Testament (Exodus 33:12; 2 Chronicles 20:7), but God never referred to anyone as His friend until Jesus, when He called Lazarus "our friend" (John 11:11). Then to His disciples He said:

"You are My friends if you do whatever I command you" John 15:14.

First of all, this was a remarkable revelation that God, in the Person of Jesus Christ, would consent to call His disciples "friends." Man, in his fallen state, God considered to be His "enemies" (Romans 5:10; 8:7), and how can enemies be friends? There is only one way—they must be reconciled. This is the wonderful thing Jesus accomplished by His death on the cross.

"For if when we were enemies we were reconciled to God through the death of His Son, much more, having been reconciled, we

shall be saved by His life. And not only that, but we also rejoice in God through our Lord Jesus Christ, through whom we have now received the reconciliation" Romans 5:10-11.

This is how God can once again be friends with His creation. This friendship, however, has conditions:

No other beloved, nor friend that men choose, beside Christ, can abide the trial; the more they are inquired into, and searched out, they will be found to be of the less worth: therefore she appeals (as it were) to all men to bring their beloveds before Christ, if they durst compare with him, as being confident none durst enter the lists, purposely and professedly to compete with him.

What sort of friendship is this if we have to obey Jesus implicitly? That describes a servant, not a friend. Jesus goes on to describe the grounds for this friendship by saying, "You did not choose Me, but I chose you" vs 16. Out of the many fishermen of Galilee, Jesus chose two pair of brothers— Peter and Andrew, and James and John. He chose a very unpopular man, Matthew, a tax collector. Jesus chose His friends—they did not seek His friendship. Jesus took the initiative, and He established the ground upon which that friendship was to be based.

Obedience was not something the disciples originally agreed to, but it became proof of their friendship. Jesus chose wisely, for when He called them, "they immediately left their nets and followed Him." Their immediate response was obedience. Had they dithered or made excuses, they would not have become His chosen ones.

"No other beloved, nor friend that men choose beside Christ, can abide the trial; the more they are inquired into, and searched out, they will be found to be of the less worth: therefore she appeals (as it were) to all men to bring their beloveds before Christ, if they durst compare with him, as being confident none durst enter the lists, purposely and professedly to compete with him . . . She has a high estimation of him—confidence in him, without fear. Satisfaction with him, and having full contentment in him, resulting in an eminent joy which cannot be shaken, all the former being in an eminent degree" James Durham, 1622-1658.

"This is My commandment, that you love one another as I have loved you" John 15:12.

While this statement of Jesus can be applied generally, it is also specific in that He is referring to the commandment He has just mentioned:
The love for our neighbor is the second most important commandment:

"The second is like it: 'You shall love your neighbor as yourself" Matthew 22:39.

It is, therefore, very important to Jesus that His children love each other:

"A new commandment I give to you, that you love one another; as I have loved you, that you also love one another. By this all will know that you are My disciples, if you have love for one another" John 13:34-35.

If we say we are friends with Jesus yet do not love our brother and sister—all of them—then our friendship with God is a fantasy, for it is a necessary requirement. It is only as the love of God flows through us that this is possible. To love the unlovely is an attribute of God, not of man, even a Christian.

"Everyone who believes that Jesus is the Christ is a child of God. And everyone who loves the Father loves his children, too. We know we love God's children if we love God and obey his commandments" 1 John 5:1-2, NLT.

Puritan quote:
"'You are my friends'—He does not mean that we obtain so great an honor by our own merit, but only reminds them of the condition on which he receives us into favor, and deigns to reckon us among his friends; as he said a little before, 'If you keep my commandments, you will abide in my love'" John Calvin, 1509-1564.

FAIR AS THE MOON

Reading: Song of Songs 6:1-10

"Who is she who looks forth as the morning, fair as the moon, clear as the sun, awesome as an army with banners?" Song of Songs 6:10

"Yes, she is like the morning! The Bride is like her Beloved: He is the bright and Morning Star. She had just returned to him, transformed into his likeness. The glory of a believer's surrendered life is beginning to appear like the glow just before sunrise. There is the freshness of a new day in her look, in her eyes, in her ways! The dark shadows of self had engulfed her, but now, a new day in her life was dawning" Esher *Shoshannah: A Devotional Commentary on the Song of Songs.*

This is one of the many questions asked in the Song of Solomon— "Where? Who? What? How? Why? It is a song of seeking; questions asked by two persons in love; questions asked by two people whose relationship is very real, yet hindered by obstacles and circumstances of a world at war with its Creator. The glorious hope and expectation of a relationship unhindered and unopposed by anything or any entity that would cause questions or doubt, is the strength, support, and comfort of every believer.

This question by the beloved Bridegroom is not one of ignorance, but of amazement and wonder—"Look at this one who is as the morning, isn't she awesome?" How different from our view when we see ourselves in the light of what we are in ourselves: "O wretched man that I am" Romans 7:24. The day will dawn, however, when we will see ourselves as Christ sees us.

"For now we see in a mirror, dimly, but then face to face. Now I know in part, but then I shall know just as I also am known" 1 Corinthians 13:12.

"Behold what manner of love the Father has bestowed on us, that we should be called children of God! Therefore the world does not know us, because it did not know Him. Beloved, now we are children of God; and it has not yet been revealed what we shall be, but we know that when He is revealed, we shall be like Him, for we shall see Him as He is" 1 John 3:1-2.

There is coming a time when all is revealed, when there are no questions, when we shall know, just as we are known.

Is there anything more refreshing after a dark night, than the dawning of a new day? It offers a fresh outlook on yesterday's problems, and a deep breath fills our lungs with fresh air, fortifying us to face the challenges ahead. This is the time to remind ourselves: "This is the day the Lord has made; we will rejoice and be glad in it" Psalm 118:24.

She is as beautiful as the moon that shines over the darkness, and the sun that pierces the clouds of the day. There are nights and days when the clouds hide heaven's lights, but the strength of the sun will eventually burn them away. Listen to the prophet:

"But to you who fear My name the Sun of Righteousness shall arise with healing in His wings; and you shall go out and grow fat like stall-fed calves. You shall trample the wicked, for they shall be ashes under the soles of your feet" Malachi 4:2-3.

As her Beloved, she will both prosper and be victorious over the clouds she will face in the coming day. When, as John in a vision saw, "a woman clothed with the sun, with the moon under her feet" (Revelation 12:1) then shall the whole church shine forth. There is no partiality with God—He sees all of His children the same in Christ Jesus.

Just as Jesus is the Light of the World, so His disciples must be:

"You are the light of the world. A city that is set on a hill cannot be hidden. Nor do they light a lamp and put it under a basket, but on a lampstand, and it gives light to all who are in the house.

Let your light so shine before men, that they may see your good works and glorify your Father in heaven" Matthew 5:14-16.

The dedicated and committed believer will be as "awesome as an army with banners." The believer marches in the army of the King of kings, with Christ in the forefront, leading His troops into battle. There is no doubt as to the identification of the army, for it is an "army with banners."

So, how do these banners read? I am sure the one carried by the King reads "Yahvahshua"—"The Lord who saves." Others may read, "The Body of Christ", "The Church", "The Redeemed"—use your imagination. This fearsome army, led by the Son of God, will make the opposition tremble with fear. Tragically, today, the opposing army laughs and ridicules the church, abolishing the very name of Jesus out of every public place. They have no fear, for too many of us hide behind stained-glass windows, cowering in the face of any opposition.

"Let your light shine," says the Commander in Chief, "Fight the good fight," "Run the race that is set before you." As the church of Jesus Christ and as individual members, let us cry out to God for help in the "day of trouble."

"In the day when I cried out, You answered me, and made me bold with strength in my soul" Psalm 138:3.

"Finally, my brethren, be strong in the Lord and in the power of His might. Put on the whole armor of God, that you may be able to stand against the wiles of the devil" Ephesians 6:10-11.

Puritan Quote:

"When the church preserves her purity she secures her honour and victory; when she is fair as the moon, and clear as the sun, she is truly great and formidable" Matthew Henry, 1662-1714

DESIRED

Reading: Song of Songs:7:1-10
"I am my beloved's, and his desire is toward me" Song of Songs 7:10

The bride has just listened to her Beloved talking about her beauty (7:1-9), and she responds with an amazement she can hardly believe, "I am my beloved's, and his desire is toward me." It is as if she is shouting it from the rooftop to any that would listen.

She has often stated "I am my beloved's," but this time it is as if the reality of it consumes her like no other time. "I belong to my beloved! I am his property, and am happy to be so." Throughout this song, her relationship with her beloved seems to an on-again off-again experience. She left him, then sought after him. He called after her, wanting her to come to him. They missed each other's company. But now, she realizes it is not only her desiring to be in his presence, but his desire is to be with her.

What an amazing truth for every born again person to grasp. Jesus desires our fellowship! He sees us as beautiful, and His heart is drawn toward us. He left the glory He enjoyed with His Father from eternity past. He left the presence of an untold number of angels who worshipped and obeyed Him, and yet, after thirty years in this world, He said, "I have come in My Father's name, and you do not receive Me" John 5:43. "He came to His own, and His own did not receive Him" John 1:11.

"He has no form or comeliness; and when we see Him, there is no beauty that we should desire Him. He is despised and rejected by men, a Man of sorrows and acquainted with grief. And we hid, as it were, our faces from Him; He was despised, and we did not esteem Him" Isaiah 53:2-3.

Not only did His own (the Jews) reject Him, but "men" (all others) rejected Him. Both Jews and Gentiles stood on the hill of Calvary and watched him die. He was "despised" and died alone. "But"—this is one of the great "buts" found in the Bible, in the history of man—"But as many as received Him, to them He gave the right to become children of God, to those who believe in His name" John 1:12.

It is these "children of God", those He has chosen to be His Bride, He sees as "fair and pleasant" (7:6), beautiful, and to be desired. This is not a fleeting relationship He desires, but an eternal one. His desire is to be with His bride in this life, through the Bema judgment, and forever on the new earth He will create only for them.

From that mass of humanity that spat in His face and pressed a crown of thorns on His head, His Father has chosen for Him a bride He can love (John 6:37). As the father of a bride gives his daughter to the one she is to marry, so our heavenly Father gives us to His Son to love and protect forever. "Therefore what God has joined together, let not man separate" Mark 10:9.

"The King will greatly desire your beauty" Psalm 45:11.

God, who knows our heart better than we do, desires to be with us. How can this be? Because we have been made beautiful with His beauty.

When Satan accused Joshua, the High Priest, before the Lord, he was clothed in filthy garments, but the Lord said:

"Take away the filthy garments from him." And to him He said, "See, I have removed your iniquity from you, and I will clothe you with rich robes." And I said, "Let them put a clean turban on his head" Zechariah 3:4-5.

Every child of God is clothed with the righteousness of Jesus (Romans 4:6). When Jesus looks at the condition of our soul, He sees nothing but His own righteousness, old things (our filthy garments) have passed away, and behold, all things have become new (the righteousness of Christ).

How meaningful are the words "Let them put a clean turban on his head." A robe covers the body from the shoulders down, but the turban the head. How important that our mind and thoughts are "clean." When Jesus healed the blind man, He anointed his eyes, and told him to wash in the pool of Siloam (John 8:6-7). "Let this mind be in you which was also in Christ Jesus" Philippians 2:5.

Puritan Quote:

"His desire is towards His people, even before conversion, though dead in trespasses and sins; that they may be quickened, called by grace, and brought to the knowledge of Himself; and, not withstanding all their backslidings and revolting from Him, still His desire is after them, to do them good; neither will He turn away from them. His desire is continually after His peoples company, grace and beauty" John Gill, 1697-1771

LEANING ON THE BELOVED

Reading: Song of Solomon 8:5-7
"Who is this coming up from the wilderness, leaning on her beloved?"
Song of Solomon 8:5

What a wonderful picture is presented to you, my soul, in this glorious passage of God's Word. It is a picture of you and your Savior, a picture depicting you leaning on Him as you travel up from the wilderness. There was a time, a long time, when you did not lean upon Him and you lost your way. How you need to lean on Him. You must lean on Him because of your weakness. You lean on Him because you need His strength, His faithfulness, His comfort. How simple yet how true is the chorus,

Learning to lean, learning to lean, I'm learning to lean on Jesus;
Finding more power than I've ever dreamed, I'm learning to lean on Jesus.

You need to lean on Him because the tendency of your heart, when left to itself, is to return to its own strength, its own wisdom. How important it is for you to adopt this posture of faith and love—leaning on your Beloved.

When you first left home to enter service for the Lord, your pastor gave you a bible which, on the first page were written the words,

"Trust in the LORD with all your heart, and lean not on your own understanding; in all your ways acknowledge Him, and He shall direct your paths" Proverbs 3:5-6.

Envision this woman leaning on and clinging to her beloved as if everything depends on it. Why? Because everything does depend on it. What does it imply? Closeness, trust, dependence, love, and a multitude of other necessities required for your walk with Jesus Christ. She depends on his strength to keep her from falling. Why do you need to continually lean on Him? Because "without Me you can do nothing" John 15:5. You need His strength in every step you take, every decision you make, every thought you think, every temptation you face, and every circumstance you encounter.

The very word "leaning" speaks of her confidence in and familiarity with the Beloved.

"Trust in the Lord with all your heart, and lean not on your own understanding; in all your ways acknowledge Him, and He shall direct your paths" Proverbs 3:5-6.

"I will go in the strength of the Lord God" says the Psalmist (71:16). The sooner we realize our own strength is too weak to walk up the hills we will face, the sooner we will learn to "Be strong in the Lord, and in the power of His might" Ephesians 6:10. Jesus told His disciples, "Without me, you can do nothing" (John 15:5), and Paul looked at His words as a positive thing when he said, "I can do all things through Christ who strengthens me" Philippians 4:13.

What a fellowship, what a joy divine,
Leaning on the everlasting arms;
What a blessedness, what a peace in mine,
Leaning on the everlasting arms.

O how sweet to walk in this pilgrim way,
Leaning on the everlasting arms;
O how bright the path grows from day to day,
Leaning on the everlasting arms.

What have I to dread, what have I to fear?
Leaning on the everlasting arms;
I have blessed peace with my Lord so near,
Leaning on the everlasting arms.

Leaning, leaning,
Safe and secure from all alarms;
Leaning, Leaning,
Leaning on the everlasting arms.
Elisha A. Hoffman, 1839-1929.

Every soul that journeys toward heaven has Jesus as its partner. He has trodden every step before us. Whatever obstacles we face, He has faced and overcome them, be they temptations, afflictions, disappointments, and challenges.

It is Christ's strength that climbs the hills, and by leaning on Him, we His strength and determination becomes ours.

Puritan Quote:

"When we least perceive him, he is often closest to us. When the howling tempest drowns his voice, and the darkness of the night hides his person, still he is there, and we need not be afraid. It is no fiction, no dream, no piece of imagination that Christ is really with his people" C.H. Spurgeon, 1834-1892.

"She is leaning on her Beloved: meaning, that believing souls lay their whole stress of salvation upon Jesus. They have not an atom of their own, but hang upon him, cleave to him, rest upon him. And this is in perfect agreement to the whole doctrine of faith (Isaiah 22:24; Proverbs 3:5; Psalm 71:15-16; Philippians 3:8-9). Robert Hawker, 1753-1857.

Other Books by David T. Peckham

Cords of Love—

Christian Poems—
Thoughts From The Heart
Written over a forty year period
reflecting the author's spiritual
struggles and victories.

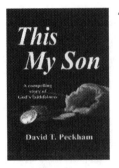

This My Son—

Testimony and thoughts from
Luke 15. A forthright and
compelling story of God's
Faithfulness

Shepherd Warrior—Historical Novel
A young Saxon's battle against
the mighty Norman Army at the
Battle of Hastings in 1066

Warrior Monk— Historical Novel
A young Saxon torn between his
duty to God and his hatred for
Normans

God's Warriors— Historical Fiction
A story based on Polycarp, an
early Church leader who is
opposed and then supported by
a young Roman Tribune.

Power of the Almighty—is the result of studying
the Bible to discover the many
ways the Power of God is both
expressed and explained.

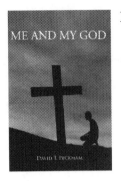

Me and My God— Written in three sections—
Section One—The Fatherhood
of God; Section Two—Spiritual
Adoption; Section Three—This
My Son.

101 Thoughts From The Word—Volume One
Devotions from Job through
Song of Songs

101 Thoughts From The Word—Volume Two
Devotions from the Old
Testament

101 Thoughts From The Word—Volume Three
Devotions from the New
Testament

101 Thoughts From The Word—Volume Four
Devotions from the
Scriptures—A book of Series